CONSTANCE MARKIEVICZ

Cresset Women's Voices

Editorial consultant
Rita Pankhurst

Black Country to Red China
Esther Cheo Ying

Constance Markievicz
Sean O'Faolain

Unshackled:
The Story of How We Won the Vote
Christabel Pankhurst

Victoria of England
Edith Sitwell

Front cover: *Constance Markievicz in the uniform of the Irish Citizen Army, 1914*
Reproduced by courtesy of the National Library of Ireland
Back cover: *Stamp commemorating the centenary of the birth of Constance Markievicz* issued in 1968 by the Irish Post Office
Reproduced by courtesy of An Post

Constance Markievicz

SEAN O'FAOLAIN

CRESSET WOMEN'S VOICES
London   Melbourne   Auckland   Johannesburg

The Cresset Library

An imprint of Century Hutchinson Ltd

62–65 Chandos Place, London WC2N 4NW

Century Hutchinson Australia Pty Ltd
PO Box 496, 16–22 Church Street, Hawthorn,
Victoria 3122, Australia

Century Hutchinson New Zealand Ltd
PO Box 40–086, Glenfield, Auckland 10,
New Zealand

Century Hutchinson South Africa (Pty) Ltd
PO Box 337, Bergvlei 2012, South Africa

First published by Jonathan Cape Ltd 1934
This edition first published 1987

Made and printed in Great Britain by
Richard Clay Ltd, Bungay, Suffolk

British Library Cataloguing in Publication Data

O'Faoláin, Séan
   Constance Markievicz. — 3rd ed. —
   (Cresset women's voices; 3).
   1. Markievicz, Constance Markievicz,
   Countess 2. Revolutionists — Ireland
   — Biography 3. Politicians — Ireland
   — Biography
   I. Title
   941.5081'092'4   DA965.M35

ISBN 0 09 172895 9

To
Anna Kelly
in gratitude for immeasurable
help

CONTENTS

	Foreword to the 1967 edition	7
	Acknowledgements	11
1	The Wild Irish Girl: 1868–1900	15
2	Social Life: 1900–1910	43
3	Politics: 1900–1910	63
4	The Poor: 1911–1913	100
5	Revolutionary Politics: 1914–1917	120
6	Illusion and Disillusion: 1917–1924	171
7	Discovery: 1924–1927	201
	Index	217

FOREWORD TO THE 1967 EDITION

This biography raises once again the basic problem of every biographer:— What is The Fair Question, or perhaps even The Final Question, that I may ask about this man's (or woman's) response to the main challenge? If the question asked expects too much the biographer is unfair to his character and, so, fails to hit the bull's eye of the whole study. If the question asked expects too little the biographer is unfair to the reader, and also fails to locate the core of the Life presented to him.

There are minor questions and major questions. Would it be fair, for instance, to question Rousseau's right to condemn Society as a corrupt force considering that he abandoned his own children to the Foundling Hospital? Or to question the honesty of Saint Augustine because, for lofty religious reasons, he abandoned his concubine, who dearly loved him, and then straightway took another? I think it would be quite fair to raise these questions – but they would not be *The* Fair, Final, or Central Question. So, I think also that it is quite fair, but not central, to compare Constance Markievicz's declared love for all mankind in general (except, alas, the English), and her love for the Irish people in particular, with her ruinous personal relations with her own family, her husband and her only child, whom she virtually abandoned as a baby in the cradle to the care of its truly-loving grandmother, Lady Gore-Booth. I think it fair, and important, because it helps us to consider certain aspects of her character.

I know well that others would say it is most unfair. Maud Gonne said so. To her Constance Markievicz was primarily a patriot forced to make an agonising choice between her love for her daughter and her love for Ireland. But this merely raises the same question in another way since there have been plenty of other Irishwomen at the time who were both good mothers and patriotically active; and since, as Maud Gonne cannot have known, Constance began the process of 'abandonment' some years before she became active in politics. The child was born in Lissadell, its grandmother's home, and Constance's home, in November, 1901. Con was not really active politically until about 1908, and in between she had her own house in Dublin, with a maid or maids, and was enjoying what would commonly be thought a good time – but it was the grandmother who looked after the child. This much even Constance Markievicz's latest and most sympathetic biographer frankly acknowledges in her fine biography *The Rebel Countess* – a complete, detailed and most scholarly book with which, on those grounds, this study of mine cannot compare – saying:— 'This child became the favourite of her grandmother, Lady Gore-Booth who virtually brought her up. Almost at once the pattern was set. When the Markieviczs went back to Paris (from Lissadell) in 1902 they left the baby at Lissadell ...' One of the saddest incidents recorded by Miss Marreco was the ultimate reunion (her word) of mother and daughter, when Maeve was twenty and her mother was fifty-three. Maeve did not recognize her mother until she was persuaded by a friend that she was really she.

On the other hand it would not be a Fair Question to ask why Constance did not devote more loving attention to her husband. For one thing Cassie Markievicz was more than able to look after himself; for another, the whole relationship between husband and wife, as will be seen in the following pages, became so comical as to pre-empt all suggestion of a marital tragedy. I have accordingly treated the Cassie-Constance story throughout as pure comedy in which nobody suffered, except their child.

Here I may as well say what I have not explicitly said in the body of this book about Constance Markievicz as wife and mother. I think she was by nature a celibate type. In this – to use a shorthand word – sexy age it is not fully recognized that there are men and women to whom celibacy and chastity comes as naturally as embodied passion does to others. I feel that Constance was one of those women for whom love was a disembodied passion, directed towards ideals rather than ideas, to Man rather than to men, and if to men, or women, to them chiefly as upholders of ideals, or as victims of the lack of them. If one could imagine such a woman as a fighting abbess Con might well have been far happier in that role than in the role of lover, wife or mother. When such a woman marries, and has a child, then husband and child had better look out for themselves.

These instances of The Fair Question, however, do not compare in urgency with the problem of what is fair to expect of Madame Markievicz when we come to her career as nationalist rebel and would-be social revolutionary. Then, she becomes a public figure. At this point in my book I felt, on the one hand, that it was my duty to weigh up the general intelligence of her behaviour and the ultimate value of her contribution to the Irish cause; on the other hand, I could not help wondering whether it was fair to ask these political value-questions about a woman who had, already, that is before the later stage of her career, sacrificed so much to help Ireland.

Nobody can doubt her growing, and ultimately total commitment to the Irish cause from about 1908 to 1926, when she died worn out by her devotion to it and, perhaps, in heartbreak at the way it had turned out, in a Civil War and, from her viewpoint, the betrayal of all she had believed in. If we must doubt her warmth as wife and mother there can be no doubt about her warmth for the Dublin poor, her selflessness in her work for them, and their gratitude to her. She gave up all the material advantages of her birth as a member of the ruling Anglo-Irish gentry. As far as anybody can ever hope to do such a thing she freed herself of all the traditions of the class that produced her excepting only, it must be said, their independence of spirit that gave her the moral courage to want to cut loose from them. One might well think that if she were alive today she could go a long way towards completely flooring anybody who asked her to do still more, by simply saying, in the catch-phrase of her period, 'I did my bit!'

And yet, it is impossible for all sorts of reasons to think of her now as a woman fighting a purely personal fight. Because of her beauty, her personal charms, her inherited gifts, not few and all of enormous help to her as a convert-rebel, because she had means, because even of her class, she stood out from the start, was never a rank-and-filer, became famous all over Ireland when she was sentenced to be shot after the Rising, one of the best-known personalities of the Irish Troubles, publicised in Ireland, Britain and the United States, and, as Minister for Labour in the revolutionary cabinet, finally accepted as one of the leaders – not a major leader, but still a leader – of that crucial period of national and social resurgence. She thus became, and remains, within her personal limits, a representative historical figure of her times. As such, surely, she must invite larger value-questions?

The reader of this biography must decide, for himself, whether they are, nevertheless, Fair Questions. I hope he will not make up his mind until he has read Anne Marreco's book

– from which I have, for this edition, quietly and gratefully borrowed several corrections of dates and facts – not only because hers is a sound, scholarly book but because she is so much more sympathetic to 'Madame's' failings and follies than, I fear, I have always been. I wrote my book in 1933, when many of Constance's and Cassie's contemporaries were alive, gathering while it could be done all the living reactions and memories of them both that were still floating around Dublin, so that, whatever the faults of my book, and they must be many, and I have deliberately left them for the most part untouched, this study has at least something of the value of a contemporary document. Yet, for that very reason whenever it has hitherto been suggested to me that I should allow the book to be reprinted I have reread it with one misgiving: namely, that just because it was so contemporary it cannot but reflect some of the impatience, even of the disillusionment, the weariness of soul with all patriotic emotion that, as we now see, looking about us at other newly-risen peoples, seem to be part of the inevitable aftermath of every nationalist upheaval. But times change, and opinions with them. Most of the impressions and memories that I here record are from her friends; some are gathered also from her enemies – and she had plenty of both. Today would the enemies be so caustic or the friends so sweet? In reading Miss Marreco's book I know I found myself saying more than once, 'That is not what he said to *me*!' – which may suggest that it is always wiser to hold back from a biography for some forty or fifty years after the death of its subject.

Now, however, that we have two biographies of Constance Markievicz I am content to believe that two points of view are better than one and that, between them, full justice may be done to this very gallant woman. For, whatever else we may think of Con Markievicz – even when we have given full weight to all her fancies, and follies and fanaticisms; and many of her male colleagues had their share of all three – we may all agree that she was one of the most gallant creatures our country had the good fortune to attract to her side at a time when only a very few supremely brave and generous-hearted men and women were, like her, glad to gamble their lives on the faith that Ireland's spirit was not dead but merely sleeping.

SEÁN O'FAOLÁIN.

DUBLIN: 1967

ACKNOWLEDGMENTS

I HAVE written this biography from the published records of the period and from oral testimony. As far as concerns Constance Markievicz the printed material is small, the oral testimony copious as a legend. While this has had the advantage of giving life, colour, and verisimilitude to the popular memory it has also, very naturally (especially in a city like Dublin), been too often inimical to cold truth. I know it is unkind to say this now that I have wearied so many people with questions. Perhaps it is as well that they have been so many – that 'too often' will never, I trust, come home to roost – though it is not in that hope, but from the mere impossibility of doing otherwise, that I express general rather than individual gratitude to those who have been kind enough to help. There must have been over a hundred people whom I have pestered during the last twelve months.

I must, however, acknowledge a special debt to Mrs H. Sheehy-Skeffington and to Miss Helena Moloney, whose personal knowledge of Madame Markievicz was intimate and extensive; to Mr Bulmer Hobson for details concerning the history of the Irish Republican Brotherhood; to Mr Martin Murphy for his vivid re-creations of life in Edwardian Dublin and his personal memories of Count Markievicz; to Mr Malcolm MacDonald, M.P., for an extract from the official records of the trial of Madame Markievicz; to Mrs G. Foden for details of the life of Count Markievicz; to Mr Rowlette for his fine account of Constance Gore-Booth's hunting days; to Mr J. Geoghegan for details concerning Belcamp House, where Madame Markievicz lived for a period; and to Mme R. M. de R. P. for personal recollections of the last years of Count Markievicz. Above all I must confess my debt to Prof. J. D. Clarkson, of the College of the City of New York, for his fine book *Labour and Nationalism in Ireland*, which I have found helpful, not so much for the information with which it is packed, as because it has been, for me, a touchstone for the history of Constance Markievicz and of her day.

I am obliged to Mr W. B. Yeats and to Messrs Macmillan & Co., for permission to print the poems which appear on pp. 13, 166, 167 of this book; to Mr James Stephens and The Talbot Press for permission to quote from *The Insurrection in*

Dublin; to Mr W. P. Ryan and The Talbot Press for permission to quote from *The Irish Labour Movement*.

The officials of the Dublin libraries have been very kind and patient; and to these, Miss C. Keogh of the Central Students' Library, Miss Roisin Walsh, Mr J. J. O'Neill, Miss B. Redmond, and Mr Michael O'Donovan, I return particular and heartfelt thanks.

Seán O'Faoláin

Wicklow
    April, 1934.

In Memory of Eva Gore-Booth and Con Markievicz

The light of evening, Lissadell,
Great windows open to the south,
Two girls in silk kimonos, both
Beautiful, one a gazelle.
But a raving autumn shears
Blossom from the summer's wreath;
The older is condemned to death,
Pardoned, drags out lonely years
Conspiring among the ignorant.
I know not what the younger dreams —
Some vague Utopia — and she seems,
When withered old and skeleton-gaunt,
An image of such politics.
Many a time I think to seek
One or the other out and speak
Of that old Georgian mansion, mix
Pictures of the mind, recall
That table and the talk of youth,
Two girls in silk kimonos, both
Beautiful, one a gazelle.

Dear shadows, now you know it all,
All the folly of a fight
With a common wrong or right.
The innocent and the beautiful
Have no enemy but time;
Arise and bid me strike a match
And strike another till time catch;
Should the conflagration climb,
Run till all the sages know.
We the great gazebo built,
They convicted us of guilt;
Bid me strike a match and blow.

W. B. YEATS

October, 1927.

CHAPTER 1

THE WILD IRISH GIRL:
1868–1900

§ 1

ON February 4th, 1868, two days after Bright, in the course of a speech at Manchester, had first questioned the divine right of England to autocracy over Ireland, thereby stirring up a minor revolution in the columns of the English press, Constance Georgina Gore-Booth was born in London. The event – the birth of the first child – was of the greatest importance; but as daughters in such circumstances were not encouraged, also a disappointment. It took place at Buckingham Gate, hard by The Palace. The locality was then exclusive, almost sacred ground. The later encroachment of shops and offices was then a thing unheard, almost undreamed in this central point of a world which was not blind to its own self-importance. It was magnificently, almost aggressively secure, all the habits of its tenants dictated and prescribed by a routine of Court and Social duty. They were born in the heart of an empire; they went to the correct Public School if they happened to be males, or were instructed by carefully selected governesses if they had the misfortune to be born 'opposite sex'; they became or married Diplomats or members of the Brigade of Guards; they gradually dozed into a reluctant retirement from the world of which for a span they had been the chosen ornaments, and finally died, bequeathing their exquisite and spacious residences to descendants who did the round of social duties in their stead.

But though she was born in, and to a certain extent into, this formal world of London society, neither she nor her people really belonged to it, and quite properly she left it without bringing from it even the faintest memory. For though the Gore-Booths maintained an allegiance to the dictates of fashionable life, as they did to King and Country – the country being the West End of London – their property, in land, was in the West of Ireland, and in houses, in Manchester. They were not only provincials, but something much more unfortunate and mid-between – Anglo-Irish. They divided the year and they divided their thoughts between the social round of London and what one may call existence at Lissadell, in Sligo; so that whatever rank fashion assigned to them in the social ledger, it was definitely lower, by however small a fraction, than the rank of families of no great age or wealth who held their property in Bucks or Wilts or any English county. (There had been 'riots' in Ireland in sixty-seven: and 'murder' in Manchester.) It was a sad position. In the eyes of fashion, whatever they might say or do, to Sligo they belonged for to Sligo they would always return, and though, in their troubles, they might turn again to Westminster or Whitehall or St. James's, it would always be because of Sligo. While in the eyes of Sligo and Ireland, they belonged to Westminster for to Westminster they would always return, and though in their troubles they might appeal to the Irish members there, or even to the Rural Council in Sligo town, it was always because of what they had in the beginning done to Sligo rather than because of anything they had ever done for her. It has always been the curse of Ireland that she has not been able to forget. It has been her source of strength, as it has been her weakness. History never becomes happy where the memory is too long.

That divided thought and life had always been the mark, as finally it was the ruin, of the Anglo-Irish gentlemen. Where it was constant it prevented them equally from being wholly assimilated by the country that gave them their wealth, and accepted wholly by the country that gave them their social rank. They were so parti-coloured that in the end their masters abandoned them, and they who had been their servants despised them. Even their very latest efforts, half-hearted as they were, to become part of Ireland only brought a smile of pity to the faces of the most sympathetic Irishmen – that odd nicely-mouthed Gaelic they sometimes learned to speak; that condescending interest, as of an antiquary, in Irish letters; that timid interest in Irish politics, so timid that no Irishman but knew the wind would turn them in a second; above all that well-meaning interest in 'the people' which was blasted and made barren by the cautious air of detachment, as of a philanthropist, that always accompanied it. The result was that nothing that they did, in their timidity and caution, availed them anything. Even their charity was accepted as a right and taken without gratitude. Paddy came sidling up their steps with his hat twirling in his hands, and in a whisper he asked the butler – often one of his own class and people – if the Missis, or if Her Ladyship, was at home; and in the hall she came to him and he whined out his wants and she, already hopeless, granted them without enthusiasm even where she could still be interested. And then Paddy went away to the crossroads where his back straightened and his eye cleared and he stuck his hat back on his head and he became a man again. He had got an inch from the people who had stolen his ell, and for the time being he was satisfied. Those two classes, the natives and the invaders (who sometimes – mainly out of Ireland – pretended to be natives) lived with shut mouths and shut hearts at one another's doors. They lived so, in Sligo, for three hundred years; a story so pathetic and so tragic and so hopeless of solution that it became like a cloud over the fields at which nobody looks but of which everyone is aware.

It must have been an extraordinary interesting experience for a Gore-Booth to come over so gradually to wakening consciousness of his or her position in time and place. At first there was just the hall and the door and the steps, and far beyond the parkland the slope of Knocknarea, and to the north the lump of Ben Bulben, and at midday, when the sun was on her southern course, the bay glancing with a million crystals of light and the Rosses or the lighthouse dark against sea and sky. The old man here and the young man there who tips his cap is, so Squidge (the governess) tells her, Pat Rourke, or Christy Conor and looking back at him she passes on. Across the fields the sun and wind catch the edge of the men's flannel bawneens and the red petticoats of the women where they rise and stoop over the turf, mixing the mud with their hands and beating it with hands and feet into turves. Down on the shore other women are scraping among the stones and rocks for carrageen. Then a shower comes battering across from Ben Bulben, a March army of ten thousand million raindrops that never fall but go sweeping over the land like a smoke in waves; under the high stone wall – how did men ever lift those great stones? – all crouch until each and every one of the passing army lights a tiny torch of sunlight; a halo surrounds the blown fur of the patient cattle; the invisible breakers of the wind begin to moan. It may be at that second that, as she hurries home, her eye falls again on the men and women in the bog, stooping and rising incessantly, unable, they, to stop and shelter from passing showers, and all that is meant by place and position touches her imagination with a little mark that chafes and irritates for ever.

At home in the drawing-room, or at table, a word – any

word, it does not matter what – fall about Christy Conor or Pat Rourke. It will be significant with a hundred assumptions; powerful in allusion and suggestion. The very tone of voice in which it is uttered took three hundred years to perfect. What with that chafing mark left by the picture of endless toil under the showers of March, and the bland satisfaction implicit in that slighting word, there is and shall always be a growing war between sympathy and indifference. In the mind of Constance Gore-Booth (and of Eva Gore-Booth) that little warfare began early.

They were lovely and gentle girls, the one fair as a lily, the other wild like a young deer. Eva's soft eyes were a little too deeply set, and Con's, much brighter and more vivacious, a trifle too prominent, as she grew older they retired just the trifle necessary for perfection. Always the younger girl was the quieter of the two – she was never strong. Her life seemed to glow behind the delicate shell of her brow like a votive lamp; so frail did she sometimes seem that one wondered that her fringe of soft hair did not strike a resonance when the wind strayed it over her forehead and about her pensive eyes. Even to her sisters she was not so much flesh and blood as a Presence.

At random one opens her poems and one finds that her verse dealt from the beginning to the end both with life and thought about life, but it was always somewhat too soft with that sense of the fragility of things and their transcience that belongs, of right, to the tenderness of youth, and a sense of the immanence of deity that comes only to the reflective or religious mind. One of her earliest poems begins:

O God, I thank Thee that all things must end
    That soon pale life shall strive and cry no more,
That Death tears down the veil Faith cannot rend,
    And wide before me stands an open door. . . .

Or, a complete poem, *Morning Glory:*

Perfectly pure and pale, a thing apart,
    Where long rank grass and common hedge-flowers grow,
Most like a star cast down from Heaven thou art,
    Here by the dusty wayside, lying low
With one brown earth stain at thy radiant heart.

Or, *Monotony:*

      Oh, poor, pale days that pass me by
        Thus one by one,

>   With neither tempest nor blue sky,
>   Nor wind nor sun.
>   Glad without smiles, and sad without a sigh,
>   Beloved of none;
>   Content to fade away and die
>   At set of sun.
>   With neither stars nor flowers nigh,
>   Nor evening breeze nor sunset sky
>   When day is done.

At random one opens her very latest poems and comes upon her sensitive lines, *Lux Umbra Dei*:

>   Blue and red and yellow still
>   Paint the sky and climb the hill,
>   Whilst the wind whispers to the trees
>   'All the earth and sky are made
>   Out of the shadow of a shade,
>   But from the shadow of God are these.'
>   When primroses are in the grass
>   And the blue waves of bright air
>   Are touched with the sunsets rose,
>   Wrapped in three colours everywhere
>   We see the shadow of God pass
>   And know what each tranced dewdrop knows,
>   What pilgrim glory through the ether flows.

And the last poem, though not latest in her mind:

>   The storm has cleared the air,
>   The sea holds the sun and the blue sky,
>   Suddenly everywhere, shining, all things are one . . .
>   Is it like this when you die?

For her, pity came early and stayed with her patiently to the end. She spent her life in the service of the poor. For Con, more adventurous, scarcely at all reflective, and never patient, that pity came late and strayed from her to the end. She saw things in the form of a drama in which she must always be hero. Her story was therefore longer and more varied. Only with great difficulty did she abandon the current of the life – that strangely divided life – into which she was born.

§ 2

The history of her family – typical of a hundred and one Anglo-Irish families – pointed the way to only three kinds of life: either she became an ornament, at best graceful, of the little social round that divided itself between the drawing-rooms of Sligo, and the drawing-rooms of Dublin and London; or she became a philanthropist, in Ireland or out of it, and with more hope of requital out of it than in it; or she might snatch, from whatever Victorian society still retained of the traditions of the Anglo-Irish bucks, as gay and unconventional a life as she dared and her allowance could afford. (Had she been born a man she might have chosen other alternatives – the pursuit of wealth or a career.) In the event she did a little of all three, but because she was a woman different from all her clan, she went beyond its traditions and broke all its traditions, and is remembered and commemorated because she broke them. She is the only woman of the Big Houses to whose memory a public monument has been erected by the pennies of the simple folk of Ireland.

She was one of a family that had been adventurous in its day. The first Gore, or Goore, to land in Ireland came in the middle of the last great rising of the native Irish – the rebellion of the two Hughs, O'Neill and O'Donnell. It was just ten years since the Armada; it was the year before Essex came on his unfortunate expedition; two years before the end of the century, 1598. The North and West was the place for men of action at that date. Gore brought with him a troop of horse, served under Mountjoy, and was treated by him with esteem. Even before the rebellion ended, he had been given grants of land by Elizabeth, and after the rising was over, and the two Hughs were fled to Spain, he got a further share of the spoils of war, from James who also made him a baronet in 1621. He married the niece of that Earl of Strafford who was so basely given to the mob by Charles in 1641. The first of the confiscators of that line, he was known as an 'undertaker' because he undertook land from its former proprietors, who became his tenants or wandered homeless and vengeful in the woods.

His fortune was augmented by his son, Sergeant-Major, later Sir Francis, Gore who ran with the hares and hunted with the hounds on the Irish front during the Civil War. Like a true adventurer he helped to hold Sligo for the Parliament but corresponded secretly with the Royalists about the possibilities of surrender. For his good will be obtained at the Restoration land in three counties. To this he added land in a fourth by marrying an heiress, the daughter of a man who had played the same game as himself during the 'troubled times'. His title died with his grandson, Nathaniel, but his methods did not.

Nathaniel Gore also married a woman of property, the daughter of one Captain Booth of Sligo who had been trusted by the Cromwellians but who lived to enjoy what he had held from them under Charles. That marriage with Miss Letitia Booth took place in 1711. By that date the large estates of Sir Paul and Sir Francis had been broken up among children, grandchildren and great-grandchildren; they were a prolific family – Sir Francis had thirteen sons and daughters (and his wife married again after he died). Nathaniel lived at Ardtermon near the town of Sligo but with his marriage he received land and property within the walls. It was he who first came eastward to Lissadell, in the seventeen hundreds. His son became in 1760, the first baronet, Sir Nathaniel Booth-Gore. (The name Booth, here a first name, was later adopted as a surname.) With him adventure died; wars were finished and done with; there were no more spoils. What property became added to the estate of Lissadell after his date was added by more genteel methods than confiscation.

With Nathaniel's great-grandson, Sir Robert, a house, large enough to be known locally as 'The Court', was built on the demesne – not long before the Black Forties. This is the house in which Constance spent her childhood; a solid impressive-looking, double building of cut limestone, faintly suggestive of the eighteenth century, a typical George IV house, plain, wide-eaved, with regular windows. There is nothing genial about the house, and one wonders if there was anything very genial about Sir Robert who built it. He was known to some as a fair landlord – probably there were worse – and as a warm-hearted man; but his name will be remembered (in the long Irish memory) only as that of the man who added the Seven Cartrons to the estate of Lissadell. It was one of those pitiful stories that are connected with the names of so many Irish landlords. The Seven Cartrons were in the town land of Ballygilgan – some eight hundred acres of what was once church land – on which lived a large number of poor fishermen and landholders. When Sir Robert arranged to take up the lease he decided to clear out the tenants, offered them land elsewhere – apparently very poor land, for most accepted the alternative of £2 per head for passage-money to America, and £4 compensation. The clearance ended, if the local folk-memory is to be believed– and the folk-memory usually is – in tragedy. The shipload of evicted tenants sank, a few miles out from Sligo, in Donegal Bay. Fifteen years after, however, in 'Black Forty-seven', he was so generous to the poor in the day of their suffering that he received an address from the parish-priest of Drumcliff thanking him for his kindness. It is recorded that he spent many thousands of his own personal income to relieve their sufferings.

Con's father, Sir Henry, the fifth baronet, brings Lissadell safely through the days of the Land League, Parnell, and John Redmond. Of him local historians have said many kind things, but none so significant as, in one case, the passing mention of the fact that, as compared with his father, he was more 'frequently at home'. It is a phrase that puts a period to adventure. Where there was kerne and Cromwellian, or rymer, or harper, or piper, and English knight, there is now Christy Conor or Pat O'Rourke ditching by the road; and there, too, under the slight seaborne shower is Sir Henry and the young ladies rolling past in the four-in-hand. 'Grand day, Sir Henry!' they call out, while the cap rises and the back stoops in humble salute. ''Day, Rourke!' The gloved hand holding the whip rises for a second. They look after him without rancour, and resume their ditching. A kind, dacant man, 'frequently at home'.

§ 3

Accepted in that way by the people, it is small wonder if she also accepted the place marked out for her in her time. And she is so pretty, how could they fail to accept her? 'The poor girsha,' they say, 'sure she's like a tame fox slippin' in and out to us, as if someone might be after her to catch her.' And when she comes with little gifts, of sugar or tea or the like, sometimes alone, sometimes with Eva, she is so natural that she might be one of themselves. She sits up on the high settle by the open hearth and talks to them simply and directly, while Eva sits for fun on the creepy stool before the fire – like a fairy queen when the sun through the small loop-hole window strikes her fair ramparts of hair and the downy fur of her neck. But as a rule she liked to go for long walks alone, calling in to a cottage if it came her way; and, as that was unheard of when she was very small, she would have to steal away from the house and the governess; and by the time they noticed her absence she was off through the shrubberies and the copses and there was no finding her until she chose to present herself of her own accord. Then she would be loud in her triumph.

She would tell the names of the children she had been playing with, the games they taught her. 'There was never a bit of the young lady from Lissadell about her,' they said, old men, now, who when they were all youngsters held her small hands in theirs.

She craved freedom from the beginning.

Quite early in childhood (an additional nightmare to her chronically distracted governesses) came the delights of ponies. To begin with, the pony was led in a dignified manner, like a dog on a chain, up and down the drive of Lissadell, with Con exercising all her considerable powers of persuasion on the nervous governess, who escorted her, to be allowed to ride by herself. After a period of this supervision, when her parents were satisfied that she would not normally fall off a gently moving pony, a man from the estate was detailed to take care of her as she rode. He used to run beside her down the drive, and sometimes on the grass beside it, holding her bridle, getting very hot and out of breath, in perpetual terror that she would escape. Con used to implore, coax, and threaten him to be allowed to trot by herself. 'I'll tell my father, if you don't let me go,' she once exclaimed. But the man, fearing rather that her father would be told if he *did* let go, and aware also, which Con was not, of the presence of a governess who had overheard her remark, then and always, refused to be moved. Eventually, however, she triumphed. One day as she was trotting down the drive, with her attendant and perspiring servitor clutching at the leading rein, she suddenly stirred the pony into a gallop. The man, taken by surprise, lost his hold and fell; and Con, freed from captivity, careered off down the avenue, pursued by the haloos and 'Hei-hei's' of the terrified stable-lad.

When she returned, assuming with childish logic that the fact she had met with no disaster proved that she was capable of controlling the pony by herself, she demanded in the future to be allowed to ride alone. Her request was, with considerable hesitation, granted; but the reservation was made that, whenever she went on the road, she should be accompanied by a groom to ride with her. Seeing that this was the best she could get at the moment, the child accepted the compromise. She was not, at any rate, to be tethered any more to a pedestrian. She merely exerted herself to secure the applause of the groom. She soon succeeded. After a short time his loud praises of her horsemanship persuaded her parents to relax even that supervision.

Free, she proceeded to employ her freedom. She spent every available minute of the day on horseback, going out as soon as she was released from her lessons, frequently arriving back late for meals or periods of further instruction. She was a well-known sight, as she careered over the country, chasing sheep or cattle whenever she met them in the fields, and urging her pony to exertions which its placid soul would otherwise never have dreamed of. She was completely fearless, but what she possessed in temerity her governesses gained in timidity. Even when her family had become resigned to her activities, they clung to their pessimism. They were always afraid that one day she would be brought back home with a broken neck. Con was fully aware of their fears, and spared no pains to add fuel to their apprehensions. She described to them, with acute relish, the ditches she had jumped, the banks over which she had scrambled, the antics she had made her pony perform. There was one of them in particular to whom she had an almost passionate devotion, and whom she invested with the endearing nickname of 'Squidge'. For 'Squidge' she reserved the accounts of her most hair-splitting adventures, even inventing them for the wicked pleasure of seeing the good soul fidget with nervousness; for 'Squidge' was much too astute to express open disapproval. She was for a time equal to the child, whom she adored, but ultimately her authority collapsed, and she retired to the more restful life of a convent where there were no Cons and no ponies to make her poor heart go palpitating with dread.

She was a curious, possibly a unique, child. In the solid, secure respectability of the Gore-Booth family she was indeed something of a freak. She did, it is true, in certain respects resemble her mother, who died only a short time before her daughter. But the kindness and imaginativeness of Georgina Lady Gore-Booth's nature were balanced always by a sense of what was 'correct'. She knew always by instinct what was the right, the inevitable thing for her to do in any situation, and did it. Georgina Lady Gore-Booth, visiting the cottagers, was always Lady Gore-Booth, the mistress of Lissadell 'out' visiting; they knew their place, and she knew hers. Constance, playing with the children of the same cottages, was a child playing with fellow children. They met on equal terms. That was the difference. And that is why Georgina Lady Gore-

Booth, charming and gracious lady that she was, belongs to the past; while her daughter belongs to the democratic Ireland of to-day.

As childhood faded, the differences between her and the rest of her family became more marked. She grew less tolerant of the routine of family life. She became anxious always to be in the limelight, always to be the centre of attention. Parties and visitors she liked, because she knew that they provided opportunities for her to show off. At home, when attention was lacking she withdrew into herself, finding interest in her painting or in reading; more generally in painting, for the contents of the library at Lissadell were not such as would quicken the imagination of a child in revolt. One feels she had much more in common with that earlier (almost legendary) Lady Gore, who chose to order her coachman to drive her about the very brim of Derk, at Knoclane, out on the crater-brim of the Atlantic where far below the waters roared and bellowed like ravening animals in a pit.

She was at her happiest out on the windy uplands, the fields rolling past her and the thud of the hoofs on the sod beneath. Of those days Mr. E. Rowlette, of Cash, near Sligo, writes:

'My first recollections of Miss Gore-Booth go back as far as the late 1870's, when as a little girl, her hair flowing about her shoulders, mounted on a small pony, I first saw her hunting with the Co. Sligo Harriers.

'I remember watching a good hunt in Ballincar, when she rode right up with the huntsman, giving him perhaps somewhat less "law" at his fences than the strict etiquette of the occasion prescribed, never indeed allowing his horse more than a couple of lengths lead during any part of the run. I remember some of the fences they jumped. I have sometimes seen them jumped since, but never without considerable self congratulation by the few who got over safely. I remember the groom who was out to take care of the child, looking far from happy as he tried rather hopelessly to get a little closer to his charge. And I remember the delighted exclamations of some of the country people on foot – "My God! Look at little Miss Gore! Isn't she great!"

'From that time on, Miss Gore-Booth quickly developed into an exceptionally high class rider to hounds. During what is now getting on to a fairly long life, I have had a good deal of experience of riding to hounds and racing, and I have some knowledge of the form of many of the distinguished and very excellent lady riders of to-day. It is, however, my considered opinion that I have never known any woman whose skill in riding to hounds equalled that of Miss Gore-Booth. I am doubtful whether I ever knew any man who was an all round better rider.

'Miss Gore-Booth always rode in a side saddle, and this would, in these times, be considered a handicap by many, more especially as regards Race Riding. It certainly never handicapped her in riding to hounds. I do not know whether her seat on horseback would be considered quite orthodox, or whether it would conform to strictly conventional standards. Indeed, I should think that it would scarcely have occurred to her to inquire into such a detail in relation to her riding – or in relation to anything else. She rode with a particularly long leather, and affirmed that it made practically no difference to her comfort whether she kept her foot in the stirrup or hanging loose. At the same time she had a noticeably free and graceful seat at all paces; a particularly strong and steady seat when riding a gallop, or over fences; and I cannot imagine that there ever was the slightest danger of her saddle causing "sore-back" – a danger that many careful side-saddle riders seem to have trouble in avoiding. Indeed she rode so easily and synchronized so naturally with the movements of her horse, that it looked as if she could ride "side-saddle" without a saddle at all! She undoubtedly excelled anyone I have seen riding in some of the rarer attributes of horsemanship.

'For instance, amongst the people – men or women – with whom I have hunted, or against whom I have ridden races, I have usually been able to form a fairly close estimate of how far he or she would be prepared to go. Although I hunted regularly with Miss Gore-Booth for about sixteen seasons, and rode, I think, in all the Point-to-Point races in which she competed, I never could set any limit as to what she would do in an emergency. Not only was she absolutely without fear, so far as I ever discovered, but her temperament as a horsewoman was wonderful. Although very keen and anything but phlegmatic when hounds were running, she never under any circumstances lost her head, got flurried, or fussed her horse. The most skittish youngster, once she got on his back, seemed at once to gain confidence and to ride and jump like an experienced hunter. Indeed her domination of her mount, and the apparently perfect understanding that always existed between them seemed to be almost uncanny. I have never seen her punish a horse, and I cannot recollect that there ever appeared to be any reason for her to do so. As to her keenness, I recollect a year in the early 'nineties when she hurried home from London, arriving in Sligo about 11.30 a.m. after an all night journey, had her horse waiting at the Meet at twelve o'clock, mounted (having changed into riding kit on the train) and started to ride a drag hunt of about five miles over a very close country. She was first home in the run in, which was definitely arranged as a Point-to-Point for the last mile, and finished as fresh as paint.

'When I say that, during all the years I saw her hunting, I can only remember seeing her get one fall (although I heard of at least one other fall she got when I did not happen to be out) and when I add that during most of that time she hunted regularly two days a week over a very close and "trappy" country, was always in the first flight – very often alone – I know that hunting people, who did not see her ride, will scarcely credit my statement. Nevertheless it is a simple fact. Some of the credit, I admit, was due to her old horse "Max", and I am certain that she would have attributed even more of the credit to him than I do.

'This appreciation of Miss Gore-Booth's horsemanship may perhaps seem extravagant to present day readers, so few of whom had an opportunity of judging her capability at first hand. I know that my estimate would have been endorsed by one of the finest steeplechase riders of his day – Captain Bidgood, an army officer, who had been a leading amateur rider in India and who hunted with her in Sligo for about five seasons. While here he made a speciality of training horses specially for Punchestown, where he had remarkable success. He used to school his young chasers over the most difficult banks he could find in our country, and used to get Miss Gore-Booth, riding Max to give them a lead over a very stiff course in their winding-up preparation. There was no other "combination" in the country at that time that could have answered "the captain's" purpose.

'I do not think that Madame Markievicz would have considered any description of her hunting adequate unless it included some details about her favourite hunter Max. Max was a "Sir George" gelding, foaled I think in 1884, and regularly hunted, usually two days a week, from 1888 to 1898 by Miss Gore-Booth. He was almost thoroughbred, fast for a hunter, and a wonderful jumper. He could not fall when ridden by his owner, though I confess I have seen him come a bad enough cropper when lent for a day to a friend, and on one occasion, when I rode him in a jumping competition for Miss Gore-Booth, after she had practically ceased riding, he jumped very moderately. He was then an old cart horse, but I think the main cause of our want of success was due to the fact that I did not in time appreciate the fineness of his mouth. He had always been ridden, during some twelve seasons, by a woman who had the lightest hands of anyone I have seen riding, and who allowed him more discretion than I found myself able to do on the spur of the moment. By the second round we were beginning to understand one another a little, but we had then gone into arrears. I remember once, while hounds were "beating" in the Cloverhill country and the field was idling along behind, we came to a gap in a high wall, which was temporarily closed by an iron bar resting from wall to wall, perhaps two and a half feet from the ground. Max walked up to the little jump, but instead of popping over, stood still and looked at the obstacle. Miss Gore-Booth patted his neck and said, "Doesn't the poor old boy like iron-fences? I wonder what he will do with it! He must soon decide, because he cannot hold up the Hunt." Max, having realized that he must get out of the way, and knowing full well that he could not turn aside, deliberately and standing quite still, lifted a front foot, hooked it across the bar, and pulling the bar gently and very carefully to the ground, walked quietly out.

'I saw the old horse when he was enjoying a leisurely old age at Lissadell. He had neither scratch nor scar nor blemish on any leg. Indeed, I do not remember that during his whole career he ever once cut himself. He was a wonderful hunter, but much of the credit for his prowess was undoubtedly due to the way he was trained, cared for and ridden by his owner. I have heard her express a hope that when she went to Heaven, Max would be there to carry her, and I couldn't have wished her a better mount.

'Some time about the middle 'nineties there was started in the Co. Sligo a challenge Point-to-Point race between the two harrier packs then hunting the country. The conditions were that five selected riders to represent each hunt should compete over a $4\frac{1}{2}$ mile course, and that the hunt which scored the least number of marks (1 mark being allotted to the horse finishing first, 2 marks to the second, 3 to the third and so on to the tenth) should be the winner. Miss Gore-Booth was of course one of the five riders selected to represent the Co. Sligo Harriers Hunt. Unfortunately at the date fixed for the Meeting Max was not available. He was, I think, down with influenza, and when the four other selected horses were excluded nothing of outstanding merit was available for Miss Gore-Booth. However, a good sportsman, the late Edward Foley, J.P., placed a useful hunting mare at her disposal, and she ultimately finished second of ten starters, being just beaten out of first place by Major C. K. O'Hara, the master of the rival hunt.

'One incident during the race is, I think, worth recording, as throwing a strong light on Miss Gore-Booth's sportsmanship as well as her horsemanship.

'About a mile from the start the course crossed a public road. This was in the comparatively early days of Point-to-Point Meetings, and courses – at any rate in Co. Sligo – were not very carefully prepared or elaborately readied for racing. Each rider was supposed to pick out his own line from flag to flag and to decide for himself where he would jump each individual fence. Miss Gore-Booth selected a weak spot in a high clipped hedge to jump on to the road – there was a fairly stiff wall directly opposite – and had committed her horse to the jump, when another representative of her own team, whose valour was beyond question, and whose mount was pulling hard, rushed up almost alongside, and a collision or at any rate a bad jostle seemed to be inevitable. Miss Gore-Booth pulled a little to one side, jumped the high hedge alongside the gap, and got safely over both road fences, leaving the easy line to the other competitor. I afterwards measured the hedge where she jumped on to the narrow macadamized road. It was 4 feet 6 inches on the field side and 6 feet 3 inches on the road side and Miss Gore-Booth was riding a mare that she had never ridden over a fence prior to the race. I afterwards discussed the affair with her, and expressed the opinion that the other rider was in the wrong, and that she would have been fully justified in holding her course; also that, had she done so, it was practically certain, from the position of the horses at the time, that *she* would not have suffered in a possible collision, and that the other rider would have had himself only to blame if he got into trouble. She acknowledged that this was so, but added: "But you must remember that it was a team race, and we all thought that Mr. —— was riding the best of the Sligo horses. Besides I was the only woman riding, and you can imagine what everyone would have said if I had knocked him out of the race."

'I am bound to admit that she also added that under the circumstances she would *never have dreamt* of pulling aside in favour of one of the visiting team!

'There was a story of one of her feats of horsemanship during her very early years – how she once jumped her horse over a cow – of which I had heard several versions. I once asked her for the true particulars and her reply, as I remember it was:

' "That was a *very* silly story. Some visitors and I were out riding near home, and we saw two cows lying a few yards apart on the grass beside the road. Both lay facing the road and X said to me: 'Con, I dare you to jump the two cows.' So of course I had to. I got over the first all right and I was just about over the second, too, when the silly thing got up. The cow and I were both knocked over. I had a collar bone broken, but luckily neither of us was hurt."

"On reading over these more or less random reminiscences I fear that they may possibly suggest to knowledgeable riding people that Miss Gore-Booth's undoubted enthusiasm somewhat exceeded her discretion and judgement. Indeed, I think that some such idea may at times have been unconsciously fostered by a section of the people who usually hunted with her, and who needed some explanation of the fact that again and again they failed to get away on equal terms or to show at the end of a run well up with her. I believe that such an impression would be entirely wrong. When riding to hounds she had a remarkably quick eye for country, and seemed instinctively to recognize the easiest line. She never adopted gallery riding; and during a run she always appeared to get away well with hounds and to stay there without special effort. If, however, there were no easier way out, the most forbidding fence never caused her a momentary hesitation. In Point-to-Point races she always took far more than the usual amount of care to familiarize herself thoroughly with the course beforehand – more important perhaps in those days than at present, when courses are so carefully prepared that little room is left for individual selection by the riders. And I have never known her to deviate by a yard from the course as selected by her except in the one case I have previously referred to. From seeing her ride training gallops and trials I know that she possessed the faculty so rare even amongst the best amateur riders, of riding a collected finish in which she never overlooked the necessity of carefully maintaining the balance of her horse.

'As indicated before, she had in this respect the advantage of tuition by an exceptionally skilful race rider – Captain Bidgood. She knew more about the theory of riding races, and about the practical points that it always pays to remember during a race than (say) ninety-nine out of every hundred amateurs I have seen riding. Her temperament and her horsemanship were, I think, entirely her own. The great difference between her and other good riders was that she could always be depended upon to remember and to put into practice the tactics she had decided upon at the right time, while so many good riders remember just a little too late.

'I remember once discussing with her the temperament of a member of our hunt, whose riding we both admired – the late James Fitzgerald. She said that during a race or a fast run with hounds, he always appeared to be just on the edge of losing complete self-control, but that one who knew him, knew perfectly well that he would be the very last to do so, and she described this characteristic as peculiarly and exclusively Irish. Miss Gore-Booth had, to some extent, the same characteristic, though perhaps, to a casual observer, the outward and visible sign of her inner tension were even better suppressed. At the same time I do not think that her temperament would have been quite correctly described as "peculiarly and exclusively Irish".

'She was a great horsewoman and a very gallant and loyal sportswoman.'

§ 4

She carried her horses into the drawing-room. When her friends were gathered for a children's party, she was more likely to be found in a corner of the room sketching horses than in the centre of the floor playing forfeits. She made pretence that she would always find more pleasure, anyway, in four-legged animals than in two-legged ones, and made it with an exasperating superciliousness that must sometimes have brought a tingling in the palm of her governess. It did not matter, perhaps, a great deal at Lissadell where everyone knew her and her ways, and where she was yet little more than a child to whom much was to be permitted. But time was getting on. And London would not be so indulgent as Lissadell, nor could she be permitted to walk for ever as if she wore ten-league boots, or talk loudly and bluntly, sometimes more loudly than a stable-boy. Her mother would find her tucked away from the romping groups and suggest as casually as she could, fidgeting ominously with her watch-chain as she spoke, that 'surely Con must want to be in this round of hide-the-slipper?' And from her stool Con would shout across the room, 'No, mother, thank you very much, just at the hind-leg now, awfully difficult, don't mind me ...' – and her dark head would sink again and her tongue curl out as her pencil manœuvred about a fetlock.

At her ordinary studies she was as good as one could expect – and governesses soon learned to be modest in their expectation of Con. At these lessons which were taught outside the regular hours, however, dancing, needlework, deportment, she was ostentatiously bored. Needlework one could understand, though when there were pools on the gravel and heavy mists hid the sea and hills, one might have expected her to be glad of any diversion. But even dancing she had little taste for; and for such elegant studies as the curtsey she had a positive hate. This was particularly odd. To be bored with the curtsey, so suggestive of everything aspired to by a young lady of class and breeding, the one piece of knowledge necessary for a presentation at court, was almost as insolent as to be bored with Royalty herself. It looked very much like a naughty pose. It was not really. Con Gore-Booth simply did not respond to the glamour of a city five hundred miles away, or of a Court that had no connection with the life of County Sligo whose green and golden world turned on its axis as by the grace of God and the force of habit.

Even when she and Eva made the long journey to London and professionals took her in hand; when really exciting parties were arranged for her and she wore really exciting dresses, the perverse girl refused to be excited. This was London, and it was fun to be there, and that ended it. But though to her it was only fun and it was only a holiday, she was about to be held in the same dilemma that had always held girls of her type; pretty little sea-fish taken out of a sea-pool and put into a glass bowl, and expected ever after to be equally happy in whichever water they swam. London, for all that it was a funeral-card, soot and Portland stone; and the only horses she saw there were either dray-horses pulling the trams or hired hacks in the Row; for all that every green patch was square, or railed and ruled; for all that it was noisy and dirty, London had a charm of its own. The nice English were pleased by her looks. They liked the natural ways of 'the wild Irish girl' – as they said too audibly. She found herself listened to, looked at, and admired, and her vanity was flattered by her success. The parties became a stage and there was often an audience. Once when she was ruling a party, and there was some discussion, she saw a famous diplomat of the day standing at the door of the room, watching her with interest. She ran up to him – there were other grown-ups about the walls but she ignored them, possibly because she was already feminine enough to detect the admiration in his eyes – and she appealed to him for a ruling. To the embarrassment of the elders he snatched her up in his arms and said, 'I wonder how many hearts will you break when you are grown-up?' After a few experiences like that, though slowly as yet, for she had a good flair for dramatic effect, and with the proper degree of indifference to the whole matter, she indicated one day to her mother that she did not mind if a party were planned for her; in fact, just for once she would rather like it. A biographer may be permitted to suppose a suppressed sigh of relief on the part of Lady Gore-Booth, suppose an inner smile of triumph because 'the girl was growing-up at last'.

So, with the widening of her little world, there came a long truce to whatever there was of conflict in her between sympathy for the cabins and indifference to the cabins. The curtain had already lifted from her stage before she came to the end of her teens and was a young lady in earnest, and as her own life began she forgot theirs. With her sisters she had already made the new generation of Lissadell famous throughout Sligo, for when she drove dashingly in the four-in-hand through the streets of Sligo town – all that is lovely in innocence and youth in her face and figure, the arrogance of unbroken will, the belief in the beauty of living, the fearlessness of unbroken strength – people felt that a wind had blown from Knocknarea where queens lie buried. Had she been a man, had she had the knowledge and the desire, one feels she could have led her people to any courage or any folly, as young Red Hugh O'Donnell had led them against her own ancestor three hundred years before. She became, instead, like his kinsman O'Neill, that Earl of Tyrone who was honoured with him and buried somewhere near him in Valladolid. She was to go in her loveliness of her twenty-one summers to curtsey before Victoria, where, so long before, her kinsman

Sir Francis Gore, had knelt in homage to Gloriana. The ancient mould was so far unbroken. Her career as a young Anglo-Irish woman was panning out in a perfectly normal fashion.

As a matter of fact, even in her more attractive adventures, she was being painfully true to type. The only things she might have done that she did not do were to be abducted by night and to ride her horse into the dining-room or up the stairs. Every other Irish wildness she repeated after the fashion of her fathers, and the people, who love and admire tradition of every kind, whether good, bad or indifferent, loved and admired her because she lived with so much traditional dash and fire. For three hundred years the Big House had kept up a reputation for 'divilment' and the folk both preferred divils to devils and divils to angels. 'The divil you know', the saying went, 'is better than the divil you don't know' – which is merely another way of saying that from the Big House angels were not to be expected, or even desired. An angel would be an unfamiliar divil.

So when one asks around Sligo, to-day, for the people's thought on Constance Markievicz, one hears not of her fight in Easter Week, certainly not of her socialist ideas, but of the picture she made flying through the streets driving a carriage and eight horses. (Dividing by half we get the four-in-hand.) One hears of the snowy night she galloped across the soft fields and on a little height found her horse come to a sudden shivering halt; as she alighted she heard muffled voices beneath her and then saw a dim light – she was on the roof of a house. Or one hears of her escapades in disguise – she was always fond of 'dressing-up'. Of these the most pleasant tells of a lesson she taught one of her men friends who was rough and unkind to the poor people. She dressed herself as a peasant girl and borrowing a cart and a donkey from one of the cabins went to meet him on a dark road near Lissadell. As he came riding by she accosted him with some simple request and was answered boorishly. She let him rail at her for a few moments and then disclosed herself.

These stories of her youth are endless – the kind of legend natural to a young high-spirited girl. All that one may observe from them is that there is never a trace of vulgarity in her wildness. She was the typical wild Irish girl.

Between that kind of existence, and as she grew a little older, the regular visits to Dublin for the Vice-Regal court, she put her childhood and her youth behind her. Then, when she was twenty, she went to London for her coming-out. She was presented at Court in 1889 and began her first London season immediately after. It was the last 'regular' thing she did. Lady Gore-Booth hovered over her daughter, with the natural pride of a mother in a beautiful daughter, and the natural expectation of a woman who was certain to be mother-in-law to some distinguished young Englishman. But to Eva and Mabel, back in Lissadell, awaiting their own turn to enter the world of fashion no palpitating letter ever came to announce the triumph of Constance. The year passed, and yet another year, and Lady Gore-Booth had to think of launching Eva, and then her third daughter, Mabel, and as she did so nothing but disquieting news came from Constance. Some sort of restlessness, from then on a recurring grain in her character, seemed to have gripped her. Having sated herself on the triumphs of the drawing-rooms she was eager for some utterly different life. She told her parents that she wished to take up art. The characteristic – legend is that she threatened, if they would not permit her to do what she wanted, to run away and earn her living posing in the nude.

Lady Gore-Booth was too kind and imaginative a woman to force any of her children to a career they disliked. She hid her disappointment and let Constance have her way. A little later she did the same when Eva wished to take up social work in Salford. And after all could she be blamed by her family? She was merely following out in all those adventures, whose news so troubled Lady Gore-Booth, the Anglo-Irish tradition of the wild Irish. She was a fine, brave, high-spirited, generous girl. If her father would not take her with him in his explorations of the Arctic; if there was nothing interesting for her to do at home – what more natural than she should be restless and dissatisfied, and in the 1890's anticipate by thirty years the unconventional Twenties?

If the friends with whom she stayed in Bryanston Square recall of her a variety of oddities, it will be noticed that most of them suggest only the most attractive spontaneity. At a regatta at Henley she was in a refreshment tent when the Prince of Wales entered; in the sudden silence following his appearance her voice was heard to say, 'Who is that very fat man who has just come in? When she was returning later from a bridge-party at Hounslow – she had won a little money – and saw the homeless creatures stretched on the Bayswater Road benches, she stopped the horses and running to the sleeping figures thrust silver into their hands, one after another, until she had no more. She had a pet snake and would wear it in her hair as a head-dress for parties, hoping, without doubt, that it would prod its fang at every gentleman introduced to her. (She kept it in a glass-covered box and naturally it escaped, and naturally she was charmed beyond words.) As she was driving in her friend's carriage one night to the theatre she saw two drunken men fighting in some West-end street. Stopping the carriage she alighted, in all her finery, and flung herself between them; and she did not leave them until the onlookers, encouraged by her, intervened also. She had odd friends – foreign students, Indians, ragged men, whom she would bring to tea to Bryanston Square and be surprised if Bryanston Square did not fall on their necks. She lived in a room all topsy-turvy with clothes, and books, and canvases – she would even leave her things on the stairs, as if it were as good a place as any other. But when a wretched 'topsy-turvy' man kept begging her, once, in Dublin for a few pence, because his liquor displeased her, she gave him a slam in the face that bowled him into the gutter and walked on with her pained and outraged friend as if nothing had happened.

If one is willing to admit that such a woman was at the mercy of her natural composition, she might be called a child of nature. If she was the natural product of her country, her country's history, and her times, another example of the fine material of the Big Houses of Ireland going to waste for lack of some force which would mould them into use, then her abandonment of fashion for art was original, significant, and courageous.

She was entered at the Slade in 1893, under Alphonse Legros; and at the same time she worked also under Anna Nordgren in a studio near the Fulham Road. Of this period A. ni G. writes: 'It was in one of a long row of London studios – The Boltons – off Fulham Road, that I first saw Constance Gore-Booth. She was in her first freshness of youth and beauty. It was still the time of the aesthetic movement and the studios were full of artists in more or less shabby blouses, gay, hopeful, chattering. One day into their midst sailed Constance Gore-Booth in some long frock of the period which I remember only as part of an enchanting picture. It was not as a pastime that she took up art. She worked hard and seriously for some hours each day drawing from the life. And later on when Miss Nordgren came to stay with her at Lissadell and they painted out of doors together her work gained constantly in technique and light and colour.' Sometimes, here, when the model was tired or ill Constance would pose in her stead, but never in the nude. That is certain, for A. ni G. shared models with Anna Nordgren and must have known if she had done.

Her name remained on the roll of the Slade for some four years, to October, 1897. By 1898 she was established in Paris where she lived in the Rue Campagne Premier, in Montparnasse and studied at Julian's, the great studio for English students in those days, just off the Rue de Rennes. The master was the great Jean Paul Laurens; he would have taught her at a woman's branch, for at Julian's classes were not then mixed. She was thus centred in the heart of Bohemianism, certainly not the original Bohemia of Montmartre made famous by such as Baudelaire and commemorated by such as Murget, but to her, fresh from the 'staid Slade' and the dewiness of Sligo, and the correctitude of the London salons, it was as exciting as it would be, even to-day, to some equally untravelled young woman from Nebraska or Ohio. She was young; she had money; she was a beauty. At night in the Harcourt, the Boudet, the Lavenue, as she walked along the boulevards, at the Concert Rouge or the Concert Colonne, wherever crowds gathered for pleasure, she must have known that eyes followed her and that men admired her. Soon it was her hey-day and her full moon. She was in love.

Casimir Joseph Dunin-Markievicz was already a practiced boulevardier when he met the dark-eyed young Irish-woman who studied at Julian's. He was younger than her by six years (he was born on March 15th, 1874), presently left a widower with one son living. He bore the title of Count by virtue of his descent from one Peter Dunin, a *comes magnus* of the thirteenth century, whose name each branch of his large family adopted to retain the title – so Dunin-Borkowski, Dunin-Korwicki, Dunin-Markievicz. The title, recognized in Prussia in the eighteenth century, was thus much older than the Gore-Booth baronetcy. Casimir was born on the estate of Denhoffovka in the Ukraine, the second son, and one of nine children. As the estates, Rozyn and Zyvolavka, were due to go to his eldest brother John, he was sent to the university at Kiev to be a lawyer. He completed his studies but abandoned his career to be a painter and so came to live and study in Paris.

Before he met Constance Gore-Booth he had already done very well at painting, and he continued to do well up to the first world-war. (His 'Amour', once in the Polish Embassy in London, was given a prize at the Paris Exhibition of 1905. His best-known portrait at that time was of Lord Muncaster. Examples of his work may be seen still in Dublin.) In Paris he had married an Ukranian girl, Mme Neymann, by whom he had two sons, Richard and Stanislaus. Count Stanislaus Dunin-Markievicz is still living, but Richard died almost at the same time as the first Madame Markievicz.

He had also lived up to the popular reputation of artists in regard to morals. He was a large, handsome-looking man, gay and cheerful, free with his money, kind-hearted, fond of company, whether of men or women, above all a man who could not live without an audience, or at least not without a confidante. Of such a man love-affairs were only to be expected. The only trouble with his friends was to distinguish between those that occurred and those that he had wished might have occurred – he was a story-teller of the first water, which is to say that he was a man for whom fiction was much more entertaining than the truth. He would have his friends believe that he had even fought duels for his loves, although listening to the details in his broken English, which he had learned mainly from Constance – with the many 'damns' and 'hells' that she told him were *de rigueur* in the best society – one never knew whether to laugh or be serious. 'Ah! I come in and there I see a man's hat and coat. I sit down at the piano in the drawing-room and I play and I play, loud as hell, the *Dead March* from *Saul*. I put my revolver on the piano. I cry out. Then the door open and out come a pale Jesus Christ – straw beard, white face. I shoot over his head – not to hurt him, you understand – just to let him know what I am. There you are! Well! Very good! *He* never come again!'

One is therefore left to choose between Cassie's loves and Cassie's wishes and Cassie's stories. One hears of his red-haired model, Martha, whose portrait he painted, and who was reputed to have been his mistress for a long time. (Afterwards he wrote a play called *Martha*.) He would have people believe that he fought a duel with the Count Guy de la Prade over a beautiful young English widow who later married the French count instead of the Polish. He loved another English girl, remembered only by the name Alice, whom he met through his friendship with Constance. That affair became rather piquant when he began to pay more attention to her friend than to herself. Cassie's kinswoman (R. M. de R. P.)

recalls:— 'Alice was Constance's friend and Cassie told me, "I could not be a pig and marry Alice – I met her through Constance." When Alice died at an unsuccessful childbirth, she sent Cassie a turquoise ring to wear in her memory. And Cassie christened his daughter, Maeve Alice.'

It was at this practised man of the world that, if tradition is to be believed, Constance Gore-Booth set her cap. They appeared to have a good deal in common, almost identical temperaments. He was full of life and she was full of energy; he joked a good deal, and she loved practical jokes; he had been reared in the country and she loved the country; they were both extremely boyish; he loved the theatre and she loved the limelight; he craved the society of women, and was an excellent boon-companion for men – she enjoyed the society of men. Like enough to appear to be a perfect match, not different enough to find out how different until it was too late. The truth is – as time was to show – they made perfect friends. The main difference between them was that in her there lurked a fundamental earnestness, while he was a born dilettante; yet even there they came near to one another, for he was serious about the most superficial things and she was superficial about the most serious things. Worst of all, she was, it is clear, sexually cold. These, alas, were things that nobody could then have realized.

For the present, however, only the gaiety of young love counted with her, the adventure and the romance. She had her will of him during those months of courting – for if he was much more practised in the ways of love and of the world she had the stronger will – he was the kind of man who would defer in his kindness, not to speak of his love, to any woman. By day they worked – a little – and at night there were the cafés, not perhaps the very fashionable ones, but as good as Cassie could afford, the Lavenue for its gardens and for its string orchestra; the Café d'Harcourt for its terrace where they could whisper and dine in the dusk; for dancing to the Bal Bullier on Thursdays, with the artists and models; at the end of the week to the concerts; for the inevitable Robinson with its huts perched in the trees, not to speak of the quiet joys of the Luxembourg gardens, or strolling happy and unaware where the trees sprinkle their leaves over the Seine.

'I think,' she wrote to somebody in Ireland – it may have been her sister, but only the last page of the letter remains – 'I think that you will like him. He fills me with the desire to do things. It is curious. I feel with the combination I may get something done, too. I don't quite know when we shall be married but I wish it to be soon.'

At first her parents were, not unnaturally, a little perturbed. She had been wont to *épater* them a little by her accounts of Paris life until on one occasion her mother sighed that 'she wished there was no such place as the continent'. Certainly, they could not be expected to rejoice at this project of a marriage to a man, and a widower at that, who came from a portion of the continent that one only heard of as an appendage to another portion associated with the idiosyncrasies of barbarians like Peter the Great or Ivan the Terrible; who, in addition, had apparently knocked about other portions of unknown Europe, like Albania, and who was now become one of those cosmopolitan Parisians than which nothing could be more different from Ben Bulben and the tomb of Queen Maeve. If they heard at all of the Impressionists they heard of them only through a slightly doubtful novelist called George Moore; if Cézanne's name then meant anything even to educated people in general, it suggested not so much pictures as the books of his friend Zolà. However, what can parents do in such circumstances? They satisfied themselves of Casimir's origins, title, and general fitness for marriage. (Constance did not mind – she assured them it would make no difference.) As to his particular fitness for their daughter, she assured them of that, too. Anyway, they liked what they saw of Casimir. Indeed one might question a hundred people who knew him and not hear one word to suggest that he was not a gentleman and lovable. So they were married – from 41 Devonshire Place, at Saint Marylebone's Parish Church – September 29th, 1900. The details, supplied no doubt by her mother, to the papers, seem phrased in order to make clear that the marriage was in every way respectable.

'Monsieur Joseph Dunin de Markievicz [*sic*][1] a Polish noble, of Zyvolavka, Poland, and Miss Constance Georgina Gore-Booth, eldest daughter of the late Sir Henry William Gore-Booth, J.P. for Co. Sligo and also D.L., and granddaughter of the late Lieut-Colonel Charles John Hill of Tickill Castle, York. The nuptial ceremony was conducted by the Rev. F. S. Le Fanu, M.A., of Saint John's Church, Dublin,

---

1. Casimir used the form 'Dunin Markiewicz' for his visiting cards. The 'de' he did not use. Constance affected it sometimes but wrote Markievicz not Markiewicz.

40

and the bridegroom was supported by M. Sichalko, of Saint Petersburg, as best man.

'There were only four bridesmaids – Miss Eva Selina Gore-Booth, Miss Mabel Olive Gore-Booth, who were gowned in dark purple satin and fichu frill collarettes of lace, and hats to match their gowns, Miss Mansfield, and Miss Mildred Grenfell, who selected green gowns (in compliment to the Irish connection) trimmed with lace.

'The bride was accompanied by her brother, Josslyn A. R. Gore-Booth, who gave her away.

'Miss Gore-Booth looked exceedingly well in a stately gown of white duchesse satin, and bodice arranged with orange blossoms. Her ornaments were a massive pearl necklace and a splendid diamond crescent and pendant, the gifts of Lady Gore-Booth, and a bouquet of rare exotics tied with satin streamers.

'Among those present at the church were Lord and Lady Muncaster, the Dowager Countess of Kingston, Lord and Lady Kilmarnock, Mr. C. Lumley-Hill, the Hon. Evelyn Ashley, Lady Alice Ashley, Mrs. Ussher, the Misses Sturgis, Miss Gilmer, etc., and after a small reception at 41 Devonshire Place, London, S.W., the newly-married couple left for a continental honeymoon tour, the going-away gown being of a pale-blue cloth, trimmed with lace; and fur and hat en suite.

'The presents were handsome and costly.'

A ceremony planned with calculated modesty, effective but without pomp. Had it been a marriage really satisfying to Lady Gore-Booth it would, one feels, have taken place at St. George's, Hanover Square, or St. Margaret's, Westminster, the reception would not have been 'small', and she would not have been content with 'only four bridesmaids'. But if she had any little secret reservations and timid intuitions, she should have based them not on the bridegroom, as she most likely did, but on the bride. That, however, would be too much to expect of so devoted a mother; as much too much as to expect her, even in her worst nightmare fears, to foresee the day when Constance would pass through London between two wardresses on her way to jail.

The honeymoon was spent in Poland, a country to which Constance immediately lost her heart. She found so much there to remind her of Ireland, the same easy-going way of life, the same haphazard method of getting things done. Yet, in some ways it frightened her. When she came back she said to a friend that she could not really see that Ireland suffered from any political grievances. 'You should see life in Poland!' She wrote home: 'I am delighted with the country – I am almost sorry we are going to live in Ireland. Yet there are tiresome things about it as well. The peasants are miserable. Yesterday we went for a long drive and passed a man lying drunk in the ditch by the roadside. I wanted to get out and help him. But the horses galloped past and Casimir said he would be all right. So there was nothing to be done.' None-the-less the Ukraine was a little jab at her conscience.

They returned to Ireland in the spring of 1901, bringing with them little Stanislaus Dunin, a child of six, the son of Casimir's first marriage. She loved him from the beginning. Her own child, Maeve, was born at Lissadell on November 14th, 1901. Then they returned to Dublin and settled down in St. Mary's, Rathgar, a wedding-present from her mother. It may be characteristic of her that she desired the house passionately; was disappointed to find that it had only a fifty or sixty years lease, and that she left it a year or so after and never lived in it again. It may be characteristic, too, that she filled it, from expensive little curiosity shops, with lovely things that she ceased to love after a few years.

CHAPTER II

SOCIAL LIFE
1900 – 1910

§ 1

THE Markieviczs came to live in an interesting but little society when they came to live in Dublin, itself one of the more interesting of the little capitals of Europe. It was a society having its last hey-day, entirely unaware that it was a hey-day, and entirely unaware that it was not what it had been. It was a self-satisfied, exclusive, limited community gathered together on the right bank of the Liffey; facing its enemies and its conquerors – poverty, business, and a rising democracy on the left bank. It had gathered itself, or rather it had been driven together, about the two last squares as yet unviolated by commerce and utilitarianism – Merrion Square and Fitzwilliam Square. Both of these elegant squares have long since surrendered to both of these inelegant forces, but even already in 1900 society was beginning to be driven from these last strongholds to the suburban roads, chiefly of Rathmines and Rathgar, outside the city.

It is the unwittingness of Dublin society in the nineteen hundreds that makes it so attractive. All through the nineteenth century, this disintegration had been going on like a cancer eating away a man's limb while he watched. Dublin society merely said what a fine limb that had been years and years ago. Across the river fashion had surrendered long since. Slums had enveloped the town house of the Dukes of Leinster in Dominick Street; a college had risen where the Belvederes once lived in Great Denmark Street; the Department of Education had invaded the town house of the Earls of Waterford in Marlborough Street; Mecklenburgh Street where those two 'lovelies', the Duchess of Hamilton and the Countess of Coventry had been born, admitted its fall when it was rechristened Railway Street. With every street on the north side it was the same, going on so long and taking place so slowly that some of the worst slums in Dublin – like those around Railway Street – had not really appeared in 1850. But by 1900 the two counterparts on the north side to Merrion and Fitzwilliam Squares on the south, namely Mountjoy and Rutland, were gone beyond redemption; and the one-time forty or fifty resident peers of Dublin reduced to less than a dozen – and even for that number one had to search the highways and byways. Ignoring it all, Merrion Square sighed at Fitzwilliam Square and then smiled down at its own bright company. Here, where Wilde, and Wellington, and (why not?) even Dan O'Connell had lived, fashion was surely safe.

This contraction to one side of the river, and to one part of that side, contributed to the ossfication of what remained. As the fashionable city was so much the smaller it was also by so much the less distinguished and the less intelligent, and like all small societies it became exceedingly complicated and subtle in its gradations and interrelations. Filled with men retired from the service of the Empire, colonels, barristers, civil servants, judges, county folk, it was a collection of people not only kept together by the common bond of that service, often distinguished, but by the acknowledgment of the unique value and dignity of that kind of career. An extraordinary mental inbreeding was the result, exceedingly tiresome to a native democracy that had little or no interest in their small-scale imitation of London.

There were good clubs, people kept good tables, everybody knew everybody else, there was excellent fellowship. If also there was a lack of general ideas (for personalities invariably become much more intriguing than ideas in small communities), nobody noticed it. In the nineteen hundreds the sun shone only for Merrion Square. If the future owners of Dublin – the men driving the drays through the streets, the popular poets and the dramatists, the journalists, the guttersnipes in the slums, the priests in their presbyteries, the politicians on their tubs, the hucksters in their shops, the artisans and clerks in the warehouses looked with amusement at Merrion Square, the Square was hardly aware of their presence.

Already when the Markieviczs arrived in Dublin the last urban centre was threatened. Rathgar and Rathmines were not merely equal to Merrion Square, but even better than it. (When Cassie returned to Dublin in 1919 Rathmines and Rathgar had almost gone – to-day there is now no select residential quarter left in Dublin.) So, being unable to afford a house outside the city, they compromised by choosing a house in Rathgar. It is characteristic of the tide in which they paddled that since their day St. Mary's has become a Catholic presbytery.

The centre of this self-important little life, they found, or rather Casimir found for she knew it all of old, was the Castle; the secondary centres the racecourses and the hunts. For racing there was Leopardstown, the Curragh, Punchestown, Fairyhouse, Baldoyle and various point-to-points within reach of the city. For hunting there were the Kildares and the Meaths, and individual sportsmen ran small packs of beagles from their houses here and there outside the city. All of them – the hunting and shooting people, the fishermen, yachtsmen, and military folk, met in the clubs or at the Castle levees, and everybody else met intermittently for dinner and bridge, and an occasional dance, in private houses; the more select at the tables of the peerage, of Meath, Powerscourt, and Monck in Wicklow, Carew in Wexford, Talbot de Malahide in North Dublin, Cloncurry and the Fitzgeralds in west Dublin and Kildare, and so forth. The rather less select, a class to which the Markieviczs attached themselves – one must count out the Dudleys in the vice-regal lodge which was, perforce, open to all degrees of society – lived behind those endless high walls that so tiresomely shut in the fields and foothills of Dublin and so often face to the north, partly because eighteenth-century architects had an idea that the south wind brings fevers, but mainly because people wished to face Dublin bay and the open sea and the dim, distant smoke of the city, and the plains of Meath below and beyond. Sometimes they saw as little as nuns in a cloister, their houses smothered in trees, mainly beech, though sometimes with a few remnants of Irish oak or that old Irish yew which is in such places always black with age and ragged from the night rain pattering down from the mountains to the south-west. Here the Markieviczs would visit at night, with the trees dropping rain on the roof of the cab, the Shaws at Rathfarnham, or, down the Naas Road, that O'Brien who was known as Peter the Packer and became the last Lord Chief Justice of Ireland.

The least select of all – though yet highly select in an absolute way of speech – were the colonels and the barristers and the civil-servants who themselves were graded by their degree of proximity to the long-faced, red-brick houses – ruby-brick would be truer to fact – in Merrion Square or Fitzwilliam Square. They lived if not in these squares, along the quiet roads and streets near by, or along the even more noiseless canals where the water between the reeds so often reflected the clouds endlessly floating above them.

As for the common people their Dublin was Joyce's Dublin. They entertained nobody but themselves, nor do they yet entertain. For their social life they supported hundreds of pubs, and for the rest they sat at home. Casimir Markievicz never 'sat at home', in that sense, but in the course of time he became familiar with some of the more reputable pubs in search of brighter entertainment than Rathmines or Rathgar or the city squares could give him – an immigrant boulevardier.

Not that Cassie did not enjoy the Castle round from the beginning; indeed, he liked certain features of it to the end. He liked the colour and movement of it; he liked dressing up in his military uniform or in his court dress; being a born flirt he liked impressing the ladies; he liked the company of the military, and the general atmosphere of wealth and good breeding. I have heard people say he was a snob, but it seems impossible in view of his very democratic behaviour from the time he started theatricals and began to be a *habitué* of the bars. He courted the company of the peerage, it is true, but that was merely to obtain commissions for portraits. If he also objected to Constance's later associations with the Dublin common folk, that was largely because he had small interest in Irish politics. He had, it is also true, an ingrained feeling for class-distinctions, but that does not necessarily make any man a snob.

One excellent story that he was fond of recounting about and against himself may illustrate much of his life and character. It should be read as if told in his own stumbling English. 'I go to the Castle, a dam big swell. Court dress, tails, white stockings, knee-breeches. And before I go I turn about and about for Constance and I say, Do you notice anything? No? Very good. I have a half-pint of Scotch under my tail in my back pocket. Maybe there be no whiskey-balls at the levee. (Whiskey-balls was his joke on *uisgebaugh*.) But there were many whiskey-balls at the levee and I send out my half-pint to the cabbie. When I come out and call my cabbie I am very tight. I lie back and I go to sleep. Suddenly I wake up and I look out. But I see no Rathmines or Rathgar. No St. Mary's. No streets. No lights. I am out in the country. I see trees and the dark fields. I shout to the cabbie but I get no reply. I shout louder but he make no reply. He is tight too. I pull out my sword and I push it through the window in the front and I stick it in his bottom. He rolls on the ground off the car, shouting murder, and the cab begin to go ahead like blue hell. I clamber out and pull at the reins. I turn the nag and I come back looking for the cabbie. He is on the grass and he is shouting that he is killed and that he is all blood. I tell him get up. But he cannot get up. So I have to pick him up, and he is all blood or wet or mud, I do not know which, and all my lovely court dress is ruined. I push him in the cab and I sit up on the box and I beat the nag with my sword and we get home after many, many turnings. I get down, then, and I am terrified that I have killed the cabbie. But when I look into the cab he is fast asleep. Very quietly I tie the reins around the pillar-box opposite St. Mary's and I go into bed. In the morning I look out. No cab. No cabbie. No more I hear about him ever again!'

His English could be much better than this when he chose to take pains, but it sometimes suited him not to: he was able to say rather more *risqué* things in patois than others dared in the King's English. When Viscountess Pirrie, later president of Harland & Wolff's, the Belfast shipbuilders, was giving a fancy dress ball to which everybody was requested to come as something connected with shipping, she asked Cassie what he intended to represent. He said, with the innocent face of a child.

'I vill paint my bottom red and I vill be a liner.' Or so he declared he had said, which with Cassie was never the same thing.

It was part and parcel of not merely his Bohemianism but of hers also that they refused to take the dry and rather wooden social round too seriously. Once she was painting a portrait of the Lord Chief Justice, O'Brien, called Peter the Packer because he had earned an unpleasant reputation for packing juries. In came Diarmuid Coffey, now clerk to the senate, a friend and kinsman of her family, with his dog Peter. 'Aha!' she greeted as she resumed her painting. 'Now I have two Peters – Peter Coffey and Peter the Packer. A little more to the right. Thank your Lordship, lovely colour on that shoulder, now. Peter Packer packed a pack of perjured jurors, so if Peter Packer packed a pack of perjured jurors how many perjured jurors . . .' etc.

These are three incidents, which even if apocryphal, suggest the attitude of the pair to the formal life they were living between 1900 and 1908. The truth is they saw that the life was too small; however much they enjoyed it while it lasted it irked always; they were too poor to do the thing in tip-top style; and neither of them were by nature respecters either of persons or of conventions.

However, they attended every function that offered, every gaiety in or out of the Season, centred on the Lord Lieutenant and Dublin Castle. Yet, even this Castle round, for example, really only came to life for a few short weeks in Easter. Then the county folk trooped up to Dublin and went into the houses of their relatives and dressed up to the ninety-nines, and the dowagers toured their grandchildren or their nieces about the houses that were open to them. Spring shopping was done between whiles (Spring cleaning was, meantime, being done at home), and, if there was enough money to go round, they either finished up with Punchestown Races, if Easter was moderately early, or if it was late, they crossed over for the beginning of the London season. They saw the opening of the Academy, the riding in the Row, the Chelsea Flower Show where His Majesty came by, shaking hands with the veterans. If the money still lasted they went to Wagner at Covent Garden; if God in his high heaven was being positively benign to be presented at Court! – and if he was merely being moderately benign to Epsom for the Derby. And then, back to the little streets of Dublin, now shabby as a star when the moon discloses, and to the bogs and the rocks and Paddy with the pig, or Biddy with the ewer; and the curate telling you all that had happened since you left, as if Ballybehindbeyond were the most important place in the British Isles. It is all recorded beautifully, maliciously and with penetrating realism in George Moore's *Drama in Muslin*.

To Constance and Cassie who had yawned at London, and for whom even Paris was no longer magical, the good souls up from the country must have appeared just a trifle fatuous. There was the time – it is her version or one of her versions – when a bunch of them came to stay at the same house as Constance – it must have been a period when she was between houses – and on their return from the levee as they alighted from the cab before the terrace (it was Hartcourt Terrace by the canal) a drunken man halted in delight to see the lovely ladies in their frills and laces and their cloaks and long cream gloves go past like a vision under the gas lamps. For a long time after he kept coming to the door, and leaning to the window and saying he wanted to see the lovely ladies, and even when they were all gone to bed he came back along the path and announced to the house that he couldn't sleep unless he saw the lovely ladies. The result was a good deal of whispering and scuffling and long faces and talk about the police until in disgust Constance put on her dressing-gown over her night-gown and shoved her toes into her mules and opened the door. She held the amorous soul by the arm and she led him along the road, propped him under the railway bridge, came home, and told them all to go to bed. The country cousins may have talked over the adventure for weeks in Ballybehindbeyond. Constance made a good story out of it; but no immense saga.

As to their not being able to do the thing in proper style, that must have counted for a good deal in their final dissatisfaction with fashionable life; and though it would be absurd to suggest that Constance became a rebel because she was too poor to be a toff, as it would be to suggest that she sought the love of the people because she could not hold the love of her husband, yet all the hundred and one things that go, unconsciously to the shaping of a life, especially so strange and wild a life as hers, should be remembered and accounted.

At any rate they lived simply enough; they always had a maid or two, but Constance often cooked or helped with the cooking – friends remember that her conversation was not above housekeeping or recipes for dishes. She had cooked for herself occasionally in Paris and liked to impart French recipes, and French economies. Their entertainments were never elaborate and there was no lavish supply of drink. One wonders how far Cassie contributed to the common fund. Less and less, no doubt, as he began to mix with boon-companions around the city. For when people say that he could drink like a fish they scarcely exaggerated. A pint of whiskey was nothing to him at a sitting. His old friend of later years, Martin Murphy, the stage-manager of the Gaiety Theatre, recalls one morning when Cassie came in complaining that Madame's Boy 'Scoots' had drunk his whiskey – a fib that he did not expect anybody to believe. 'Rubbish!' cried Martin. 'You are a big Boy Scoot! But there's my keys and you know where my desk is. There's two half-pints there. And you know where the watertap is.' Cassie came back in about ten minutes slapping his stomach comfortably. 'Good man, Martin. Boy Scoot better, now. You will get the two half-pints at two o'clock.' He had polished off the whole supply within a quarter of an hour. Or so Martin said, who could also tell tall yarns. Still, money cannot have burned the pocket of so convivial a son; he cannot have been able to add much to Constance's income.

She never seems to have taken up any of those dutiful offices which occupy the time of some ladies of fashion. Her name never figured on the committees of philanthropic societies, which, considering her subsequent career, is puzzling. But the most interesting thing of all, in this connection, is that she began, if one may say so, to abandon her daughter gradually. At first Lady Gore-Booth in her kindness paid for a governess; then she began to have Maeve to stay with her at Lissadell; the periods of the child's absence lengthened until the time came when she did not live with her mother at all. A very shrewd remark by a man who worked side by side with her in her revolutionary days, the late P. S. O'Hegarty, hit her off well: 'a woman of great kindness but no natural affection'. And another friend recounts an illuminating little incident which occurred during one of Con's visits to Lissadell to stay with her mother and daughter. In the big drawing-room she undertook one morning to teach Maeve how to sing. She put the little girl standing on the grand piano and began to tap a note on the keys, persistently, monotonously, while the mite above her head tried to get the correct note. When she had managed to record it in a small, tremulous voice, the mother went on to another note, and so to another and another, until the child in tears, rebelled. On Sir Josslyn Gore-Booth's marriage in 1907, Lady Gore-Booth retired to a small house, Ardeevin, a mile or so from Sligo town and Maeve was entrusted to the care of governesses, to one of whom, an Englishwoman, Constance endeared herself for life by calling her, in the heat of argument, a 'bigoted bloody Sassenach'.

Cassie, on the other hand, did find other things to occupy him besides his painting and his social life – before, that is, he reverted whole-heartedly to Bohemianism. Always fond of young people, he helped boys at their clubs and games wherever he got the opportunity. He founded a Dublin Fencing Club, which met in Merrion Row, and became president of it; there he was always ready to help as instructor, and he gave small prizes for tournaments. His humour, like his wife's, was boyish and simple, and he enjoyed the young men's horseplay and simple jokes. Indeed they almost patronized him as if he were their junior. One of them says they just thought of him as a big, fat child – something to tease and romp with.

It was from this club, apparently, that Cassie got his idea for one of his better pictures, 'The Fencer', a picture of which Dublin painters still speak in admiration. It was reproduced in the *Irish Review* – a man with waxed moustaches and in a bright jersey holding a foil between his hands. Like most of Cassie's portraits it is workmanlike, very talented but without verve. She also painted, and exhibited. There are many examples of her work in private possession in Ireland. It is generally agreed that she was, simply, not a real painter. She also gardened, which I find both gallant, and warming and just a little sad – this keeping faith with the wide skies of Sligo and her happiest memories of Lissadell in her suburban plot. But, then, gallantry and loyalty were two of her most endearing qualities.

Very naturally in the circumstances, these two full-blooded, energetic, young people – Cassie being the full-blooded one, and Constance the energetic (Was not one of her later homes, Surrey House, known as Scurry House?) tried to squeeze more out of fashionable Dublin than Dublin was accustomed to give. And when they could not get what they wanted there, they very naturally began to explore further. They became known as a gay and merry pair who were up to every 'divilment'. Twice while gathering personal recollections of their early Dublin days I was told of the famous Markievicz scandal of 1909 when the Count shocked all Dublin by going to a fancy dress ball as Christ, with the Countess on his arm as the Magdalene. The scandal did occur, but it was not the Markieviczs. It is illuminating that it should be ascribed to them. The actual culprit was a foolish young lieutenant of the Rathmines Fire Brigade named Lewis, who appeared in a white mask, blood-stained, and a white robe bearing the letters I.H.S. at the skating rink carnival in Earlsfort Terrace, in the October of 1909. The papers made a great to-do over it, especially the *Daily Sinn Fein*, and for some time, no doubt, the names of all sorts of unconventional people went echoing about the Dublin whispering gallery. In the end the lieutenant was forced by an angry populace to flee by night to England.

The story of a small scandal caused by Cassie, later, at a fancy-dress ball, possibly true, is a better measure of their 'divilments'. This was at a carnival in the School of Art when Cassie arrived on the floor, dressed – or rather undressed in the opinion of some – as a sans-culotte. 'But, a sans-culotte!' remonstrated Cassie. 'He have no trousers. How can you know what I am unless I undress the part?' His expostulations only made the greater furore. The company divided on the question, and as it was after the date of Madame's entry into Sinn Fein they divided, not on morals, but on politics. Cassie was sent away to a little gallery with a cloak about him and a vote taken as to whether he had or had not enough clothes on. The Sinn Feiners won. I give the legend as I found it.

There was one other reason why the fashionable round proved unsatisfying. When the Liberals came in under Campbell-Bannerman in 1905, there was a changeabout in the vice-regal lodge. Lord Aberdeen returned as a 'liberal' Lord-Lieutenant; he had been there many years before, for a brief period, and had been very popular with the mass of the people. Under the new regime all vice-regal functions became much more democratic and less exclusive, but inevitably, what had ceased to be selective ceased to be desirable. Even Lady Aberdeen's interest in anti-tuberculosis campaigns seemed to bring society too near common earth. Merrion Square began to speak of the Lord-Lieutenant, flippantly, as His Ex.; and of Lady Aberdeen, as Ishbel. The usual little stories began to creep around among the snobs – the Aberdeens were Scotch, and close-fisted; Ishbel kept the purse-strings; they entertained poorly; the Lord-Lieutenant was weak and vacillating. When in 1913 he invited Jim Larkin to the vice-regal lodge, the Unionists said he had destroyed the dignity of his office. He put it in jeopardy at any rate, for Jim Larkin did not respect any office and he subsequently made such piquant references to that meeting as, 'The viceroy said to me. Would you mind shaking hands with me, Mr. Larkin?' – and, 'Only for that duffer of a judge you would be out long ago.' (The Aberdeens made a good impression on the bulk of the people however who voted for the party and lived in hopes of Home Rule.)

Lastly, other interests became necessary when Constance and Casimir had ceased to love one another with that first passionate love which makes young married people so completely and, to some, so maddeningly self-sufficient. Having exhausted the pleasure of finding worlds within themselves far more wonderful than any world outside, having drained the delights of companionship, without flaw, perfect and of endless variety, the triumph over time, the power over satiety, the armour of endless joy, the joy of endless solitude – suddenly the pot began to go off the boil. People who had smiled benignly to see them walking up and down the drawing-room of Saint Mary's, hand in hand, just as they stood hand in hand like shy children in their lovely, if rather too lyrical, wedding photograph, now heard Constance say – 'I don't know why Casimir married me'. And looking at Cassie, found him silent. Should one pay small attention to so trifling an incident? It might have been no more than a form of humble love, as if she were to say, 'I am not worthy of him,' and his silence the embarrassment of an undemonstrative man. He was always so respectful to her, and kind, and he always liked her so much, and she him, that there never was any more definite outward indication that the lovers had become friends. Still intimates will learn an immensity from such trifles, especially women, for whom trifles can mean a world of happiness and unhappiness; and one or two did think that she should make that remark so frequently.

She made it once-too-often. 'I don't know why Casimir married me.' Cassie rapped back – 'He didn't.' Which, of course, closed the subject. This singular incident occurred in the presence of others. One very close friend of both (G.F.) remembers it well. 'I asked him why he was so rude to her and he replied that he was getting tired of this remark of hers, and that in desperation he made the reply he did. And said at the same time that it was perfectly true she did marry him, and not he her – though out of the admiration and respect he had for her he never retaliated till now. He did not love her with that passion he was capable of, but he was tremendously fond of her, spoke of her always with the admiration one would give to a friend, though he was not as faithful as a husband should be. Since the birth of their child she did not require him as a husband – this she told me herself. Though in all matters where his fidelity as a husband was concerned, he never at any time flaunted his infidelities in front of her. He was always a perfect gentleman though he was, as Yeats said, a bit of a barbarian. Yeats is a poet with a poet's mind, but he does not see through a woman's eyes that some loved the barbarian in him – myself for instance. I loved him very much.'

No scenes, then – nothing that anybody could be surprised at; merely little touches so small as to be without meaning if one were not attending. So that people do not remember now anything to record the fall of Love's temperature, and nearly all reject as impossible the idea that they could ever have separated. But, then, 'nearly all' means men and women who were living active, external, sometimes rather dangerous, lives – men and women not practised in reading the language of the *demi-mot*, the tragedy in a sigh, the misery in a shrug. And Maeve Cavanagh, a poet, and a fellow-rebel of Constance's, does, somehow, remember just such a weary Hey-ho, a gesture, a hand limp-falling, an untranslatable sad smile, when Cassie was mentioned. And her friend, Helena Moloney, remembers how Cassie and Constance would meet from breakfast to breakfast, and he would be 'old man' to her 'Con'. Little by little, some people noted, too, he would be away for longer periods and still longer periods, until she flung herself into politics and he became the man-about-town.

She had tried, in marriage, to turn her back upon the storm of the world; but even within the sealed chamber of love its east wind had found her out. Back to your regiment, madame! – it seemed to say – for you are one of life's adventurous souls. You are, forever, undoomed to rest.

Certainly, most women would have refused to acknowledge even to themselves that the dream was over. Out of those who would have acknowledged it, few but would have languished for the rest of their lives in the hollow below that wave unable to climb again. But Constance Markievicz was a rushtip that beats back after every wind. A friend (L. ni G.) speaks of her, even when old and worn, as always remaining in the mind's eye with 'an unforgettable and enduring measure of grace and beauty'. With so much to spare even in her last years she was well able, now, to retain from the brilliance of her love a glow of comradeship that held the wayward Cassie almost to her death. That fire of her youth never showed any sign of dying of its accord. At the age of fifty-nine she died young.

§ 2

Her active political life began around 1908, her fortieth year, her prime and moritural summer. I deal with it in the next chapter, but here must mention one possible influence in that direction: the literary side of Dublin life, reflected in so many books and names of the period that it must be unnecessary to mention more than a few – *Joyce's Portrait of the Artist as a Young Man*, or Moore's *Hail and Farewell*, plays like *The Suburban Groove*, novels like Lennox Robinson's *The Young Man from the South*, Æ holding court in Rathgar or at the Hermetic Society; Colum vehement in the Arts Club, James Stephens talking without rest, Yeats chiming the organ note, Seumas O'Sullivan and Seumas O'Kelly, Synge dying, Ledwidge coming of age, and the Abbey Theatre flourishing on high-minded poverty and minute audiences. Most of this young literary group she came to know, her taste for such friendships whetted by her time in Paris, and newly encouraged by her sister Eva, who had been writing continuously since her girlhood, publishing many of her poems in *The Irish Homestead, The New Ireland Review, The Nineteenth Century, The Yellow Book, The Savoy*, etc., and who had begun to publish her verse in book form since 1904. Since her girlhood she and Eva had known Yeats. His lovely lines *In memory of Eva Gore-Booth and Con Markievicz*, printed at the beginning of this book, recall those early days of which he wrote to Eva, in 1916, 'your sister and yourself, two beautiful figures among the great trees of Lissadell, are among the dear memories of my youth'. This connection with the new national movement in literature must have been of the greatest effect in drawing her into the political movement of Sinn Fein. Æ was no admirer of the Irish Party; Yeats had written *Kathleen ni Houlihan* in 1901-2; Colum, Stephens and the rest were all allies of Arthur Griffith, editor of *Sinn Fein* (later first President of The Irish Free State), and wrote, then and later, for his papers.

It was the theatre, however, which gave her most pleasure. In those days before the cinemas it was in a healthy state, what with the Theatre of Ireland, the Hardwicke Street Theatre, the Little Theatre, the Celtic and National Players, the Abbey, the Trinity Players (under the Lion and the Unicorn) not to mention the regular, commercial theatres which were only on occasions as interesting, for it was the usual run there of fifth-rate plays like *Mrs. Wiggs of the Cabbage Patch*, or *An Englishman's Castle*, or *The Light That Failed*, unless now and again a star fell on Dublin and Pavlova or Maud Allan filled the plush chairs.

This irregular theatre-life has not hitherto been described (nor the teeming life of the pubs). The Markieviczs, between them, began to relish it from about 1916 onward. It must be granted that, artistically, they did not always take to it on the most serious level, but it had one important effect on her on the social level – it brought her somewhat closer to the populace at large and to popular Dublin life.

It is almost impossible to avoid the elegiac note here. We know of the poet Little who dressed in sackcloth and ashes – not too many ashes for comfort, nor too many sacks – and who foretold Gehenna in the trams and blighted the flowers of the Parks with the brimstone of retribution. But few now remember the Toucher Doyle who was familiar with earls and marquises but could only read betting slips and count in odds. The professional flaneurs like The Bird Flanagan we know about; but the bloods unconscious, like Wagger Macdonald, and Tommy Furlong, Ray Molloy, and Martin Murphy (Markievicz Murphy), the hosts of the taverns, Neary's and Joyce's and The Old House of Laurels, The Red Bank, Davy Byrne's, the 'Old' Bailey, all those poor men's universities have passed into a dimness that is almost oblivion, who were centres of life in their day. We hear from time to time of novels that will chase Muttonhead and Pat Hoy and the Dublin Vigilance Society, and Pat Kelly and little Dubronsky and John Wyse-Power, and The Jew, and the Doctor, and the rest of that vanished or vanishing tribe down the boreens of the Styx, but only one real novel has been written, that emetic not too aphrodisiac masterpiece of Joyce's and that great book which is sometimes thought to contain the essence of the Dublin of the early 1900's is in fact as remarkable for the many sides of Dublin life that it ignores.

Cassie's part in the Dublin theatre of the period went by the name of the Dublin Repertory – almost inevitably rechristened by him, the Dublin Reformatory. His headquarters became Neary's snug in Chatham Street and Joyce's in King Street. Here with his new friends he would plan out his scheme of production. Generally it was Neary's – because that was the 'nearyiest way,' from Grafton Street, by a back lane to the Gaiety. But past Joyce's was the 'nearyiest' way out – it is opposite the Gaiety Theatre's entrance.

Cassie first began to put on plays at the Gaiety on May 23rd, 1910. And he wrote his own play *The Memory of the Dead*. He called it 'the bloody play'. It was a 'ninety-eight play, sufficiently adept and well-knit, with heroics and action in plenty. It was a popular success and he took it to other centres – to Bray in the Moorish Mosque which had once been a Turkish Baths and later became a cinema, to Cork in the Opera House. Constance played in it under a stage name, Constance Gore ('Of the Theatre of Ireland'). Her appearance was magnificent and her voice was an agony. She thought herself a great actress and Cassie told her quite bluntly she was rotten. Though she did not resent his frankness she would expostulate; and he would insist, 'No, Con, you were rotten in that part.' She would laugh an appeal to the company and go her way unbelieving. Everyone agrees she was a poor actress; as she was a poor painter. An incurable dilletante, the only art she excelled in was the art of living, splendidly and with grace. Other plays produced were *Monna Vanna, Seymour's Redemp-*

tion, Strife, John Bull's Other Island, The Devil's Disciple, Eleanor's Enterprise.

All these gave Cassie opportunity to exercise his talent for naturalistic production. He would go to any lengths to be realistic – sometimes too far. In his realism he had a strong ally in Martin Murphy, the resident stage-manager and carpenter of the Gaiety. With *Eleanor's Enterprise*, for example, they had a real thatched cabin, using the straw-casing of wine bottles for the thatch; a real donkey; a real creel-cart; and even real hens and ducks. Unhappily the actors sometimes disapproved of the emphasis on properties and production, and in this play Ashley, a good actor, resented seeing his best scene – a love-scene with Constance – spoiled by the movements of the donkey. On the second night he decided to lead away the donkey at this point. But the donkey refused to leave the limelight and the harder Ashley pulled the more did the animal resist. All the time Cassie in the wings growled furiously to see his realism interfered with, delighted when the reins suddenly gave and Ashley tumbled head over heels off the stage. 'Dam good actor, donkey!' hissed the count. 'Only one ass on the stage now.' For *Strife* nothing would do Cassie but to have real labouring men, straight off the quays, at one and six a night apiece, to act in the big scene. Cassie foolishly paid them beforehand so that their blood was up when it came to the fight scene. In Martin's words – 'There was murder on the stage.' The squad of supers was smaller for the rest of the week, what with Cassie's chastened ideas about realism and the expressed opinion of the men, 'I dowan't miund bein' an actor for a nighut or two. But, bejase, I wowun't be kilt for wan and sixpence!'

What with the 'Reformatory' and his own private drama Cassie was now fast becoming one of Dublin's well-known characters. And like them he paid the price of the atmosphere he wove about himself. If with him a pub could change magically into a palace and every meeting become an adventure it is true also that his life became like a hero-tale where every vestige is as good as the next and any one meeting becomes typical of nights upon nights of vagabondage. Like all the rest of the Dublin playboys he has become in the memory not so much a personality as a symbol. In that sense all 'characters' are only half-real. In their lifetime they have dramatized themselves out of the *corpus mundi*.

In his character as 'character', he liked particularly to hunt

with little Dubronsky, the Polish tailor, who never learnt to
speak English and who hated being called a Jew. With the
warm-hearted Martin Murphy, of the Gaiety, they made a
wonderful trio, the count, the tailor and the carpenter; the
count with his English that he had learned from a Sligo girl
in Paris, and perfected between the drawing-rooms of R*awth*-
mines, and the *baacks* of the Dublin pubs; Dubronsky with his
vills and his *vonts*; and Martin with his rich vernacular varied
by persistent imitations of his two friends. Dubronsky was a
man whom no novelist could resist, and the pity of it was that
no novelist seems to have met him. He was so tiny and the
count was so huge; he was so pertinaceous and so *vif*, so like
a young rabbit in his gestures, and the count was so heavy and
so sly and so suave; and Martin, their ally and their bozzy,
enjoying them both. It was the little tailor's ambition to be
everywhere and in everything. You might open the paper and
not be astonished to find him in the front row of some Gaelic
League group; he was photographed among the past-pupils of
the Christian Brothers in Synge Street; he went to Kingsbridge
to welcome back John Redmond from the United States; he
was furious not to have been with the Count and Martin to
meet Pavlova at Kingstown.

For Pavlova's visit Martin and the count went off in a first-
class carriage to Kingstown. The Count had known her in
Saint Petersburg and he instructed Martin on the way how to
welcome a Russian. Say, *Ztradtswite*, he instructed. Martin
said *Ztradtswite*, until he had it pat. 'You must greet her just
as I do,' instructed Cassie. 'What do you mean?' asked Martin.
'Oh, you must do whatever I do. You will see,' said Cassie impatiently. At the pier many distinguished people were waiting
– among them the directors of the Gaiety. But the Count found
a front place at the gangway and when Madame Pavlova appeared he stepped forward and addressed her in Russian.
Behind him Martin waited with his *Ztradswite* tripping over
his tongue. But to his horror he suddenly found the Count
laying his arms about Pavlova and kissing her on both cheeks.
Bracing himself Martin kissed her likewise on both cheeks.
Afterwards he had to meet the infuriated manager. 'What the
hell are you up to here?' stormed the man. 'Yeerha, what?'
remonstrated Martin. 'Don't you know yet how to greet a
Russian lady?' And to prove his superior knowledge he and
the Count arranged a real Russian welcome in the dancer's
dressing-room – a cloth of unbleached linen, a jug of water,

plain bread. Pavlova was delighted. The Count's fame rose another peg.

Another small incident, eloquent of the to-and-fro of Cassie's life in the years before the war, was the departure of Pat Hoey. He was a friend of the Joyce of earlier Dublin days and sums up a good deal of the atmosphere of the ways and life of the wits and wags. At that time the favourite pub of the clique to which Cassie belonged was a tavern in Fleet Street, christened by Cassie, in his usual infantile manner, as 'The House of Laurels' because it had a laurel in a tub on each side of the door. Lady Aberdeen ('Ishbel' to the world) was taking one of her anti-tuberculosis plays to the Sloane Square Theatre in London, and Hoey was going there in connection with it. In the Laurels they had always foregathered and in the Laurels they drank his health and planned a send-off party. It was a useful tavern because it housed one Muttonhead, the curate of the place, a bartender who loved to listen, mouth agape and eyes wheeling, to the palaverings of the intelligentsia, and could, therefore, never refuse them credit. For the farewell party 'Jimmy' Montgomery (later the Irish Free State film-censor) wrote a ballad, so local, that almost every line needs annotation:

VALE

The desolation of emigration enshrouds the nation in palls of woe
For employment agents, or such expaygents, has forced the Hope of the Hoeys to go
To Bloody Britain, our hearts are splittin' to know this flittin' is takin' place,
For on to-morrow – to our deep sorrow – he'll make his home 'midst the Saxon race.

The 'Man from Lusk,'[1] with 'Jem Roche'[1] and 'Rooney'[1] must share his exile from Granuaile,
And stolid Saxons won't undherstand them, nor lend an ear to 'The Turfman's Tale'[2]
The 'Iron Road',[2] where the 'Last Tram'[2] rushes, with merry men from 'O'Connor's Bar',[2]
Has passed at last from Bohemia's borders, through Calathumpia and 'Mullingar'.

1. Sporting characters of Edwardian Dublin. The 'Man from Lusk' was the challenger of Youko Tani, the famous wrestler.
2. Favourite recitations of Pat Hoey.

John Bull – the Vampire – has bled our counthry, and lured our
    best to his noisesome lair.
And now he's takin' our 'Gifts of Nature', and that charmin'
    crayture 'The Girl from Clare.'[1]
We chant the dirge of our lamentations, our shattered hopes,
    and our blank despair,
And the 'Crossest Guns'[2] of our friend McGuinness boom
    punctuations to that sad air.

No more at eve in the 'House of Laurels',[2] no more at noon
    by the Scottish Weir,
Will Red Bank Knights[2] emulate his morals, when quaffing
    goblets of ginger-beer.
Now London Johnnies will ape his costumes, his hippy coats
    and his creased pants;
They'll grow moustaches like hairy walnuts, and swap their
    canes for his neat ash plants.

But we hope that Vaynus, contimporaneous, with Ireland's
    freedom will waft him here
'In the no far distant . . .' (Asquith consistent, and we persist-
    ent, perhaps next year (?)[3]
When the Dhrum of Ulster, and the Harp of Leinster, are
    played by people of pleasant mien,
And the Irish Wolfhound hunts ould King Billy[4] from the
    emerald pastures of College Green.

                The Calathumpian Out-Lawreate

Not very witty, perhaps, but pleasantly easy-going and sociable, redolent of the unembittered Dublin before the Troubles.

But it was not, however, the first time Pat Hoey had been sent off, with a subscription raised for his benefit, only to turn up a week later in Davy's or the Bodega, the subscription money better spent. This time the crowd arranged to meet him at Westland Row and see him off to Kingstown and the boat. But again there was no sign of Pat. By pure chance Martin and the Count found him, ten minutes before the train was due to

  1. Another favourite recitation of Pat Hoey.
  2. Favourite pub of Edwardian (and modern) Dublin.
  3. One of Asquith's more ambiguous phrases with regard to Home Rule which produced much hilarity in Ireland.
  4. The Statue of King William in College Green; since decapitated and then blown-up.

leave, rolling joyously down King Street. In mad haste they lifted him and laid him in a taxi and rushed off to Westland Row. There, as they had to be back to see the curtain up at the Gaiety, they laid him, not too tenderly, on the platform among the crowd. 'Do as much for him now,' said Martin, 'as I have, and bad luck from him.' All that remained to do – for all such affairs of the pubs were conducted according to an accepted etiquette, as rigid in its own way as any Castle etiquette – was to send a congratulatory telegram to Lady Aberdeen and to Pat on the first night. It was not sent. Instead Hoey found among the sheaf waiting him at Sloane Square on Monday night, the message: 'Muttonhead and entire staff sacked. Consternation general. Wire fullest instructions.' (Poor Hoey died so poor that his only worldly possession was 'one glass of malt left to his credit at Davy Byrne's.')

The end of this Dublin round came for Cassie in 1913 when he went as war-correspondent to the Balkans. In the best accepted traditions he was sent off to his fate. Tommy Furlong gave an 'American' wake in his benefit, with coffin and snuff and drinks 'and candles all nate and complate'. There ended, too, the Dublin Repertory Theatre, and the easy days of Edward and George. None of its lights are now as much as glowing; no old ladies tottering about Ballsbridge or Rathgar who had once been kissed by a Lord-Lieutenant, or old gentlemen in the Kildare Street Club, still reading *The Times*, a little perturbed at the liberalism of the *Spectator,* still giving the toast of 'The Flag' or 'The Fox, gentlemen,' or 'Ad finem esto fidelis'. Were Cassie back among us now he would find the life rather thin and colourless, though the pubs are more full than ever and the poets and the novelists write on. He would have to be told – 'Tommy Furlong? Ah, yes poor fellow. He died in Mercer's Hospital. The Wagger? Went into the Hospice for the Dying – God rest him. Little D.? Died in the lunatic asylum. The Toucher? The Bird? Are there none alive? John Wyse-Power? No. There's only just a few left. There's good old Martin, for one. There's Jimmy Montgomery,[1] as busy and active a man as ever he was. Paddy Kelly, away back in Connemara among the twilight pools and the rocks, a poet of the people gone back to live among them. There's the Doctor. (Do you remember, Cassie, the first time we saw his big yellow Rolls-Royce bowling down Grafton Street?) and there's little

1. This was written in 1933. The last of these to go were 'the Doctor' (Oliver St. John Fogarty) and Miss Helena Moloney.

Miss Moloney hard at work among the workers. (Do you remember the night you mixed a sup of whiskey with her sherry and you couldn't get her off the stage? And Martin shouted from the wings – 'The cow is in the corn. Turn her off, Mary.' And you said – 'Dam good line, that! We'll keep that, Martin?') Willy Orpen? No. But his drawing of himself and his brother is still on the wall of Davy Byrne's back-snug. Do you remember ould Clinton? (We put him up on a horse in the Saint Patrick's day procession, dressed as Brian Boru. He got his death of cold out of it and he died the week after.) Pat Hoey? Jim Plant? Gone, Cassie – all gone. Best ask no more.'

It was perhaps as well for him that he did not come back to live where, of his day, there would be nothing left but the memory of it. He had come to know and enjoy the people – but, truly, only the more gay and light and superficial aspect of them.

For her it was different. While he had been setting the pubs aroar she had been probing into the life of these same people with other instruments. For all that she was of the Ascendancy, for all that she was of the old landlord class of usurpers and undertakers, for all that she never came to know them as intimately as only one of their own number could know them, she did get to understand them far better than either Cassie or even they themselves ever suspected. Perhaps it was that while he merely enjoyed them she loved them; which, seeing that she did not apparently deeply care for her mother, her child, or her husband, is not, if one considers it, so very surprising. There had to be someone on whom she could expend the warmth of her being.

CHAPTER III

POLITICS:
1900–1910

§ 1

ONE must put it that way, for merely to say, of the beginning of the century, that a Gore-Booth began to take an interest in Irish politics would be an injustice to a family and a class. The Gore-Booths had always taken an interest in Irish politics. Better say even that she began to take an active interest in Nationalist politics; which is different.

For, ever since Parnell and Pigott, Davitt and the Fenians, the Invincibles and the Land Leaguers, not to mention Tim Healy snarling over the mace at the 'Shpaker', Nationalist politics had become the prerogative of the mere multitude. Politics in Ireland led to jail, broken fortunes, even broken heads, insults in the Irish press, libel in the English press, and (since the Irish party had set its face against accepting office from any government) offered a career to no man. Indeed when one thinks of Parnell's life with his uncouth and uncultivated army, from Flutther-britches Dillon, and 'Non-stop' O'Brien, to Jo Biggar the pork-butcher, and Tim Healy with his knotted tongue; and thinks, then, of how much of their secret hearts they revealed when they got Parnell down and could kick him, one shudders to think of some of those bland and mild gentlemen from the Big Houses trying to lead and mould Irish democracy.

Even when Parnell was not merely down, but dead, his followers at one another's throats, the Fenians and the Land Leaguers rotting in jails all over England, the priests still harrying the very ghost of adultery, and the unfortunate people utterly lost in the darkness and the storm, it is still unthinkable that somebody like, let us say, Sir Henry Gore-Booth should step into that nest of vipers. Nor did it become a whit more thinkable when, a little later, Redmond, in his role of snake-charmer, quietened the brood; for nothing could stop the intractable Healy, and the visionary O'Brien from perpetually hissing either at one another or at Redmond, or in the south, at least, a foolish populace from tearing itself into factions year after year over the phantom of a cause. To have touched even the hem of all that was impossible for anybody who did not know Ireland and the Irish through and through, their passions and their qualities, their vices and their cunning ways, their complicated background; and to say that people like Sir Henry could have known only very little about such things as these is to understate. They were times when even the most unselfish idealists, as Redmond was in many ways, or insuppressibles like O'Brien, had to drive themselves on to take part in public life. But if it was inadvisable for wise men to take part in that kind of politics around the nineteen hundreds, what word is there for a woman, still more for a woman of the Gore-Booth class, who took an interest in the politics of those forgotten victims of 'Parnellism and crime': the politics of the non-political allies of the Parties, the politics of that extreme minority that raised the storm for Parnell and were flung aside by him for a woman – the politics of the forgotten Fenians and the condemned dynamitards now suffering the agonies of hell in Portland and Chatham, like old Tom Clarke who came out sane and unbroken to fight again, in 1916; not to mention the politics of the 'unspeakable' Invincibles, of whom one or two (like that poor old wretch, Fitzharris, known to infamy as Skin-the-Goat) went to jail in '83 and were never heard of after.

It took time before the daughter of Sir Henry Gore-Booth reached down through the entanglement of the wilder jungle undergrowth of Irish politics to the inheritors of these men's faith and hate. But that she should, from the beginning, have chosen the road that led to that type of politics, rather than to the at least moderately legal politics of the Parliamentarians, marks her off at once from her class. But that she should ever have been accepted by the common people is quite extraordinary – so much so that we must examine with some little care the political situation, around nineteen hundred and after, that made an entry into even the antechamber of these regions possible for one of her type.

§ 2

First, one must remember what atmosphere and what memories of politics melted into all her other vital girlhood memories of the older Ireland. The young child of fourteen, famed already as a horsewoman, cannot have closed her ears and eyes to everything but horses in the middle of all the pother of the eighteen-eighties. In '82 there was *The Times* on the lunch-table and her father and mother talking in horror of the murder of Lord Frederick Cavendish and Mr. Under-Secretary Burke; the sudden, strange fall in the conversation when the servants entered, the glances downward to watch the heavy feet moving towards the door, the expelled breath of suspense and the renewed rush of talk. And then, in the afternoon (it was early May) her father walking alone in the garden, or in the woods, unwilling to meet his tenantry that evening, trying to drive the horror of it from his mind. No matter what other things came to drive such a scene from the memory, nothing can have expelled it wholly – not with so much mystery about the assassination, and the excitement of the arrests and trials, and the revelations that followed; not when, even to this day (whose young folk will never again hear a first-hand account of what the older people had to live down during those months), there is hardly a person in Ireland who has not heard at least the odd names of Skin-the-Goat, and Number One, and Carey the Informer, and O'Donnell who shot him at Capetown. It must have been the same with the Land Leaguers. On the mind of that child who was always going and coming among the huts of the people, a warm, impressionable, and kindly child, there must have been left many reflections of the tenants' struggle to live. There were wild days, too, and wilder after the Phoenix Park murders when O'Brien, Healy, and Davitt were all before the courts and Parnell only a little while out of Kilmainham Jail. It was at this time that the Joyce family, not so far from her home, were tried and hanged for a Land murder, and O'Brien fighting tooth and nail to save the innocent man among them. Could she pass a chapel or thread a way through a fair in '83 that she would not hear talk of the pennies being collected for Parnell? In '83 or '84 was there not a dynamitard found at Greenwich with his hair clotted in his own gunpowder and gore after a futile attempt to make London bridge come falling down in earnest? In '85, when she was seventeen – how lovely she must have looked at that time! – Sligo and all Ireland was in the throes of a General Election and boiling over with sedition. What talk there must not have been after it was all over, in the drawing-room of Lissadell, when they found that Parnell held a balance of power that could make or break Gladstone, and when for the first time since the Union an English minister brought a Home Rule Bill before the House! All that was assuredly moulded into her memory of her people at the most exciting period in their history since Emancipation.

Even her origins connived later with the effect of these memories, for she avoided the debacle and the disillusion of Parnell's fall. She was in London preparing for her coming out when the Pigott letters, associating Parnell with the Invincibles, produced the *cause celèbre* of the decade; in the middle of her London season when the Royal Commission proved Pigott to be a forger, and, doubtless, she was a little relieved because the Irish leader was after all a gentleman who had no connection with such disreputables as Skin-the-Goat or Mr. Patrick Ford. She moved farther away from Ireland when she entered the Slade just as the O'Shea divorce scandal was threatening to split Ireland from top to bottom. And then came Paris where Ireland faded out completely. She was left with nothing but a memory of uplands and storms, a place where the struggle for existence made life tempestuous and terrible, a remote place where her father and mother lived, a dickens of a long way off when at Christmas and Spring, she had to plan her visits home. She was a lovely, a supremely lovely young woman of thirty years, full of vitality, full of humour, full of mischief, full of pride at having emancipated herself – in love with at least one man, and possibly loved by others, living, whether it was a wild life or not, a gay round in a gay city. How was such a girl to pore over these thrice-folded and dog-eared newspapers from Ireland, merely because a Department of Agriculture and Technical Instruction had been established in Dublin, or Local Government had replaced the Grand Juries, or O'Brien with his patriarchal beard was calling Healy with his black face, 'a renegade and an impertinent thief?' She had her coloured picture of Ireland and nothing intervened to cause her to destroy it.

True, when she returned it was not to her memories of politics she came but merely to the picturesque Ireland. For if memories cannot be destroyed they can be overlaid. She must have often been one of many unattached *revenants* at the Broadstone Station around Christmas and Spring, with a porter bustling before them, as by instinct towards a second-class carriage, loading the racks with their wraps and their monogramed hatboxes, and touching his cap to the sixpence that drops from a safe distance into his fist from a neatly-gloved hand? She, being a kind young woman, and an emancipated young woman, would doubtless have smiled or even joked with him, and he would have blarneyed her and winked at his chums because she was such 'a damn fine-looker'. Then, because she was a would-be painter and must be conscientious as well as emancipated, she would look with eagerness at the country-folk in their coloured shawls hastening down the gloom of the platform; and, as the train moved out, watching as eagerly for the little fields that follow on the backyards, and the little pools of water in the fields, and then by degrees more and more grey rocks, all changing colour under the shifting light. She would rejoice in the small white cabins, the horses shying away from the clank and blown steam of the engine, the shadowless and quiet dusk. But then her type would always sink back, toy with the *Spectator*, or the *Tatler*, smoke, try to sleep, grow restive, until in the evening they were met at some little station by a boy with a trap and be swallowed up in the dark as the train rolled on, swallowed up and lost to the rest of us gabbling about politics in the third-class carriages, swallowed up and lost because they were no more part of our lives or of the life of Ireland than the tourist who goes and leaves no mark behind.

It was in that mood of half-detachment that she had returned to Dublin as a young bride, though one notes with pleasure that there was at least no question of her not returning at all. If Casimir had been French she might not perhaps have come back to us; if he had even been German or Italian. But one feels that for Casimir a choice between Poland and Ireland left very little to choose. To that gay soul, gay as a peasant or gay with the cheery, if rather heavy bonhomie of a commercial-traveller, Ireland was well enough – as well as Poland anyway, it would do very well – possibly it even did 'bloody well' ('Constance teach me my English.') It was this natural mood of detachment, in both of them, children both of harassed countries, that sent politics into a very dim and distant offing.

§ 3

She did well to enjoy the glory of her first year of love, the excitement of her first child, the swinging in Casimir's arms about the throne-room of the Castle to the sound of the best Dublin bands. There could hardly be anything of interest seeing that the Nationalists were only just composing their differences under Redmond after ten good years of disunity. In 1903 things did stir a little with Wyndham's second Land Bill – a revolutionary measure that in time altered the face of Ireland, though in appearance scarcely dramatic enough to excite anybody but a social reformer. Then occurred, still 1903, an incident that created such an immense rumpus for so little reason that it may be taken as a fair measure of the dullness of parliamentary politics during those years of her abandon.

What happened was that some thirty of the more important Unionist landlords, such as Lord Dunraven and Colonel Hutchinson-Poe, making a first and last (and painfully feeble) effort for the leadership of the people among, and on whom, they lived, had formed an Irish Reform Association which in August, 1903, proposed a Devolution scheme of the mildest type; it would give Ireland a limited fiscal control and Parliamentary powers of a local nature. Mild as it was, it aroused bitter opposition among the Ulster associations, and, judging by Redmond's pronouncement on hearing of it, jubilation in the Irish Party.

As far as Wyndham was concerned the scheme had been developed during his absence on holidays but the brunt of the blame fell on him because it had been fostered by his Under Secretary, Sir Anthony MacDonnell (later Lord MacDonnell), and blessed by the Viceroy, Lord Cadogan. Immediately he heard of it he repudiated it and all knowledge of its progress, but MacDonnell proved that he had at least referred to it in his correspondence with his absent chief, and Wyndham fell under suspicion among the Tories.

Normally, no doubt, the thing would have blown over and been soon forgotten, but as things were the Government was already in deep water. Chamberlain's Fiscal Campaign of 1903 was splitting their ranks, and the Nationalists used the MacDonnell-Wyndham controversy as a wedge for the growing split. Already (1904) hoping for a Liberal Government they pressed their attack on the Tories. Wyndham fell before them early in 1905 and there the incident may be dismissed, unless for the sake of fuller vision and as an illustration of the slow tempo of things in Westminster through the first decade of the century, one prefers to lose it in the comings and goings, the lobbyings and the caballings that went on all that year, those endless meetings and wire-pullings that in such assemblies as Westminster are calculated to wear the vigour out of even the most active men, and in the case of the Irish members seem to have worn away all sense of perspective. For when the Liberals did come in, under Campbell-Bannerman, they fulfilled none of the hopes of the Irish Party. Though Redmond did excellent political work of one kind and another, whether over an

English Education Bill, an Irish Land Bill, or the Reform of the Lords – whose rescinding power always loomed ominous for Irish hopes – nothing of his work did more than touch the hem of the real question of Irish liberty.

So the dancing went on in the Castle, and the gossips hummed over the tea-tables, and as far as Ireland's essential question was concerned, this kind of talk was just as effective as Redmond's kind elsewhere. Yet if people had the wit to see it the truth is that Wyndham's Land Acts were doing far more for Irish prosperity than Home Rule was ever likely to do. That conclusion to the long, and often brutal and always unjust, landlord system effected a revolution in the life of the countryside. It gave property to men who had had no property; it gave hope to men who had lived fighting despair; it encouraged thrift and enterprise where the landlord system had discouraged both by raising rents for every improvement effected by a tenant on his farm. It took time before this became apparent. Only Parnell, tutored by Davitt, in the last century, and Mr. De Valera tutored by the farmers themselves in this, have been able to realize that in a farmers' country the farm is the storm-centre of the political fight.

But the men who had made the Land League fight serious and real were no longer behind the Irish Party, the type of men, that is to say, who were ready to risk the gallows for a cause. It is hard to say who was behind Redmond. He was leading men who had dethroned a giant. He was representing a people who had wasted all the fighting spirit of two generations in fighting among themselves. And because of that, because he had no sword to rattle – even if he were the man to rattle it if he had it – he spent those three futile years squabbling about a little matter like the Wyndham business, making more fuss over the affairs of a Chief Secretary than Parnell would have made over a Flogging Bill; and the people blamed him for it.

The secret of Anglo-Irish relations, as we can now see it, is simply that no reform, no concession of any importance was ever gained from the British Parliament except under the threat of force. One sees it clearly in the effect of Grattan's Volunteers, of O'Connell before and after the Monster Meetings, in the comparison between Butt and Parnell, in the comparison between the treatment of Carson and the treatment of Redmond, not to mention events of recent years. Once the extremists abandoned the Parliamentarians the Parliamentarians were always finished.

So much we see clearly now. But around the nineteen hundreds others saw it, too. Those of the mass of the people who were losing faith, with good reason, in the Irish Party, saw it with a vague sense of shame. The very tiny secret cabal of extremists who were preparing the way for direct action with a slow but deliberate patience of mine-layers, saw it quite clearly. The somewhat larger body of middle-class, mainly lower-middle-class, clerks and teachers and skilled artisans, who worked openly under various banners against Party methods and who later came, or were urged, into public view as Sinn Feiners, saw it in honest anger. So did the growing body of young men and women who deliberately renounced all political affiliations to work for the revival of the Irish language, Irish folklore and Irish customs, in the Gaelic League; while the intelligentsia, bored with the futility of Westminster, devoted their energies to the creation of a national drama and a national literature. Only those Big Houses who took no interest whatever in their country, and for whom the political, cultural, and social centre was 'town' – by which to your surprise, you found they always meant the city of London – were satisfied and happy, and since nothing was to be expected from them they might just as well be happy while they could. Their time was drawing to a close.

Of this list of the disgruntled the really important ones were the underground extremists, and the men who contributed to the founding of the Sinn Fein movement. It must not be thought, however, that these, or any of the others, worked in isolation. Discount makes for fellowship. The secret extremists burrowed their way according to policy and, in a manner that will be described later, into every circle of disaffection and disloyalty. The *littérateurs* wrote for and worked with the Sinn Feiners. The Gaelic Leaguers were interested in the work of the literary revival. Some of the literary men, like Joseph Plunkett, the son of Count Plunkett, or Thomas MacDonagh – both executed in 1916 – walked through the salons, revolutionaries incognito. Some men were socialists, revolutionaries, and Sinn Feiners all at once.

In a sentence, there was a Parliamentary Party that could make no headway, and a scattered number of unbelievers, waiting for the man or the circumstance to weld and lead them;

and outside all, the passive populace whose support was essential to the final success of either.

Such, very roughly, was the ostensible condition of Irish politics on the night – frankly, an hypothesis – when Madame Markievicz kicked her silver slippers from her feet and resting her toes on the fender decided that all this Castle business and all this chin-chattering, would-be-witty, scandal-mongering life was a hollow sham, a slavery in fact, because if you compared it with the deliberately chosen slavery of the atelier or the Art School it was ineluctable without being profitable. Nor is it entirely a legend; for 'hollow' was her own word afterwards to describe that gay life when it had ceased to thrill her. 'I saw the hollowness of all that Castle business and I wanted to do something for the people,' were her words to one of her earliest colleagues in Sinn Fein, old Alderman Tom Kelly.

§ 4

If, then, she was to become interested in politics that she should have chosen to be interested in Sinn Fein rather than The Irish Parliamentary Party is not surprising. One must remember, that in the nineteen hundreds Sinn Fein, like Socialism in the eighteen hundreds, was, for the liberal minded, a respectable interest, more respectable in some ways than the Irish Party, for it had no past to live down, and no apparent future to tempt any but the disinterested. It also had the merit of being connected with the literary revival. One was in good company with Yeats, Edward Martyn, James Stephens, Padraic Colum, Edward Bulfin, Frederick Ryan, Æ, Alice Milligan, or Susan Mitchell. On the other hand, for those who, like Constance Markievicz, wished to dissociate themselves from the ultra-respectable, this very literary connection smacked of an idealism, an earnestness of purpose alien to the bohemianism of the Arts Club. Excepting Martyn, moreover, all the literary men interested in Sinn Fein were young and poor, and all were commoners. The movement was, in addition, against all forms of government accepted by the respectable – especially and particularly government from Westminster; and from 1905, even against the idea of the most temporary representation in Westminster. Finally, it had, from the beginning, been disloyal enough to rouse the anger of the law. The *United Irishman*, the organ of Sinn Fein, was seized by the police twenty-three times in its course, thrice publicly suppressed in 1900, the printer threatened by the Secret Service in 1905, and the paper ended with a libel action in 1906.

One feels that it was such things that drew Constance Markievicz to Sinn Fein, rather than any intrinsic merit in its constructive ideas. She need hardly be censured for this since for a long time there was no such organization as Sinn Fein: it was in the beginning not so much a movement as a man, and not so much a man as a little halfpenny weekly, observed on the bookstalls. *The United Irishman* began to appear there in 1899. Its editor one gathered was a journalist named Griffith. Its policy, so far as one could understand it, was one of dissatisfaction with Parliamentarianism, and for the rest, a desire for a more virile nationalism. If this was something easily understandable to the native Irishman whose blood moved by instinct, in response to such words, for a woman like Constance Markievicz, it was merely something that vaguely awoke old memories of midnight tar-barrels glowing and smoking at the cross-roads of a black line of helmeted police resting on their carbines in the Sligo streets during some political meeting long, long ago.

Even when she began to peruse this little ha'penny paper and read that Mr. Griffith accepted 'the nationalism of '98, '48, and '67 as the true Nationalism, and Grattan's cry, *Live Ireland – Perish the Empire*, as the watchword of patriotism', apart from her ignorance as to what '48 and '67 really stood for, she must have felt that very similar words had been flung wide over the country by Mr. Healy or Mr. O'Brien in their more enthusiastic moments. Moreover, Mr. Griffith was impartial in his attacks – disconcertingly impartial. He belaboured not only the Irish Party, but the Dublin Labour Party (edition of Sept. 7th, 1901), the Dublin Trades Council, (Sept. 14th, 1901), the United Irish League (Jan. 3rd, 1903), the Irish Republican Socialist Party (Nov. 19th, 1904), the Republican Nationalists, the *Freeman's Journal*, Strikes – he gave no help to Larkin – and even advocates of high wages who were told (July 5th, 1902) that 'Irish workers must make a sacrifice in money for the moral and social gain of living among their own kindred in their own land'. All of which, neither wholly understandable nor wholly agreeable to those who were initiate of his brand of nationalism, must have been more than confusing to those who, like Madame Markievicz, read him at first from curiosity or in mild sympathy.

Really, only two things were clear about Griffith; he wanted the restoration of the constitution of 1782 under which Grattan's Parliament sat in College Green; he hated the Empire, and loved his own people.

By the time she was beginning to be seriously interested in Griffith it is true that his ideas had clarified themselves somewhat, or perhaps it may be, merely, that in requiring an organization to supplement his paper, people began to clarify his ideas in discussion among themselves.

First, as to the ideas, at the third annual convention of a body known as Cumann na nGaedhal, founded with his blessing in October, 1900, but really run by William Rooney – it was almost purely a local body – Griffith outlined his Hungarian policy, so-called because in imitation of the Magyar leader, Deak, he advocated abstention from the parliament of the oppressor. Late in 1905, another important date in the history of Sinn Feinism, Griffith, seeking a new platform, revived the old National Council, a committee originally called into being to consider the nationalist attitude to a Royal Visit, and had the satisfaction of hearing it pass a resolution along the lines of his abstentionist policy. It favoured,

> 'National self-development through the recognition of the rights and duties of citizenship on the part of the individual, and by the aid and support of all movements originating from within Ireland instinct with national tradition and not looking outside Ireland for the accomplishment of their aims.'

Here for the first time is the doctrine of self-reliance, which is the core of the Sinn Fein idea, stated by a body, admittedly local, but purporting to be widely representative. As to the organization – it was supplied by the energy of the secret extremists who felt that Griffith should be helped. As a result of their activities, the National Council and Cumann na nGaedhal were amalgamated with other smaller bodies and the result was the Sinn Fein movement.

That phrase, 'national self-development' – coupled with the ideas implicit in his Hungarian policy and the old formula of the Constitution of 1782, was as near as Griffith ever got to the clarification of his ideas. For, it will be noted, that when the declaration of 1905 goes on to speak of the utilization of various other movements 'instinct with national tradition' it is content to refer to the 'accomplishment of aims' which it does not define. Perhaps this is not quite just, for one may be expected to go to the pages of the new *Sinn Fein* for the definition here and there, in various articles and pronouncements on social and economic questions, rather than in an orderly programme.

But here, in considering the wisdom of Madame Markievicz's relations with Griffith, one is obliged to take a definite stand, since all depends on the agreement of their ideals, not to mention their mutual satisfaction with the ideas that were supposed to implement their ideals. And here, too, one begins to wonder if revolutionary movements ever move towards defined ends, whether all such movements are not in the main movements of emotion rather than of thought, movements arising out of a dissatisfaction with things as they are but without any clear or detailed notion as to what will produce satisfaction in the end. How else can numbers of people come together and work together? How else could two such very different people as Arthur Griffith and Constance Markievicz come together at all, except by the agreement of their emotions, and the disagreement of their minds?

The basic emotion that welded so many disparate personalities during the period of the revolution was so powerful and so ancient that it needed no defining. It was the emotion of a country bitterly conscious that its individuality had been suppressed for a long period by brute force. It sufficed to draw thousands of people together. It did not prevent their falling apart, in a rather sudden realization of the differences between their personalities, when the origin of that emotional impulse towards comradeship disappeared. To have attempted at the beginning to agree not merely as to the general, but the particular end, would have produced disruption at the outset.

Griffith had many ideas as to what he meant by such words as Liberty. He had more ideas than most. The trouble with him was that they were always vague. Patrick Pearse, later the leader of the 1916 Rising, had no practical image of Freedom at all until Connolly by sheer force of personality, hammered it into his dreamer's head that there is such a thing as a 'material basis of freedom'. Constance Markievicz, in her woman's way, had no intelligible ideas but many instincts. It both annotates Griffith's influence on her, and measures her instinctive wisdom that she abandoned Griffith as soon as she met Connolly. For she saw in Griffith not only the politician who hoped and believed that the establishment of a native parliament would in time solve all problems – a view she shared up to a point – but saw in him also a man who had no defined attitude to those problems. Whereas she saw in Connolly a man who also relied on the native wisdom of his people and the healing power of Freedom, but who had a very definite attitude to the problems which Griffith tended to shelve. And she liked definite attitudes. It was her strength and her weakness.

She drew naturally away from the man with the long view to the reformer with the defined ideas. She drew away from the cautious politician to the warmth and enthusiasm of the Labour evangel. She felt that Griffith had no interest in the Teigues and Molls of the kitchen unless he could make them part of the battalions of this Liberty he did not define. She felt that he was a man who could think of only one thing at a time, and that all such questions as a satisfying social policy (even a social policy that would express the individuality whose suppression energized him throughout twenty years of active and unrequited political agitation) would be always pushed aside by him until the one big question was finished with – to wit English interference – *and that then there was no guarantee that he might not continue to shelve it for ever.*

That Griffith had good reason to shelve the matter of a social policy is not to be denied. The unifying element in his movement was Nationalism, not Socialism. He trusted, too, that the natural humanity of his people would in time face that question bravely; and he was also content to allow the people to solve their social problems in their own way. He was a working politician and he believed genuinely in the 'will of the people'. Being, therefore, neither a reformer nor an evangelist, and a revolutionary only in a limited sense, he could not at any time hope to hold for long the interest of such impatient and ardent souls as hers.

At first he had hopes of using the working class, though his main hope was in the middle class, the skilled tradesmen, the small shopkeepers, the humbler professions. But that 'large and respectable class, the men of no property' who had been the hope of 18th century Tone and the trust of 19th century Mitchel are naturally the enemies of all moderates, as Griffith soon discovered. It is no exaggeration to say that Connolly distrusted him, and that Larkin, who found himself attacked by him without restraint, must have definitely regarded him as an enemy. For his part he wasted no effort in palliating any lacks or failures observed in official Labour and being entirely ignorant of and unsympathetic to the difficulties facing Labour in the nineteen hundreds, he, in turn, soon came to mistrust and even hate it.

His paper, for example, was full of such sneers as the following: 'We observed the Labour Party on Christmas Day going to mass at the pro-Cathedral in state. It wore an unctuous smile, a London tall silk hat and kid gloves, a Leeds suit and Nottingham boots and leaned on the arm of the Publican.' Taken as propaganda for clean administration that would have been cogent criticism from anybody; taken as an appeal for finer Labour ideals it would have been cogent from Connolly and accepted from him in that spirit; it was actually propaganda for the Irish Industrial Revival, and the point is that Griffith was almost indifferent as to the conditions under which the Industrial Revival was to take place.

It was not that the editor of the *United Irishman* did not wish heartily for all possible improvement in the conditions of Irish life. His difficulty was that there before him was always the warning of such as Parnell who had been swallowed by the Land League when he thought he was using the Land League to fight for Home Rule; earlier, the example of O'Connell who had postponed Independence to agitate for Emancipation. It made Griffith go rigid with tension to think that any section of his battalions should be bought, or deceived, or worked upon by any cause, however praiseworthy in itself, to the detriment of the one great cause which would solve all causes in the day of its triumph. He felt the Irish Party was being bought by palliatives ('Killing Home Rule with kindness', was what John Dillon called it); he feared that Irish Labour might be deceived into a friendship with the enemy through the fraternal spirit of socialism; he definitely declared that the Irish workers were being worked upon, used as a tool, by their own unions dictating from England in the desire to try out costly experiments on Irish soil. So during the railway strike of 1911 he mocked bitterly at the 'admirable Englishmen who had authorized the Irish people to fight' while they keep their own countrymen out of the fray. 'The prospect of an Ireland with its transit held up, an Ireland in whose cities factory after factory will be compelled to shut down, and wherein, to the hardship of enforced unemployment will be added a rapid advance in the price of food, forms a black picture. It has a bright comparison. It is that of the English railwayman whistling at his work . . .' (*Sinn Fein*, Sept. 23rd, 1911).

Again during the height of the 1913 struggle when the Irish workers were fighting for their very lives, for the merest principle of justice in their conditions of work, he had no good word to say for the conduct of the English unions; even when these sent over two food-ships to the literally starving strikers in Dublin, he mocked: 'the function of the Irish brother is to fight. The function of the English brothers is to stand behind him' (*Sinn Fein*, Oct. 4th, 1913). He had no time for these interruptions in the struggle for freedom; he had some sympathy for them but he considered them politically inexpedient.

It was always the same cry with him: Freedom first and everything else will naturally follow. For a time Constance Markievicz took it up. And not unnaturally. She was neither poor nor helpless; she was not of the people; neither of their class nor their religion nor their political faith; their traditions were not her traditions; she was part not of their history but of the tail-end of the history of their exploitation. She had every reason to distrust both the Irish Party and the Irish Government; they had both been tried for a hundred years and, to her mind, the results were meagre. All she knew was that she wanted to do something for James Malone of the Coombe and to do it she did the only thing she could think of. She did not join Sinn Fein – she never joined anything – she flung herself into it. When she came to the surface – some would say after three or four years, some fifteen – she found that Sinn Fein had every desire but no plan for doing anything at all for James Malone in the Coombe. 'She was,' Æ observes mildly, 'a little breathless in the pursuit of her ideals.'

She was, it may also be observed, not deceived by her instincts. Griffith, when he came into power, continued to shelve the problems he had always refused to face.

§ 5

By March, 1908, she was a declared Sinn Feiner. In that month, instead of being in the Castle ballroom, she was on the draughty platform of the Rotunda with the reformed National Council, or Sinn Fein. The year after she was on the executive of Sinn Fein. We may be perfectly certain that she got every possible ounce of enjoyment out of that experience, and equally certain that despite her genius for enjoying herself, the thing must at all times have been very trying indeed. She had been through a series of contrasts; the social round of London after the huntin' and shootin' of Lissadell; the Slade after the social round of London; Paris after the Slade; the social round of Dublin after Paris; and now the greatest contrast of all – humble people, endless arguments, dusty committee rooms, men with strange accents, and sometimes with strange manners, a kind of humour quite foreign to her, a seriousness such as she had never felt before, the oddest mixture of commonsense and nonsense, the aroma of a strange religion over everything, and above all a constant allusion to a whole corpus of tradition and opinion, a reference to a world she had never really known, an acceptance of everything to which not merely her life but the life out of which she came had always been opposed. It was as refreshing and as shattering as travel in a strange land. She began to exploit at once the emotions of the explorer, and her discoveries were both exciting and discouraging.

The Gaelic League, for example, was a weird and wearisome hinterland. When she first wished to join the national movement she had gone quite simply to Griffith – the only name familiar to her – and asked him what place there was for such as her in that movement. Griffith, who was no feminist (who was even opposed to giving the vote to women) took her coolly. She was, possibly, not the first society woman who had come to him in search of a new thrill. Knowing the difficulty of learning Irish – having failed to learn it himself – he sent her off to join the Gaelic League, which, obediently, she did. But learning Irish was scarcely Madame's meat. She spent several months pounding away at *Is bó é*, It is a cow, *Is bó é*, It is a cow, *Is bó é*, It is a cow; and *Táim*, I am; *Tair*, Thou art; *Tá sé*, He is, and all the rest of it; declensions of all types, verbs irregular and verbs anomalous, and then she gave up the ghost.

'If you were to ask me,' says one of her most intimate and most loyal friends, Miss Helena Moloney, 'what was the greatest·defect in her character, I should say it was a childish love for the limelight. It never prevented her from doing good, hard, and unpleasant work. It never seriously misled her. But the work she did always had to be of a dramatic, or even of a glamorous kind. Her character was made that way. She could only express herself in terms of action and gesture and drama. It never prevented her from going down to the very bottom of the kind of work that did appeal to her and learning the rudiments of it and becoming efficient at it. But it had to be work of a certain type.'

Not even the more spectacular features of the Gaelic League campaign satisfied that side of her nature, not even the fight for Irish in the National University which gave a great fillip to the League in 1909. There was something too deadly solemn and evangelical about the Gaelic League, and she was not moved even by the monster procession and mass-meeting in that year with tableaux on lorries and endless ranks of singing school children and hairy-legged men in kilts, and Douglas Hyde with his moustaches like a mask, and men carrying banners bearing unintelligible symbols spattered with diacritics. The women in Irish costume looked so very earnest; and she had enough humour to observe that some wore buttoned boots under their poplin gowns and some carried umbrellas. Not even with the best will in the world could she make any headway in that atmosphere. To the end of her days she could only write a sentence or two in Irish, and these Gaelic Leaguers, being deplorably unbending people, could never accept a woman with a name like hers, and a past like hers and a voice like hers – to hear her trying to speak Irish was an agony – and she had waltzed and quadrilled far too much ever to be able to wind and hop through the convolutions of the Waves of Tory or the Four Hand Reel.

There was a kind of tradition among these people, too, that to be formal, or to be polite – even with some to shave or to wear clean linen – was to ape the manners of the sophisticated and decadent Saxon. Having, by vow, eschewed all political affiliations, sacrificed everything, as it were, to the vocation of the language-revival, all the energies of the Gaelic Leaguer went into other forms of extreme action. One of the sacrifices she made, and – there is no other word for it – *sportingly* made, was the sacrifice of the formality in social behaviour to which she had been bred, and which, for all her Bohemianism, meant a good deal to her. To the Gaelic Leaguers she was none the less impossible. They were a cult, not a movement; they lived for one idea and to no other idea did they attend, not even to ancillary ideas. In fact ideas of any sort were as much a distraction to them as ideas of any sort but those connected with Independence were a distraction and an annoyance to Griffith. Into that one Lhasa the explorer never penetrated.

The nearest she got to it was to make the acquaintance of a Patrick Pearse who had edited the Gaelic League organ since

1903. In '99 he had been teaching Irish classes in the old Royal University, with such students as Hugh Kennedy, later first Chief-Justice of the Irish Free State, at this time aged twenty; John Marcus O'Sullivan, later Minister for Education in the Irish Free State, then eighteen; Arthur O'Clery, later Professor of Law in University College, Dublin – which replaced the Royal; and, so one report has it, James Joyce, then seventeen. At the time she joined Sinn Fein, Pearse was starting the school that was to implement his ideals and perpetuate them after his death, at Cullenswood House, Rathmines.

With the women she made better headway than with the heavy-handed idealists in the Gaelic League. Women are kinder (when they are kind), more immediately opportunist, and less suspicious (when they have decided not to be suspicious) than men. And they appreciated (where the men had only derided, or even suspected) her good efforts at conformity – her rejection of formality in behaviour, of distinction in dress or speech. Perhaps it was because some of them felt a little snobbish at being associated with a real countess that, to her great delight, they treated her as if she were not a countess at all.

They were found in a little organization called *Inghinidhe na hEireann*, or The Daughters of Ireland, and they were in the main extremists, and in the main opposed to Griffith's compromise of a national constitution under the English Crown. They wished to 'establish the complete independence of Ireland, encourage the study of Irish, of Irish literature, History, Music and Art, especially among the young, to support and popularize Irish manufacture, to discourage the reading and circulation of low English literature, the singing of English songs, the attending of vulgar English entertainments at the theatres and music-halls, and to combat in every way, English influence, which is doing so much injury to the artistic taste and refinement of the Irish people.' In 1903 they started a monthly paper, called *Bean na hEireann*, or the *Irish Woman*, mainly through the initiative of Miss Helena Maloney, who became later Madame's most intimate friend; for this paper Madame Markievicz wrote, sometimes under her own name, sometimes under the pseudonym of Macha (a fighting queen in ancient Irish legend). Among these women was Maud Gonne who had helped to found the organization in 1900. With these she found herself much more at home than with the Gaelic League, but with the womenfolk she met in the Irish suffragette movement, she never made common cause. She sympathized with them, as she was always ready to sympathize with anyone who had courage enough to fling a brick through a shop window and go to jail after, but there was nothing in her character to be moved at the thought of injustice to woman *qua* woman; if she was not, or perhaps because she was not a masculine woman, she was not a militant feminist. She could not see herself sewing banners and talking endlessly with women gone rigid with a sense of personal injustice, and being jailed indecorously for so unglamorous a cause as theirs; any more than she was content to sit at home or in a classroom over an O'Growney textbook for the sake of being able to speak Irish in a country where nobody, outside the Irish-speaking districts of the West and South-west, wanted to talk Irish except as a hobby among intimates. The limelight was not strong enough in either case.

This refusal to devote herself to the suffragette movement is of some significance. Speaking in Dail Eireann in the days after the adoption of the Treaty, when everybody was given to apologias and personal confessions of one sort or another, to a proposal for the extension of the franchise to women, she said (March 2nd, 1922):

'I rise to support this just measure for women because it is one of the things that I have worked for wherever I was since I was a young girl. My first realization of tyranny came from some chance words spoken in favour of woman's suffrage and it raised a question of the tyranny it was intended to prevent – women voicing their opinions publicly in the ordinary and simple manner of registering their votes at the polling booth. That was my first bite, you may say, at the apple of freedom, and soon I got on to the other freedom, freedom to the nation, freedom to the workers.

'This question of votes for women, with the bigger thing, freedom for women and opening of the professions to women, has been one of the things that I have worked for and given my influence and time to procuring, all my life whenever I got an opportunity. I have worked in Ireland, I have worked even in England, to help the women to obtain their freedom. I would work for it anywhere as one of the crying wrongs of the world, that women, because of their sex, should be debarred from any position or any right that their brains entitle them a right to hold.'

The reference to England is to the Manchester election of 1908 in which the question of women in public bars was warmly discussed. With Eva she defended the girls' right to serve in bars and opposed Churchill's candidature. On that occasion she drove a four-in-hand through the streets. A working-man, who disapproved of the exhibition, shouted out: 'Can you cook a dinner?' 'Yes!' she shouted back. 'Can you drive a four-in-hand?' As to her 'work' for the rights of women in Ireland she is remembered to have visited suffragettes in jail. She fought with them for a flag when Trinity students raided the rooms of the Franchise League. She so far forgot her sense of humour on one occasion, in 1913, as to plan a tableau for them at Molesworth Hall in which Joan of Arc came in shining armour to a suffragette in Kilmainham. But otherwise their passion was not hers.

The woman who said Constance Markievicz was a boyish woman and that everything about her was boyish, her sense of fun (that rocked, for instance, at the thought of somebody tripping over a carpet), or her sense of adventure (which made her love every madcap kind of foray) was saying merely, in another way, that she was not made to be happy in the company of solemn women – or men. In after days, in other organizations, she was to meet a great number of women who were definitely not of her sort, especially in the provinces, women who were anything but boyish and to whom she would be handed over bodily at meetings by her men colleagues – the local mayoress, or the local commandant of Cumann na mBan, or the local patroness of Sinn Fein. Simple, astute, effective within their limits, warm-hearted or cold-blooded, she could talk to them of politics, but of politics only and even on politics she once said they were 'as solemn as blazes'. For the rest they could talk to her of housekeeping of which (their sort of housekeeping) she knew little; she could talk to them of horses of which (her sort of horses) they knew less; she could talk to them of art, travel, personalities, and on personalities she could be very entertaining – but it was, again, not always wise to be entertaining in Limerick, let us say, about personalities who were a joy to Dublin but disembodied heroes out of it.

After the first rapture of finding herself accepted by the people and passed, she must have found little to entertain her in these excursions into the small towns of Ireland, in those awful Saturday-night welcomes at the little railway stations where not even the warmth and the earnestness of the welcome could make up for the hours after it in which there was nothing to be done but talk over nothing or walk about the streets meeting the local worthies, or sit in the little poky parlours being introduced to an endless stream of callers, all equally shy, all equally earnest, all equally tongue-tied. There was comradeship in plenty but how much close friendship? It must have exhausted anybody but a woman of the finest heart and the most genial warmth of soul. There was only one escape and most people in her position availed themselves of it – to talk business, even to invent business, without ceasing. She did not avail herself of that escape. She just smoked endlessly, chewed gum, stood with her back to the fire, and blathered away like a machine-gun; and those silent provincials simply loved her for it. But if one doubts that it was an exhausting life one has but to look at her photographs of around 1908 and her photographs of the period just after the Insurrection, when, at forty-eight, she is already an old woman.

For the rest she found that there existed an Irish Socialist Party – and 'existed' is the word for it – in 1908; and that a strike-organizer, Jim Larkin, was stirring up the workers in Belfast and founding a new Irish Trade Union, yet to become famous. She heard vague and inaccurate rumours of the underground extremists; and two years later when they boldly published a weekly paper to express their attitude she heard a little more. Yet it was between these two, the socialists and the extremists, that she was to divide the rest of her life, once she had proved to both that she was not just another dilletante playing, like a child, with fire. Lastly she came to know, one by one, the various literary and debating societies, such as the Students' National Literary Society, or the Celtic Literary Society, that were sometimes merely in sympathy with the Sinn Fein idea, sometimes a cloak for more serious activities. She spoke at or addressed such societies from time to time, measuring her thoughts and theirs, learning bit by bit to know her own people, to become more and more like them, and to persuade them to accept her as one of themselves.

As an indication of how unprepared she was for membership of any extreme Nationalist movement in 1908, it is interesting to advert to the ambitious Christmas and New Year Carnival which she and Casimir helped to organize in Sligo in that year.

It was typical of everything distasteful to Sinn Fein and the Gaelic League. It was parochial and provincial because it took its ideas and its standards from second-rate Dublin concerts, if not second-rate English provincial concerts that in turn took their ideas from second-rate London concerts. With the exception of the Glee Club's singing of Moore's 'Avenging and Bright,' and the actors' Sligo accent, there was nothing in the entire seven-days' entertainment that could have told a visitor that he was not attending a Christmas carnival at some big house in Bucks or Herts. There were four plays – *After the Fair*, the scene Whirligig Hail; *The Dilettante*, by Casimir, a play in three acts, with the scene laid in Major Deering's Shooting Lodge, Scotland, in the Library at Longhurst Hall, and in the 'parlour' of Mrs. Watt's cottage – Constance played the part of the heroine, Lady Althea. The third play, by the members of the Sligo Catholic Institute, was 'The magnificent Tragedy' – *Pizarro*, the scene Peru and the time 1531; the fourth play, alone, suggests that a National Theatre had been in existence for nearly ten years – *Home, Sweet Home*, a comedy by Nora Fitzpatrick and Casimir, the scene Belfast and the time the present. During the entire week only one word of Irish was spoken – and that was in introducing Miss Owens, 'the Dublin soprano, and *Feis* gold medallist'.

And yet there was a great deal about that gay week of entertainment in the west of Ireland that was attractive. It suggests a happy, self-contained society – if not a self contained culture. Catholics and Protestants joined in it, the big house and the cottage, Dublin and Sligo. Of the fifty or sixty women on the ladies' committee, O'Rorkes, Maguires, O'Connors, M'Donaghs, Gilmartins, M'Hughs, M'Canns, Gallaghers, and so forth, there are not more than five or six names that are not the names of the people. And there was much that was artistically ambitious. They had tableaux vivants from pictures by Fra Angelico; a scene from *King John*; the Glee Club sang Webbe's 'When winds breathe soft,' Auer's 'Ave Maria,' Balfe's fine arrangement of Moore's 'Avenging and Bright.' For amusement, too, they had planned liberally with 'Campkin, the champion trick cyclist, and Madame Campkin, the sensationalist Empire trapeze performers, a most delightful and daring act of physical skill'; a ventriloquist, roulette, a shooting-gallery, cards, cinematograph, a marathon race, a tug-of-war, comic songs and sketches; 'Miss Louie Thunder, the juvenile comic'; and Madame Fanny Bauer, the soprano from London; and from Dublin the Markieviczs brought their theatrical friends, Sealy Jeffares and C. J. Browner, to sing; Carré the sculptor; Frank Lowry, Marie nic Shiubhlaigh, Stamer O'Grady, Miss Nora Fitzpatrick, Miss Nellie O'Brien, George

Nesbitt. There was something almost legendary about it – like those folk-tale feasts where 'there was the best of every food and the finest of every drink, and the fun did not stay nor stop nor halt for a year and a day.' The only thing wrong about it all was that it was in no way distinctively Irish.

§ 6

The kind of work for which she was fitted, she always invented for herself. Her first, finest, and last piece of creative work – work not undertaken as a follower but an originator – is testimony to the truth of this. She took the idea of a Nationalist Boy Scout movement mainly from Baden-Powell, who had, in 1908, the previous year, founded his Scout movement in England. She was encouraged to emulate him, in Ireland, by Bulmer Hobson, at that time one of the most energetic and enthusiastic of the secret revolutionaries, the Irish Republican Brotherhood. She simply said – 'Why shouldn't we do that?' and asked him to help her to do it. He told her of his own previous attempt to found such a movement in Belfast, as far back as 1902; at her request and at her expense rented a hall in Lower Camden Street, a poor quarter bordering on the Coombe, and helped her to call an inaugural meeting with Sir Roger Casement and some others on the platform. From then on the Republican Brotherhood kept a fatherly eye on the scouts, or Fianna as they called themselves – taking the name from an old Irish legendary or, it may be, actual force of fighters who had also lent their name to the ancient 'Fenians.' The extremists sometimes gave them help with money, and there is extant a letter from Casement, from somewhere in Africa, sending a gift of ten pounds for 'kilts for the boys'.[1]

1. The Scouts were still in existence in the 1930's, though in a much attenuated form. Rather late in the day efforts were then made to stress their educational value; but it is probably too late since in both the main Irish churches strictly non-political scout movements have meanwhile been founded.
In March, 1934, some 'sixty delegates representing all parts of Ireland, including Northern Ireland, attended the annual Ard-Fheis of Fianna Eireann (the Boy Scouts of Ireland) held at the headquarters, 19 Ely Place, Dublin.
'The Chief Scout (Mr. G. Plunkett) presided, and said that the Fianna Eireann was founded twenty-five years ago by the late Madame Markievicz as a non-political and non-sectarian organization. It was, he said, primarily an educational movement.
'Resolutions were passed deploring "the sectarian spirit which is being

As far as Madame was concerned, half-boy herself, the boys could not have been in better hands – apart from the admitted fact that she had no desire to make them a permanent or lasting movement; they were to contribute to the cause of emancipation and then, presumably, die – as, practically speaking, they have died. She had no wish to found a Scout movement that would last as a Youth movement divorced from that political end. She might have done so – but she would not have been Constance Markievicz had she thought along those lines. So, even here, where her work was useful, and, more than useful – an integral part of the revolution – little but the memory remains. Every other element of the revolutionary period had been merged into the institutions of the new Ireland, and, in one way or another, continues to influence it, except hers.

Her work with the scouts consisted in training them to grow up as soldiers. And one of the more useful things she did with them was to train them to use guns. It was very difficult at that time to procure rifles and revolvers and there was as yet no precedent for openly flouting the law to practise with them. Later when, thanks to Carson, the country was flooded with armed Volunteers, whole companies of men would march out to the mountains, throw out their scouts, and crack away for an hour or two. The police were too few to stop them, and the Castle was playing the game of letting barking dogs bark. But in 1909 the thing was unheard of. She had, however, discovered a law that permitted the use of guns on one's own property, and availing of it she took the little Balalley Cottage in the foothills of the Dublin mountains and brought her Fianna out there. She was a good trainer. She began with small Winchester rifles, then went on to the service rifle and small bulldog revolvers. She was strict in her methods. She made them carry their guns with care; gave her instructions briefly, made them repeat them after her, and supervised their use of the weapons. If she caught a boy pointing a revolver in fun at a comrade she soundly clouted his ears. She did such good

fostered among Irishmen," condemning sectarian Scout organizations, and calling on the youth of Ireland to sink all political and sectarian prejudices, and that Catholics, Protestants and dissenters should unite now as Irish Republicans.
'The question of the Fianna Eireann affiliating with any military or political organizations was discussed, and a resolution was passed against any such affiliation.' *Irish Times*, March 20th, 1934.

work in this way, training the boys to care for guns, clean guns, drill with guns, and generally respect guns that when the Volunteers were founded a few years later there were trustworthy drill-masters available immediately.

If all this was exciting and enjoyable for her, for Casimir it was rather painful. They were living at number fifteen, Garville Avenue, Rathgar, when she started the scout movement, and from then on the scouts or the 'Sprouts' as he contemptuously called them, 'sprouted under thee bed and they sprouted over thee bed, and thee little devil-sprouts drink whiskey, Martin, even locked whiskey!' They were day and night in the house and they ended his peace and ended his painting. It is the greatest pity that he left no record of those days when the sight of Constance Countess Markievicz, of Lissadell and Rathgar, walking down Grafton Street at the head of her scouts, and Cassie standing at the door of Neary's pub in Chatham Street with a big glass of Scotch in his hand, watching them march past, proclaimed finally to Dublin that time was at last taking its revenges on the gay liver; proclaimed, too, to the brick-faced houses of Rathgar and Rathmines, Dartmouth Square and Fitzwilliam Square and Merrion Square, that the time had come to decide whether the Markieviczs were to be invited or not in future. He had no desire to break finally with the Castle folk. He had less desire to be associated, even indirectly, with politics. A Pole, an aristocrat, a member of the Imperial Russian Army, he saw in politics Siberia and chains, and he had no wish for whatever corresponded to either in the British prison system. Even apart from all that, Bohemian and all that he was, the incursion of the ragged-breeches into his home – it was really becoming her home and his hotel – was in itself unpleasant. That big, able-bodied man must have felt that one house was not big enough to hold him and his work and Constance and her work, and felt grimly, as a French journalist said later when he visited them in Leinster Road, 'Ce n'est pas un salon, c'est un quartier general.' (The place is not a salon, it's a General Headquarters.)

One saw him more and more at the Arts Club, dining solitary, or taking refuge in the company of his male friends, Gogarty, Seumas O'Sullivan, Willy Orpen, Martin Murphy, Tommy Furlong, and the rest, cracking his *risqué* jokes at the bar of the Gaiety where he once cracked an English stage-manager's head for being insolent to him, or in his other hundred and one haunts of conviviality, Davy Byrne's, Joyce's, the Bodega, the Bailey, the Winter Gardens of the Royal where the crowd clustered around 'Miss Morissey, the Queen of the Royal Bar'; or Corless's Bar that became Jammet's Restaurant; or you found him up at Lamb Doyle's at Stepaside on a summer Sunday for a drink and a glorious view back at Three Rock, or out over the whole of Dublin, its chimneys coldly smoking or plumeless, and the dark sea fading beyond into the clouds behind Skerries, and somewhere even far northward into County Down.

A gentle, easy going man, it was not fear of contact with life that made him dislike this invasion of his home. He was as willing as Constance to let his front door open of nights lest a stray dog or tramp or any homeless creature might want shelter from the rain. But what was Ireland to him or he to her that he should weep for her? He had no vocation about knowing his own people in Poland; why should he want to know his wife's people in Ireland? He had something of the feeling of Wilde when a friend in a rowdy café marched before him crying, 'This is Oscar Wilde, my friend, and whoever touches him will deal with me!' – 'You are protecting us at the risk of our lives.' 'Is there no one,' asked Cassie, 'to appear in a burning bush to save me? She offer me to Ireland as a sacrifice.' And off he marches with his troop to another snug and another reviling of Fate. If she were logical, he might have said, she should have sent him back to Poland to fill his mother's house with the ragged-breeches of Zyvolavka. He had gone off there so often and for such long periods already that in her new exalted mood she would probably not have minded.

And when, as usual, he did go in the spring of 1909 – to earn his year's income – she does not appear to have minded even less than usual. A new enthusiasm had seized her.

§ 7

It all started with the reading of Craig's book on the famous Ralahine experiment in Co. Clare, *The History of Ralahine*, which Bulmer Hobson lent Madame. Here she read how, as a result of a number of lectures in Dublin, in 1823, by Robert Owen, the English socialist evangel, Arthur Vandeleur, a member of a well-known Shannon-side landlord family, resolved to establish a co-operative colony among his tenants. For a time the project flourished until the originator helped to ruin it by losing his fortune at the gaming-table; the law finished the downfall of the commune by refusing to recognize the right of such a community to hold property and the whole thing was swallowed up without mercy by the bankruptcy courts.

Who fathered the wild idea of resurrecting this commune in Dublin is now hard to say. Nobody is ever particularly anxious to own an abortion. Undoubtedly a good deal of the enthusiasm came from the ever-enthusiastic Madame. Bulmer Hobson is also, at least partially, responsible in that he put the idea into her head. Casimir was away in Poland at the time, happily for his peace of mind. Only Miss Helena Moloney is left of those who took an active part in it.

Hobson, was not, at first, without enthusiasm for the idea of reviving the utopia, and as Madame was enchanted by it, and could talk nothing else for weeks, he obligingly went into figures with her, explained the scheme in detail, and agreed to be one of those who would join her if she found a suitable house and farm. Sick to death of the little suburban house in Rathgar, and eager to live again in the country as she had done when a child in Sligo, eager, too, to have larger premises for her Scouts. Madame pushed on the scheme with her usual energy. The first thing to do was to gather in ten or twelve people who would share the expenses and the losses, if they should, as of course they would not and could not, be. Had not Vandeleur succeeded until he threw away the scheme on faro! The next thing was to find a small farmhouse or some eight or ten rooms with six or eight acres of land. But the disciples were not easy to find – not in cynical Edwardian Dublin. 'Oh, no!' they said. 'We know Madame! And Cassie! Not to mention the Scouts.' Nor was a house easy to find. In the end the only place available proved to be Belcamp Park, Raheny, a fine, big, roughcast-limestone house about six miles north of Dublin off the Malahide Road, for their purposes a barrack of a house (it has about twenty rooms) and its land, stablings, and walled-garden, itself almost as big as a small farm, were all in a shocking state of disrepair. With it went seven and a half acres of land. Its rental, then, was about one hundred odd pounds a year. Madame was delighted with it and fought tooth and nail to get a five years lease.

It is certainly one of the most attractive houses in that part of County Dublin, hidden away among the flat winding side roads, west of Raheny, that lead to nowhere in particular. In the eighteenth century the place was a kind of rural Rathmines where the muddy and dusty boreens thrust here and there by inconsiderate demesnes, existed only to link gate-lodge to gate-lodge, a place where gentlemen played at farming when labour was as cheap as slave-labour, and all the privileges of wealth were as yet unimpeached by the lower orders. Swift built a glebe-house nearby, a red brick building so solidly temperate in style, apart from its odd lantern on the roof, that one almost looks around instinctively for the appropriate Flemish or Dutch canal and the frail line of poplars against the low sky. Grattan lived over the way in Belcamp House. In the grounds of Belcamp Hall there is a tower to the fame of George Washington, erected there by an admiring Irishman who corresponded with him in spite of the immense distance between.

Flat, drowsy country stretches away to a horizon broken only by hedges of magnificent beech clustered in soft domes against the pale summer air, or black and ragged and erect against the cold winter clouds. It is the landscape of the pictures of Nathaniel Hone who lived across the fields from Belcamp Park in Madame's day. From the drawing-room windows there is a magnificent view over the cropped fields to the hill of Howth, the sea sparkling here and there between the trees, at night the lights on the hill wavering in the pulsing air. Artane, the little village to the south-east, measures the low level of the countryside – in Gaelic 'the little height,' the one protuberance seen between the house and the distant smooth flow of the Dublin mountains or the peaked sandstone top of the Sugarloaf miles way in Wicklow across Dublin Bay.

Up to the beginning of the century the place had scarcely altered its character of leisurely and profitable toil – servants' toil. Then Belcamp Park was owned by Lady Farren, an absentee landlord, spending the easy profits in Cheltenham. Under the Wyndham Act of 1903 the tenant-right was bought by Sir John Jervis-White-Jervis. All about, the very names of the houses retain, still, that same flavour of absenteeism – Priorswood, Cameron Lodge, Bonnybrook House – the flavour of, to be sardonic, Griffith's constitution of 1782 and Grattan's 'patriots' parliament'. Perhaps that was why she liked the place; it reminded her of Lissadell – it was not unlike the house at Lissadell, and in her time the place was fallen into that raggedness that is more common far from Dublin, hedges left uncut, lodges squat and sagging, gates once more useful than ornamental by now becoming things more of ornament than use. It was ideal for the scouts, for it had many outhouses, decrepit as they were, plenty of yard-space, quite practicable in summer if there was not too much rain, and it was really in the country though within walking or cycling distance of the capital whose pale night-glow so lit the clouds to the south that it was never really dark about the tents. By day the city smoke hung like a dust over the distant woods.

Not even the pleasant aspect of the place however sufficed to attract disciples. Besides it was nearly the end of summer, 1909, before she got clear of Garville Avenue and lumbered out with her furniture to Raheny. In the end the commune was reduced to four people and one of these was an expert agricultural instructor from Glasnevin College. This, perhaps, was the last thing needed to assure the little band of the certainty of success. It almost set the seal of a government scheme on their Utopia. Dublin watched with interest, a grin hovering about its lips.

At once the 'barrack' swallowed up the enthusiasts. It seemed immense and cold after the three storey house in suburbia, 'with all modern conveniences.' It sweated damp on rainy days. Seen in the cold light of October the place was a wilderness. For four years nature had run riot over the walled garden. The rain and frost and fog indicated, far from mildly, that the only solid thing about the outhouses was the wall against which they leaned their weary bones. The drainage had not been cleared for years. The fields were sodden when the autumn passed and there were lakes in the yards. The hedges were excellent hedges; there was plenty of wood in them. Belcamp Park was a testimony to the utility of the Wyndham Act and the methods of absenteeism.

Still, they were only beginning. Up at sparrow-call, bed at sundown, that was to be the rule – once they got going, once the lamps came and they need not stick candles on the mantelpieces, once the expert got all the implements he wanted, once the baker and the butcher and the grocer realized they were really expected to call, once this and that and the other. Then out came the Scouts – in their millions as it seemed to the commune. Only the expert was free and in the walled garden he seemed as lost as a snail in a jungle. The others, Madame and her friend, that is to say, cooked and washed up from eight in the morning to eight at night. Bulmer Hobson, who, finding the scheme was not being worked according to plan, had nevertheless come out against his better judgment, had to leave them daily to attend to politics in town. The commune was virtually reduced to the expert in the walled garden.

Even Madame soon began to see that things were not going quite according to programme. Her own word for it was that things were a bit 'thick'. However, they encouraged each other by saying that once things got going . . . And meanwhile by degrees – of course admittedly by degrees, the expert in the walled garden was getting things ready for serious work.

So things dragged on well into the Christmas period and then suddenly Casimir arrived back from Poland. In Joyce's and Byrne's and Neary's he soon heard the ripple of laughter over the Raheny commune and many sly jokes and tip-o'-the-wink smiles set him hot-foot out to see what the hell Constance was up to now. It was really too good a situation even for Casimir and he made the utmost of it; it appealed to all his sense of drama, and being a man whose mind at the most slight and tenuous cobweb of a suggestion filled at once with fantastic visions of intrigue, three-cornered situations, assignations, and what-not, he exploited to the full the possibilities for drama in the domestic arrangements at Raheny. One really begins to be sorry for poor Madame at this point. For once in her life she was getting far too much of the limelight. She was sure to lose money over the scheme, as also were her friends. And here was Cassie spreading the most unscrupulous stories about her all over Dublin.

Casimir's own account of his arrival was probably not quite gospel truth but it has all the marks of a general veracity. 'I have great trouble to find this house but at last I find it and I send away the cabbie. I find the house at the end of the avenue, all dark, all silent. I knock and I knock but not a sound. I go around the back and I call out, "Constance!" No sound. I come around to the front and I knock and I call out, "Constance!" After a while a window goes up and a dirty little ragamuffin puts out his head and say "Who da?" I say, "I want to see Countess Markievicz." He go away and I wait. No sound. I knock again and I call, "Constance!" Another window go up and another dirty little ragamuffin say, "Who da?" I say, "I am Count Markievicz and I want to see Countess Markievicz." I hear much scuffling and running and at last the door open. It is all dark but I see Constance. "It's very dark, Constance." I say. "We have only one lamp," she says, "and the gardener is reading with that." We go into the drawing-room and there I find the gardener with his legs on the mantelpiece, and he is smoking a dirty, filthy shag tobacco. He does not stand up when I go in. I say, "I am hungry. Cannot I have some food?" And they scuffle and they whisper again while I talk to the gardener. At last they bring me cold meat and bread and butter. That is how I return to my home.'

His, too, the account of the only coup the gardener ever made. Cassie had badgered and bullied the poor fellow until in the end the man decided that he really must show some return. As it was nearing Christmas time he cut down a holly tree in the front of the house and rattled off with it at dawn to Dublin where he sold it for thirty shillings. He was quite proud of himself until the landlord's agent observed the naked stump and billed the Countess for five pounds compensation.

To the end of the adventure Cassie harassed them. Perhaps he was having his revenge for the scouts. His method was simply to tell absurd stories about the scheme – often against himself. Once he came into Dublin of a morning, very hoarse. 'What on earth has happened to your voice?' they asked. 'It is this way,' explained the *flaneur*. 'Last night the expert woke us to say there was noise of sheep in the kitchen-garden. "You must get up and hunt them out," says Constance. So, I get up and I go to thee window in my pyjamas, and I see thee sheep in the moonlight. And I bark at them like a dog. And when I bark they go and when I stop they return. "You must go out and hunt them," says Constance. "I will not go out", I say. So I stay there all night and I bark and I bark. And my voice is quite gone,' he hissed, 'when the morning come.' It was surely he too who started these stories, which there is no reason to believe, that the scouts were often on such short fare that they raided the larders and left Cassie without his supper; wherefore in his wardrobe, really a built-in closet of tiny proportions, with his trousers and his boots he would secrete pieces of bread and meat, and he, huge man, crouched inside this dark hole would devour hastily what he had salvaged from the hungry horde, while Madame stood guard outside the door in the bedroom, asking him impatiently if he had yet finished. Occasionally, too, they went across the fields to dine with Nathaniel Hone, the painter. It is recorded that he said that the two Markieviczs ate like tigers and confessed that it was really for the food rather than the company they came.

Having exhausted the possibilities in one direction Cassie now began to turn the dinners at Raheny into board meetings. He asked leading questions about the scheme itself, primed by

Æ, ignoring Madame, who ought to have known her husband better, when she was uncommunicative as from scorn. Miss Moloney, who only knew Cassie as Dublin knew him, for a good liver, a good companion, a Bohemian, a painter, a dilettante, and man-about-town, leaned back and smiled over his efforts to be business-like. For Bulmer Hobson, torn between his sense of loyalty to Madame, and his common sense that told him the scheme had never panned out according to programme, with its attenuated numbers, attenuated capital, and the unforeseen complications of the scouts, the thing must have been extremely painful. Besides no two such opposite types as the deadly-earnest revolutionary and the cynical Bohemian ever met as met there over these dinner-table discussions.

Despite their scorn and to the rather painful surprise of Madame, indeed to her dismay, Casimir shewed himself to be an astute man of business. With the help of Æ's figures he pricked the balloon of their enthusiasm – already a rather sagging balloon. Hobson left for Belfast, the expert left the walled-garden, and Madame and Miss Moloney stayed on until they could dispose of the rest of the five years lease as profitably as they could. This they managed to do in April, 1911, when they moved back into Dublin, first to a five-roomed flat in Mount Street, and then back again to suburbia, to Surrey House, Leinster Road. The experiment cost, in net loss, two hundred and fifty pounds.

§ 8

In all the Raheny co-operative commune lasted for at most two months. The remainder of the year and a half spent at Belcamp Park was devoted wholly to the Scouts, whose organization she began to make as perfect as possible. Gradually her ragamuffin army began to look presentable. She made the boys work under their own General Staff, inventing an Executive Council to advise on policy. Of this she was elected President, took part in the Staff meetings, and became *ex officio*, Chief Scout.[1]

They had small taste for woodcraft and the rest of the picturesque and harmless skill which the Baden-Powell scout

1. On the staff at one time or another in the initial stage were:— Liam Mellowes, who took command of Galway city and county during the 1916 Insurrection and was executed by the Free State government during the Civil War; the first captain, Con Colbert, executed in 1916; Sean Heuston, executed in 1916; Joseph MacKelvey, executed by the Free State government.

loves to learn, but they revelled in Signalling, Drilling, First-aid, Shooting, and all such forms of militaristic training. They gave the local police a worrying year while they were at Raheny; they would play such pranks on them – very Markieviczian in tone – as lying in ambush for the patrols and then with bicycle-pumps making noises like rifle-bolts loading. It was fun, then, to see the cautious pause on the part of the police, and the mummery of their sudden decision that it was 'looking like rain', and time to return home. It would have been a very dangerous prank in later years, but at this period the country police were taken seriously by nobody – easy going folk whose sole occupation was reading the *Weekly Freeman* and creasing their polls in the sun.

They did all the other usual things that boys do. Madame had a dog, Poppet, which some of them disliked intensely and regarded only as 'an ould dog you'd love to root', and behind her back Poppet did get an occasional 'root'. They armed themselves with her best cutlery. For all that they liked her, they sometimes laughed at her accent and imitated her high shrill voice. Boys at school do the same thing with their teachers. And some of them would tell her over-pathetic stories – or their mothers would. That was something from which she always suffered, but though she knew it and was told of it she could never risk disbelief in any appeal from one of her protégés.

On the other hand, though everybody, now that she is dead, pays tribute to her, it is also evident that many of these boys adored her without reserve from the beginning and that some of her most loyal friends were found among those youngsters. After all she had to have some recompense for the sacrifices she made – the surrender of the outward code and manners of her class, her delight in dainty and beautiful things, food, dress, possessions of every kind, though some people did not sympathize with these surrenders, or her adoption from this on, of unkempt clothes, or such habits as gum-chewing. They either dismissed it all as affectation or dismissed her for an insensitive, strident, raucous woman, who had let herself go to pieces. It was probably a little of both in that cottage among the hills, for example, you now saw her in any old skirt and jumper, barelegged striding through the whins; yet if you asked her to dine she came in all the tasteful dress of earlier days. But is it not, sufficiently, simple carelessness and formality both in the same woman? Instead people asked, petulantly,

Why can't she be herself? Forgetting that in that case they merely meant, Why can't she be like us? For if she were herself she must inevitably behave just as she did – a white blackbird.

Poor soul, neither white enough for Lissadell, nor black enough for Dublin – she came more than once to friends in a moody and downcast state. Desmond Fitzgerald, who was afterwards Minister for Defence in the Free State cabinet, and possibly took part in the unpleasant task of ordering her commitment to jail during the civil-war, recounts one such visit when he, too, lived in the hills, and he remembers how utterly despondent she was, thinking of her daughter, Maeve, thinking of the fewness of her friends, thinking over many things that she had done and could wish undone in her life. She put down, afterwards, some of her impressions of those days, admitting that the work of organizing the movement was such very uphill work that she often felt depressed and almost hopeless. 'A branch would start up spontaneously, crowded with enthusiastic kids, all wanting to start fighting at once; and then they would gradually disappear one by one when they found they were not to go out fighting the English the next week. But out of each branch started, a couple of really sincere, clever boys would come to the surface and these boys formed the nucleus of the real Fianna.'

Young Mellowes was such a boy. He had a job in Dublin which was paying him adequately when he came to Madame, and told her, rather with a twinkle in his eye, she records, that he was thinking of giving it up for a better one. The young man went on to explain that he had a bicycle and a good new coat, and his idea was to sally out, with this equipment, on the roads of Ireland, as an evangel for the scouts. All he asked her to do was to raise thirty shillings to set him on his way and to guarantee ten shillings a week after 'in case of emergencies'; but he would never really need that ten shillings a week since sympathetic people would be sure to offer him food and lodgings wherever he went. Bulmer Hobson, who was then the most active member of the Irish Republican Brotherhood, believes that Mellowes was much more than a Fianna boy, at this stage, and that he was really cloaking his more serious activities as an I.R.B. organizer under the less serious ones of the scouts – in which case Madame did even more than she imagined when, after much troubled consideration, she sent the youth on his way. From that day Mellowes' life was one of endless struggle and strife. It ended with the inevitable calvary of the devoted revolutionary. He was shot, in 1923, by his former comrades.

Her comment on his life and death (published in a typescript pamphlet during the civil-war) is worth quoting as being typical of her own more exalted moods, and the more intense and exalted moods of her boys: 'He earned the fear and hate of (here she mentions a cabinet-minister of the Free State government) who knew that in the end Ireland must stand for Liam and for the honourable and courageous who care more for honour and integrity than for life; so he had him killed. But Liam, dead, will conquer and the Republic, for which he died, prevail against her enemies.'

§ 9

Roheny helps to define the atmosphere about the rebel countess; the commune – the scouts; the count – Hobson; play – serious work; comedy – the tragic note. Surrey House, to which she came from Raheny, defines the atmosphere about the rebel's husband as one of good-humour become exasperated.

For Surrey House was neither a home nor the mansion that the name suggests. Its postal address of 49B Surrey Road, gives a much better idea of its extent and appearance – a red-brick villa chequered with yellow facings, fronted with a small garden-plot and approached through a creaking iron handgate. She made small effort to build up a home here; she was possibly weary of the struggle to make a home according to her taste on an income inadequate for it. She could have made a home in a big country house where she would have a butler and a gardener and servants; but not in a row of suburban houses, on a few hundred a year.

In a few months the place was untidy, unkempt, and next to uncomfortable, a house where you found in the hall a hatstand leaning under its weight of hats and coats, parcels all over the tiles, pictures askew, and you hung your own hat, more than likely, on a nail driven into the cracked plaster. Constance had begun, too, to dislike or to pretend to dislike carpets – she said they were fusty-musty things, and she went so far as to leave even the bare board unstained. 'Why bother?' was her point of view. 'It's clean. If I stain it people will leave bootmarks on the polish and the maids will begin to complain. It doesn't show on the naked timber.' And yet the place was filled with good pictures, bric-à-brac, tapestries, books, fine furniture. The result was bizarre, and even invigorating for its originality – as she, through her histrionic side, possibly knew. A frequent note from her would read something like: 'Come around to-night and meet so-and-so. The carpets are up and the gas off. But we'll talk.' Or, if you came in around supper-time, she would cry a welcome of, 'I doubt if there is anything in the house to eat. But we'll have some bread and butter anyway.' It was just a trifle embarrassing to the good Dublin bourgeoisie who were unaccustomed to sailing so close to the wind. To them to have one's gas cut off by the company was a disgrace. To her, a joke. Or she made it a joke – much, one suspects, in the same spirit as she made a joke about Cassie's 'lovely ladies'. One knows these people. 'Come into our hovel,' they say, disarming your criticism. 'Cassie is a gay dog,' may have been one way of hiding a wound. In polite society are not fictions commonly treated as realities and realities passed off as fiction?

She may have enjoyed it, nevertheless been glad to abandon appearances too tedious to preserve. She filled her house with an endless crowd of visitors, for Irish people love that kind of house where you just lift the latch and call in – the manners of the country brought into the town. If you did call on her in that way you might find candles lighting the drawing-room, somebody thumping gaily on the piano while heel-and-toe merrily rattled out a jig on the bare floor. Over by the fire you saw the countess, a little dishevelled, a cigarette hopping on her lips as she gabbled away to her latest 'lion'. Rarely, now – 1911 onward – was it a literary lion; rather some social or political revolutionary like old John Devoy on a visit from America, or Jim Larkin down from Cork, and just out of jail. It was June when Devoy visited Dublin, the June of the coronation celebrations: with him she addressed a wildly disloyal meeting from the custom house steps. Cassie might be there, too, watching the couples whirling by him in a set or a barndance, keeping up a witty conversation with some city clerk or disaffected civil servant. If the place got on his nerves he just went off to town for a drink and conversation. If that was not possible he got cross or morose at this deafening gabble about him. Once when a Citizen Army man (a year or so later than this date) was insolent to him about people with titles he suddenly caught the man by the neck and trousers and dropped him out of the window. 'So!' he grunted at the roomful of people, fallen into a sudden silence at his rage. Then Constance laughed and he dissolved into laughter too and the dance went its way.

It was much worse for him than Raheny. There were scouts everywhere now, more obvious in this small house; there were so many people coming and going that he did not know what the half of them did or wanted. Heaven only knew what was going on in his own drawing-room if he opened the door and had to retire with apologies before some conference or other. If he rang his own front-door bell, the door was, likely as not, opened by some Scout who demanded the password before letting him in. While as for painting – it was a thing of the past. Every inch of space here was required, now, for Con's schemes, everything was subordinated to them. She, too, had definitely given up serious drawing and had taken to writing pamphlets, songs, speeches, drawing political cartoons. She bought an old printing-press and from it she reeled off seditious handbills that piled up on the dining-room table, on the settees, on the chairs, mixed with scout equipment, blank paper, carbon, typewriters, the overcoats and hats and umbrellas of the visitors. Worst of all, from Cassie's point of view, the house was now constantly under the observation of 'G' men from Brunswick Street, the centre of the British secret service squad in Ireland. Little wonder he began to stay away from the place, losing himself in his plays.

In her abandon to the cause of Ireland she had become oblivious of self, husband, child, and home. It was only a question of time before her child became, in return, oblivious of her; before her husband virtually left her; and her home, and all in it that the two of them had put together, stick by stick, in their golden days, disappeared in ruin. Yet once again, even if she had foreseen it all, she would probably not have greatly cared. Then, at any rate, she did not, held by a new excitement and a new personality, one of the most dramatic of all who had so far come her way. It was the excitement of the Dublin slums crying out for bread and blood, urged to the barricades by a man with the lips of a woman, the tongue of a Danton, the eyes of a child and the heart of a tiger, named Jim Larkin.

CHAPTER IV

THE POOR:
1911–1913

§ 1

That year of her return to Dublin and the years following – 1911 and 1912 – were years of terrible misery for the poor, not merely of Dublin but the United Kingdom. In England, where national politics readily assimilated these economic problems, everything passed off more or less smoothly, but what started in Dublin as a series of Labour troubles ended in a revolution. That merger between socialism and nationalism she was to symbolize when she fought, in 1916, with the Citizen Army under the flag of the Plough and the Stars.

Even through the merest outline one can sense the excitement (and the suffering) of those years. It began in the July of her return with a strike of seamen and firemen that crippled the port; accompanied by the already 'usual' sympathetic strike of dockers and carters, and the (also usual) sympathetic lock-out of other workers by the masters, in this case of some eight-hundred men controlled by the Coal Merchants' Association. This strike was barely settled when the London dockers and the Liverpool railwaymen downed tools. In London eighty thousand men were out by the second week in August, and in Liverpool alone, by the 15th, thirty thousand dockers had been sent home by the employers. Rail trouble spread to Ireland just as things were being settled in England, and out of this Irish trouble there arose a bitter fight between the men and the employers engaged in the Irish timber trade. For as the rail-strike began to fizzle out and people were breathing freely, it transpired that the timber merchants had locked out five hundred of their men on the 21st owing to the dislocation of the rail-services. This fight was the first preliminary to a crisis.[1]

Early in September the goods-workers of the G.S.W. Railway executed a lightning strike in sympathy. The thing spread

1. This account follows Clarkson, q.v. p. 240 f., but there appears to have been a minor wages dispute as well. The definition of a 'lock-out' as opposed to a 'strike' is always difficult; often depending on nothing more tangible than a point-of-view.

until a general strike seemed inevitable, but the English unions refused to co-operate adequately, the railway directors locked out thirteen hundred men at Inchicore, and in October the men capitulated under humiliating conditions. They had been through a bad time and they had not even the satisfaction of a partial victory.

The real issue which made this particular fight significant was only implicit there. In a bitter struggle that was meanwhile going on between the ironmasters and their foundry-workers in Wexford, the issue was clear. What had happened was that two firms of ironmasters closed down their foundries, locking out five hundred and fifty men. 'The men had made no demands, had made no trouble, *but had joined the Irish Transport and General Workers' Union.*' The local organizer, P. T. Daly (to be heard of again as a member of the Irish Republican Brotherhood), was willing that the men should join any other bona fide union but insisted on their right to join the I.T.G.W.U. if they so wished. Refusing every effort at intervention the masters stood firm and one by one closed down their plants. They saw the menace of what was already being called Larkinism. The rail strike spreading from England made it a favourable time for a fight; they filled the little town with hundreds of police, and as the arrival of the police was always the signal for disorder in Ireland – due partly to a feeling of resentment among the people, partly to the over-officiousness of the old Royal Irish Constabulary – the local organizer was soon arrested and jailed for inciting to riot. James Connolly took Daly's place in January and six months after the outbreak of trouble effected a settlement on Daly's original offer. The masters agreed to recognize an Irish Foundry Workers' Union and reinstated the men without victimization. As the new Union was affiliated with the suspect I.T.G.W.U., and two years later was absorbed into it, this effort to smash the new menace, that had come on the heels of Larkin into Irish politics, was hardly a success for the masters.

That fight, the second major preliminary to the crisis of the following year, was in fact directed not so much against a Union, or even a man (for all that Larkin typified, as he had created, that movement) as against a vague stirring, a menacing restlessness that had for the first time in the history of Ireland begun *from below*.

But if it was Larkinism to the employers it was also Larkin to the workers. Unready to understand a movement, they had no difficulty in understanding a man. And not surprisingly so, for Larkin was a remarkable man, a born leader if there ever was one. His personality fired all Ireland in those days and it was his personality as much as his ideas that attracted Constance Markievicz.

He was everything that she would have liked to be and he had done everything she would have liked to do. He had spent his life among the down-and-out and for the down-and-out. He was a man who could produce swift results by direct action. And, looking back at his life and hers, she must have realized that between the two of them, she with her politics apparently taking the long view, and he with his strikes the short view, it was he who produced lasting results, and she who – as far as the people she wished to help were concerned – produced no practical results at all. Larkin gave her the one and only opportunity she was to get of doing something practical for that part of Irish life which, one feels, was her true vocation. She seized it readily without – as so often happens to all of us – realizing what she seized. So that when Larkin departed for America in 1914 she turned back to other things. That has always been the fate of the Irish underdog – to be swallowed by the hounds of Nationalism. Even as Pearse could speak of 'Ireland poor and lowly and low in the dust' – and had as little to say for the poor and lowly Irish, sunk in the mud of misery; she, too, hypnotized by the same rich-dream-colour of the Poor Old Woman, could not see, for more than a little interval, that the poor old women of the Dublin slums were, in their rags, a dream beyond even that panoply of ancient vision. That brief interval of lucidity she owed to a man whom her class and blood called and treated as a yahoo.

§ 2

Larkin had come out of the dark netherworld with the eyes and face of a poet. He burned with a fiery simplicity of belief in his fellow-man and his speech to them was like a lava. When he came to work among them, in Ireland, the year Constance Markievicz 'went native', he was a young man of thirty-one just beginning to realize his own powers; he had mild but wide, clear eyes, questioning, almost staring; a long nose; sensuous lips; a sombre lock of hair across his forehead; the hollowed cheeks and high cheekbones of an ascetic.

Born in Newry, in Ulster, and taken to England as a baby, he grew to a hard but pitying wisdom in the Liverpool slums. At seven he was working forty hours a week for two shillings and sixpence, with the perquisite of a current bun and a glass of milk on Saturday nights. At nine he was earning three shillings as a full-time apprentice to a bibulous paper-hanger whom he left, quixotically, when he realized that he was keeping a grown man out of a job. He served his time to a French polisher, lost that job also, and found himself at the age of ten and a half wandering and starving on the London road. He got odd relief jobs; he worked at the docks; he was left fatherless at fourteen. Thereafter he did anything and everything that would put a bite of food into his belly – stevedoring, portering, carting, coal-heaving, carrying bags, bushelling – in brief every conceivable job afloat and ashore. Then with ten others he stowed away to the River Plate and among his group of vagrants (employed on discovery, as trimmers in the stokehold) he began his career as a 'menace.'

'After we had broke bulk I called them together, pointed out that we had only one change of clothing, and it would be destroyed working coal; they were giving us burgo and molasses for breakfast instead of hash, and those of us who smoked had no tobacco. I suggested writing out our demands and that a deputation be sent to the skipper about it. Some said we would be shot for mutiny but they agreed that an old shellback named White, and I, should go. Our demands were, "no watches, work from six to six, regular meal-hours, same food as crew, each man to be supplied with one set of dungarees and one shirt, a plug of tobacco a week and no work on Sundays". The captain, Evans by name, was a little chap and refused point-blank. We told him we would work no more and he replied we would get no food. Knowing some of the firemen I had them posted and the first thing next morning, as soon as the sailors turned out and the forecastle crowd were coming forward with the grub, we waylaid them and relieved them of the grub, returned to the forecastle and had breakfast.

'Then the row commenced; the firemen refused to work without breakfast and the upshot of the affair was we gained our point. White and I were sent for by the old man. He tried bluffing us, putting us in irons, said he would get us jailed on our arrival at Monte Video, and then not only conceded all we asked but granted us an allowance also of one bottle of square-

faced gin each day. It is unnecessary for me to say I had no
gin and further I got the crowd to give the gin to the firemen
who had stood by us. Before arrival at Buenos Ayres I was
agreeably surprised by the mate giving me twenty-five dollars
Argentine – worth at that time 1s. 2d.

'On the way up to Mobile I again got at loggerheads with
the Chief Engineer who was always wanting me to assist the
greaser. One night about two bells after I had turned in he sent
the donkey-man forward to tell me I had to take one of the
firemen's places. I refused; pointed out that I had been working
hard all day at coals and refused to do any more. The chief
sent for me and as I was entering the alley-way I was seized
by the chief donkey-man, second engineer and third mate, who
with other assistance carried me into No. Three hold and
ironed me to a stanchion, leaving me only a tin of water. What
a night I passed. The rats came around me in hundreds. They
ate all my fingernails and toenails. It makes me shiver even
now. . . .'

It is worth while giving that incident in full, not for its
own sake as a picturesque adventure but because it illustrates
the man, his pluck, his belief in men, the return of that belief
in their trust in him.

So his youth went on. Back in Liverpool, he became, after
several years more of hardship, foreman in a shipping firm.
Then after a strike, in which he lost that job, he began his
career as organizer for the National Union of Dock Labourers,
and so back to Ireland in 1907, beginning with Belfast. From
that on, Irish Labour began to fight and to close up its ranks
while fighting. He led it in strikes at Cork, Wexford, Dublin,
Waterford, Sligo, working among the poorest and the least
skilled, trying to discipline men who had broken every previous
attempt to organize them, fighting a lone hand, opposed constantly by the cautious and conservative members of his own
executive – it was this that really made him found in 1909, the
purely Irish 'Transport and General Workers' Union' – getting
small encouragement from the better-class trades in Ireland,
hindered, especially in Belfast, by all sorts of racial and religious prejudices, victimized on at least one occasion by the law
– which acknowledged its injustice later by releasing him from
the term of imprisonment to which it had sentenced him –
often directly opposed by the church, a heart-breaking, uphill
job, year in and year out, with weapons that had grown so

rusty from lack of use that he never knew the second they would break in his hand.[1]

The methods inevitable to such a warfare did not please everybody. They are best described by giving the example of Connolly's work in Belfast with the I.T.G.W.U. Going there in 1910, on Larkin's release from jail, he found the men again fallen spiritless, and powerless, since Larkin's departure, exploited almost without knowing it. On the docks, for example, in order to extract the last ounce of energy out of the grain-labourers, a system of bonuses had been introduced, by which, for an additional fifth of a day's work, crowded into a ten hours' stretch, a man got a tenth of a day's pay. As there was always a surplus of unskilled labour polishing the quay walls with their ragged shoulders, and as none or few could stand the pace for more than three days running, it was nothing less than a merciless using up of the unfortunate wretches' human energy after which they were thrown, weary and idle, on the quays until they had recuperated for another bout of hell-for-leather. 'By tips to winchmen, firemen, etc., the situation was made worse. The pace was kept up on the fillers and carriers by curses, obscene language, even physical violence, along with the ever-present threat of dismissal, while tally-men and checkers were forbidden to reveal the actual tonnage being done until the day's end. Hence while one hundred tons had been taken as a day's average, one hundred and sixty, one hundred and eighty, and two hundred tons as a day's work came to be regarded as in no wise remarkable. One man had to carry this weight over his back from hatch to shiprail in each gang. All day long other men toiled in the suffocating hold, barefooted, half-naked, choked with dust, while tubs rushed up and down over their heads with such rapidity that the men's muscles were strained to breaking point and the feverish recklessness was a constant menace to life and limb.' In other

---

1. The number of times the law has been used against Larkin is interesting. The briefest search has noted that he was charged with wounding, July 24th, 1907; fraud, August 20th, 1909; false pretences, June 18th, 1910 – the sentence was remitted in September, 1910 – voting before expiry of five years from the date of a criminal conviction, March 1st, 1912; assault, September 28th, 1912; for once as plaintiff when one Peter Sheridan was given six months for assaulting him in North Frederick Street, Dublin, during the 1913 strike; seditious libel and revolutionary conspiracy August 29th, 1913, for which he was sentenced to seven months in October, 1913; and he has been in the lawyers' hands almost as often in recent years.

words the workers exploited one another with the astute help of the bosses.[1]

Plenty here, surely, for a Larkin or a Markievicz to weep at; good reason for strikes, sudden and sympathetic, guerilla-work of all sorts, 'scorn for agreements', contempt for all 'legal and parliamentary' methods of attack. At any rate so Connolly thought. Once at Dixon's timber-yard in Dublin the men were locked out; by his orders the Transport Union struck in Dixon's Belfast works; the Dublin men were, at once, reinstated and given their wages for the lost day. Another time a dock-labourer named Keenan was killed at the unloading of a ship in the Belfast docks, and the employer's solicitor suggested he had been murdered because he was a non-Unionist. At dinner-hour Connolly called out the men working on the employer's ship, the *Nile*, and they refused to return until the insinuation was repudiated; within an hour 'everything was arranged.' On another occasion the Ulster linen mills decided to curtail output by fifteen per cent, and as a result the mills were put on short time. Individual millowners, however, began to cheat their own federation by speeding-up output within the limited time – thus reducing wages without reducing results; new rules began to fine employees for such crimes as laughing, whispering, bringing in sweets, a newspaper, darning or knitting-needles, fixing hair. 'The whole atmosphere', Connolly reported in the *Irish Worker* (October, 1911), 'was an atmosphere of slavery.' He called the girls out on strike, and because the other union leaders would not help them, they voted for a textile branch of the fighting I.T.G.W.U. As it proved to be a bad time for a fight Connolly had to order the girls back, but he sent them back with instructions to break systematically every one of the objectionable rules. 'If a girl is checked for singing,' he instructed them, 'let the whole room start singing at once. If you are checked for laughing let the whole room laugh at once. If anyone is dismissed all put on your shawls and come out in a body. And when you are returning, do not return as you generally do but gather in a body outside the gate and march in singing and cheering.' They did so. 'The girls went in singing and they came out singing again.' And when the bosses capitulated they went in singing again.

Clearly these were methods which could not but lead to a

1. *The Irish Labour Movement*. W. P. Ryan, p. 203 f. See also Clarkson, op. cit., and Connolly's *The Axe to the Root*, Dublin, 1910.

final clash. For if Labour employed shock-tactics so could the employers. They were methods, and these were circumstances, that could only produce either complete disorganization of industry or amelioration of the conditions under which industrialists made their money. Often, as in Wexford at the Pierce foundries, it ended in a drawn battle; often, it ended in a defeat for the men. But it all served to organize Labour. The crisis came in 1913 – for Labour and for Larkin – and it was a critical year in the history of Constance Markievicz. In that year the employers, sick to death of the guerrilla methods of the I.T.G.W.U., went on strike themselves.

§ 3

It is, admittedly, easier now to see that 1913 was a year of crisis in the history of modern Ireland than it was to see it then, and one cannot blame Constance Markievicz if she did not feel that her fate was being born. One has to remember that people were even still, at that late date, squabbling over Parnell. A row at a public Board was enough, yet, to fill columns in the daily papers, if his name was but mentioned. Or if the British Navy sent its Home Fleet to Kingstown all Ireland was capable of forgetting everything else in its excitement. Or, if Home Rule was taking up too much time at Westminster the whole body of Anglo-Irish loyalists went pale with anxiety and called meetings to protest, beseech and threaten. One can almost feel grateful when George Moore murmurs through his window at Ely Place, that overlooks the nuns in the convent grounds beneath, that the multitude in Ireland are fit only to dig the bogs; as one is glad when some recluse writes to the papers that he has observed a magnificent meteor over Killiney. For if people will not be serious about serious things it is better that they should not be serious at all.

If one turns from the newspapers of the day to the weekly periodicals, certainly the Labour weeklies, one wishes, on the other hand, that people could be serious without being filthy-mouthed. Not that one easily condemns Labour, for if scurrility reached its lowest level in the workers' organs of the time, brutality also had its day out. If the *Irish Worker* stank with insult, the innuendo of the *Irish Independent* – owned by the leader of the Dublin employers – was slimy with cant. The trouble was that, as in most Irish fights, the personal element was, by this date, too much felt on all sides. It was not so much Labour against Capital, as Larkin against his chief antagonist among the employers, William Martin Murphy, Perhaps it was the most effective way of engaging the emotions of the workers and the public, but it ended by confusing the issue – an issue which only the employers saw clearly. For in their hearts to them it was not a question of the Transport Union but of the menace of Trades Unions in general, and behind these the menace of the general European uprising of Labour.

So while the employers prepared to oil the thumbscrew, Labour lashed, without restraint, scabs, police, the bourgeois Sinn Feiners under Griffith, all political parties without respect of hue, and all employers without distinction.

The police, to them, were 'skulking bullies,' 'a savage breed of Cossacks', 'a gigantic column of ignorance', 'most detestable creatures'. A man who took a striker's job was not merely a scab, but 'a miserable scab', 'a deserter', 'a traitor', and the limit was reached when the *Irish Worker* of August 19th, 1911, declared that if the British Army was justified in shooting deserters then 'we are also justified in killing a scab'. Opponents at the Corporation elections of 1912 were described as 'corrupt and inefficient creatures'. One was named for a 'notorious libertine and one of the most foul-mouthed blackguards whose every word is an oath, whose breath emits blasphemy, and who, if the public knew a tithe of his guilt would be hounded out of public life, aye and private life, too'. He was called, furthermore, 'a beast', and 'a stain on the earth's surface,' and dismissed in scorn for saying that Home Rule would not be granted if he were not elected councillor. Of another the paper said that 'the name of X. would bring a blush of shame to any man's face, never mind an Irishman's face'; of Y. that he was 'a pimp, a lying slave-driver, a thing, not a man'; of Z. that he was a 'lick-spittle, a time-server, a place-hunter, and official hangman'; and that his colleague had to be carried home dead drunk. As for the employers, 'slave-drivers' was too mild for them; they were 'earwiggers', 'lugbiters', 'wily crawlers', and William Martin Murphy was a 'blood-sucking vampire', a 'whitened sepulchre', 'the most foul and vicious blackguard that ever polluted any country', a 'mountebank,' a 'tramway tyrant' – until, at last, hoarse with abuse, the paper pictured him as an octopus sizzling on the hobs of hell. ('Octopus' was a favourite term with both sides in those days.)

Capital, meanwhile, set itself to its genteel methods of

cornering the law, and cornering the politicians, and starving-out the recalcitrant poor, always disclaiming responsibility for the conditions that made the poor so unaccommodating. Thus when a Departmental Committee of Inquiry into the Housing of the Dublin Working-classes reported so gloomily on conditions in Dublin, that even the *Irish Times* had to say: 'We had suspected the difficulty of living decently in the slums, this report proves the impossibility of it,' the *Irish Independent*, Murphy's organ, pushed off the onus on the 'citizens in general' – whoever they might be – saying, 'The strictures which are passed upon the administration of the sanitary laws cannot fall upon the employers as a class, though they certainly do imply censure upon the general body of the citizens for failing to return the right class of man to the Municipal Council.' The foremost contemporary historian, apologist, and partisan of the employers adds a highly interesting example of the art of conscience-drugging: after remarking on the physical shortcomings of slum-dwellers he says, 'At the same time, the thought of all that is implied in the way of demoralization and decadence of physical powers, should make us chary of playing the role of critic to the employers who have to utilize this damaged material. Inefficiency carries with it a penalty which cannot be altogether avoided while industry is conducted on commercial lines.'[1]

It cannot be denied that the employers were at the limit of their endurance around 1912–13, they had tried to parley with Larkin and Larkin had replied by fighting them tooth and claw. By lightning strikes, broken promises, contracts repudiated, sympathetic strikes, he had harassed them beyond all patience. For he was not merely there to support men striking against a grievance; he encouraged them to seek for grievances, to be awake to every effort to exploit them, to fight on any pretext for the conditions of work to which they were entitled, to force the pace. And when he had his men out his method was to isolate the enemy by calling out now this, now that ancillary trade until he had beaten his man to a surrender.

'To Hell with contracts' was his famous slogan and it

1. *Disturbed Dublin*, Arnold Wright, London 1913.
In 1911 the death-rate in Dublin was almost twice the death-rate in London; as compared with England the number of those who died in asylums, hospitals, prisons, and workhouses in and about Dublin was about two and a half-times as many; and of the total death-rate in Dublin almost half died in such institutions. A quarter of the population was living in one room tenements.

summed up his moral attitude to the entire question; and he acted on that principle until the employers felt and said they felt they were dealing with an unprincipled demagogue. They had organized in Cork with effect against him. They now gathered under the leadership of Murphy, the founder of the Dublin Employers Federation, Ltd.' It was this man who ultimately faced Larkin, and smashed him – but not before Larkin had done what he set out to do – not before he had founded a Labour Movement that with leadership equal to his could have in time done almost anything it liked with Capital. That it did not use its strength when he was gone was no fault of his.

§ 4

Murphy was a man who from humble beginnings had come to control railways not only in Ireland but the Dominions, tramways in various towns in England, two newspapers in Dublin, a large drapery business, and the Dublin Electric Tramway Company. He was a Cork-man, one of the most pertinacious and acidulous tribes in Ireland; he was a Home Ruler of the old school – believing, that is, in the commercial value to Ireland of a place in the Empire; he was seventy years old or more at the time Larkin faced him – a tall, white-haired, kindly-looking old business-man.

It was against his Tramway Company that Larkin struck, choosing the opening morning of the Horse Show, Tuesday, August 26th, 1913. At ten in the morning he called out every motor-man in his control; they simply stepped from their trams wherever they found themselves, pinned up the badge of their Union, the Red Hand, and then either stood by to watch results or trooped to Liberty Hall for orders. There was nothing unusual about that kind of strike in Dublin at this date. People grumbled merely because such a day had been chosen and hoped the affair would be settled by the morrow.

But both Labour and the employers knew that with such a man as Murphy things would not pan out so easily this time, and they both soon communicated their feelings of apprehension to the public. At once Murphy locked out one hundred and twenty men and boys in his parcel depot – he said he knew they were Larkinites only waiting for the word to come out as strikers. He had the motor-men charged with holding up traffic by abandoning their cars. He dismissed the men on track and pavement work whom he did not trust; he had for weeks before employed more men than he needed, specially for such a contingency as this. He sent his clerical staff and all his odd workers to man the cars. Larkin called out the fitters and boiler-men at Ringsend. Murphy had the power-house guarded by police. The strikers howled at the faithful men and attacked some cars with stones and that night in Beresford Place, beside the custom house and under the shadow of the great iron railway-bridge of the Dublin loop line, Larkin addressed a huge mob that swayed with excitement as they listened and cheered him on to wilder and yet wilder threats. But what he did say before he ended that night, his thin hatchet face white with passion under the arc-lamps, his long hands clawing the air, his voice hoarse with fury, simply took their breath away. It was an incitement to revolution.

'Carson is arming in the North,' he cried. 'If he can arm why shouldn't the Dublin workers arm? Arm yourselves, and I'll arm. You have to face hired assassins. Where ever one of your men is shot – then shoot two of them.'

By the custom house railings stood the dark line of police, heavy coated to their shins, stub-legged, their hands fingering the batons at their hips. The mob looked towards the 'hired assassins' with apprehension and hate. The reporters scribbled madly. Very naturally Larkin was in jail within twenty-four hours, less naturally out of it the same day, and most naturally back the same night (the 29th of August) to the arc-lamps and to an audience doubled in size and thirsting for fresh incitements to violence. He gave it to them.

'Starve us?' he shouted. 'Starve us out? If they lock out the Transport Union we'll pay no rent. If they lock out the Transport Union, then, in Kruger's words, we'll stagger humanity. Starve us, would they?' he besought the beast of many heads growling beneath him. 'Any man who starves when there's food in a shop window is a damn fool.'

He had promised to hold a meeting the Sunday following in Sackville (i.e. O'Connell) Street, and while he was in jail it had been proclaimed. Now he lifts up the sheet bearing the printed words of the Royal Proclamation. Holding a lighted match to it he defied the powers by whose virtue it was declared.

'People make kings and people unmake them,' his voice carried over the listening crowd. 'I care as much for the King as I do for the magistrate who signed this paper ... We have a perfect right to meet in O'Connell Street. We are going to meet in O'Connell Street.' The flames ate through the uplifted paper. 'And if the police or soldiers are going to stop us, or try to stop us, let them take the responsibility.'[1]

His face was in the dark as the last glowing ashes floated down on the faces upturned to hear him. Out of the dark his voice came, strident:

'If they want a revolution, then God be with them.'

Some ten thousand voices soared in a wordless cheer. But, then, a mob will cheer anything spoken by a man of intense feeling. The real acceptance was with a navvy-like man listening quietly in the room behind the orator, and he did not cheer at all. He was James Connolly. They shot him in 1916.

Of course it was all like a mad vinous drug to Constance Markievicz. And the man had set fire to the emotions of many far less excitable than she, people of all grades of understanding and society, a magnet that set a dance afoot among the coldest fragments of the Dublin populace. It is not too much to say that she flung herself into his arms; perhaps a cynic might say that she wrapped her arms about him, for there was something of the octopus even in her.

The danger alone was enough to rouse her. All over the city and at all hours riots sprang up without the least warning. Murphy had rallied the employers to him, man by man, boasting that Larkin had been able to control only a fifth of his men. 'I have set him on the run,' he challenged. 'It is up to the employers to keep him going.' The employers soon did, but meanwhile the Dublin mob had its say. It became the order of the day to hear the crash of breaking glass, the screams of the lane-women as they hurled bottles and bricks through the air, their hair flowing about them like Maenads, the children crying with fear and pain as the rabble trampled them underfoot, to hear the hoarse breathing of the police as they chased them, to hear the thud of baton on flesh and bone. After dark no trams were safe on the streets and pedestrians were wise to stay indoors. Between that Tuesday and what was known long after as Bloody Sunday – until a Bloodier Sunday in later years outstepped it – there were riots at Ringsend, Brunswick Street, Beresford Place, Talbot Street, Marlborough Street, Earl Street, and up and down the quays about O'Connell Bridge. No time, surely, for peaceful citizens to be abroad and yet a time when day and night Madame Markievicz found

[1]. Constance once tried to burn a Union Jack in public but it would not take fire. Larkin, asked how he could be sure his Proclamation would take fire said, 'I had it well soaked in petrol!'

herself with delight wandering among the back streets and the
rabble. A man was killed (the finding of the inquest) by a blow
of a baton on Eden Quay. Another labourer died of wounds
received later in a baton-charge on Eden Quay – the finding
of the Dublin Disturbances Commission. It was a time of
excitements. A whole house in the slums crumbled to the
ground. When they were burying the dead workers and the
immense *cortège* was in the middle of O'Connell Street the
mourners suddenly fearing a baton-charge scattered on all
sides and left the coffin in the centre of the street. A time that
gave rise to bizarre stories, apocrypha of history no doubt,
like that which pictures Maud Gonne, walking with Yeats
along some little shopping street, the poet head aloft, the
loveliest woman in Europe fondling a brick in her muff, eye-
ing the police and the shop windows for a target. It was said
that Larkin, who was wanted by the police since his defiant
speech of the 29th, was staying at the Vice-Regal Lodge with
Lady Aberdeen. Madame Markievicz was reputed to be carrying messages, disguised as an old woman, to and fro between
Liberty Hall and Larkin's hiding place. A wild story said that
Murphy engineered the strike deliberately because he was
nearly bankrupt. But whatever was believed or not believed,
everybody believed that Larkin would keep his promise and
speak in O'Connell Street on Sunday.

Certainly Madame believed it; for Larkin was staying with
her out in Surrey House among the pamphlets and the Fianna
and the rolled-up carpets, and they spent hours together planning for Sunday's coup. Cassie was, naturally, dragged into it.
His best Saville Row frock-coat, his best top-hat – these she
offered to Jim, and she and Dudley Digges, the actor, would
make him up as an old bearded parson. There was the difficulty
of his height? He must stoop. Of arranging a platform? He
must speak from the window of William Martin Murphys'
hotel, the Imperial (now Clery's). Of getting there? He must
be led there as a prospective guest. Of his Liverpool accent
which would at once be recognized? He must be stone deaf
and a 'niece' would lead him by the hand, past the police at
the door and the possible watchers at the reception desk. It
was all her metier – disguises, risk, humour, dramatic effect.
She revelled in the plotting of it. As for Cassie, just back from
Albania (it was the period of the Balkan War, and he had been
acting as war-correspondent there), she gave a reception in his
honour at Surrey House, which flattered him immensely until

he found that it was intended purely as a blind to hide the comings and goings of the conspirator's agents. (Perhaps, too, he did not like seeing his best coat used in this way; afterwards when a pressman reported that Larkin was dressed in a frock-coat 'of obviously proletarian cut' he was furious.) But being a good fellow he joined in the fun with the best grace possible, even if, being a many-sided man and sorely-tried he did say to another reporter who tried to interview him on Sunday evening: 'What can you do when your wife ees a damned fool?'

That Sunday was the first direct clash with the law; it put her name definitely on the list of 'suspects' at the Castle. All that Sunday morning she was busy preparing Jim for his public appearance, and one can imagine that if she was a woman entirely without nerves, for Larkin, highly-strung and over-worked, it was more than trying. Reports came frequently to them that O'Connell Street was 'black with police'. There were in fact over three hundred police in the street when Larkin drove up to the hotel door, and at the Depot an unknown number of mounted men. Guided by his 'niece' (a school-teacher, Miss Gifford) and announced as the Reverend Mr. Donnelly, he was led by the page to the room booked for him in advance. It opened on a balcony from which he was to address the crowds scattered expectantly up and down the street below. Unhappily he found the window blocked by a huge window-box of flowers. Dashing out through the lounge he made for a better window, and as he ran, to the horror of the people seated here and there on his way, the old man tore his whiskers in handfuls from his jaws. At twenty-five minutes past one, while Madame and Cassie waited below in a state of the uttermost anxiety, a window was flung open on the second story and Larkin began to cry out to the mob. From end to end of the street his name rang and the crowds converged to the hotel door. At the same time police rushed upstairs and dragged Larkin inside. Below, outside, the police charged. Rush and counter-rush continued for several minutes. Madame and Cassie, in a carriage, succeeded in approaching the hotel as Larkin emerged and standing up she cried to him: 'Well done, Jim!' – then calling on the hustling mob to cheer him. The coachman was ordered to drive to a side street; in the excitement a policeman tried to pull him from his perch; another rush was the result and another baton-charge. Finally the pair were led out of the danger zone.

But up and down O'Connell Street one saw a pitiful sight.

The police do not really appear to have behaved as badly as they were reported to. All the week they had been under a terrible strain. One had seen them lined up against the shop windows, very much indeed like Cossacks in their long coats and domed helmets, itching to be at the mob; one saw such things as a woman come reeling from a pub with a bottle in her fist, stoop to the kerb and crack the neck of it on the stone, drain the liquor through its jagged neck, and then hurl it with an oath at the dark, stalwart line. The only reply would be a 'Steady, now, men – steady!' from an old Head Constable plodding up and down before his angry men. The crowd would always run as the missile crashed, then halt at a distance, and from its front line might fly a hail of stones; then the crowd would return nearer and nearer to the police and the old tide of growling insults would taunt the silent giants on the kerb. Little wonder if, when at last, this Sunday afternoon, the order came to charge they charged with a will. Even then nothing might have happened if one of the many exits from Sackville Street were not, by order, blocked to all traffic. Here when the melee began after Larkin's arrest, the flying crowds were met by a sergeant and a dozen men, met behind as they tried to recede by another advancing wave of spectators and police; hemmed between the two they were hammered without mercy. That Prince's Street bloc produced the disasters which ended in a Government Commission.

Some of the things that happened afterwards are pertinent because of Madame Markievicz's attitude when one spoke to her about them. In the evening riots were frequent throughout the city, and the unfortunate police, now thoroughly hated, had a thin time among the poorer districts, such as Inchicore or Redmond's Hill, where the lanes and side-alleys were uncontrollable. Often attacked by converging crowds they stood small chance against the flying brick and bottles, or the flowerpots flung down on their heads from barricaded houses. An incident at Inchicore is typical. Here a Sergeant Mincaid, a Constable McMahon and another man were so foolhardy as to arrest a rioter out of a crowd of one hundred and fifty men. They had to pass on their way to the Police Station a hall of the Transport Union where another crowd surrounded them, separated the three police, released the prisoner, knocked down the sergeant and kicked him into unconsciousness; he was taken by some samaritan into a house where he came to after two hours. One of the policemen was levelled by a blow of a heavy stone, kicked also on the ground; while the third policeman was also knocked down, rose, fought his way to his comrade, was again felled and fought his way into a house, here the occupant in fear of the rabble howling outside let him out by the back, whence he took refuge in another house and so, when things calmed down, by devious back ways to hospital.

When one spoke of those things to Madame she was without pity. 'Served them right,' was her answer. And in that attitude all the strange unwomanliness which seems, as it became intensified with time, so alien to her nature, is again apparent. She was a woman who became fanatical when she took sides.

§ 5

With Larkin in jail, Murphy now began to marshal the employers against the Transport Union. Acting on a pledge to employ no member of the hated union, firm by firm shut down its works until by the middle of September fifteen thousand men were idle on the streets. Actually that is a measure of Larkin's power, not of the employers', for the men could have remained at their posts by agreeing not to support the Transport Union. The result was that by the end of September, when the weather joined forces with the employers, one saw everywhere women and children shuffling about the streets in search of food. No wonder Æ lashed the employers and the politicians. 'You determined deliberately,' he wrote in an open letter to them, 'in cold anger, to starve out one-third of the population of this city, to break the manhood of the men by the sight of the suffering of their wives and the hunger of their children. We read in the Dark Ages of the rack and the thumb-screw. But these iniquities were hidden and concealed from the knowledge of men in dungeons and torture-chambers . . . It remained for the twentieth century and the capital city of Ireland to see an oligarchy of four hundred masters deciding openly upon starving one hundred thousand people, and refusing to consider any solution except that fixed by their pride. You, masters, asked men to do that which masters of labour in any other city in these islands had not dared to do. You insolently demanded of these men who were members of a Trade Union that they should resign from that union; and from those who were not members you insisted on a vow that they would never join it.

'Your insolence and ignorance of the rights conceded to the workers universally in the modern world were incredible, and as great as your inhumanity. If you had between you, collectively, a portion of a human soul as large as a threepenny bit, you would have sat night and day with the representatives of labour, trying this or that solution of the trouble, mindful of the women and children, who at least were innocent of wrong against you. But no! You reminded Labour you could always have three square meals a day while it went hungry. You went into conference again with the representatives of the state, because, dull as you are, you knew public opinion would not stand your holding out ... Cry aloud to Heaven for new souls. The souls you have, cast upon the screen of publicity, appear like the horrid and writhing creatures enlarged from the insect world, and revealed to us by the cinematograph ...'

In his sympathy with the workers he was joined by well nigh every intellectual in Ireland – James Stephens, Daniel Corkery, Joseph Plunkett, Thomas MacDonagh, W. B. Yeats, Mr. and Mrs. Sheehy-Skeffington, Patrick Pearse, Laurence Kettle, and others. Griffith, almost alone, stood out. It was in the effort to do something practical for these unfortunate women and children that Constance Markievicz abandoned her Boy Scouts for the time being and organized a food-kitchen in the basement of Liberty Hall. Here the warmest and best side of her character came out. She cadged food and money from her friends, roped in her Surrey House 'gang' to work long hours cooking and cutting and buttering and ladling out for the endless procession of tatterdemalions that stormed hungrily down to the gloom of her kitchen. Once a scab's child stole into the procession – for even scab's children could be hungry – and with much trembling lest she should be discovered the mite managed to reach the spoon of Providence – only to be observed at the last moment by some urchins before her and driven into the holes and corners of the basement before their screams and fists. Happily with these children, at least, Constance could not be bitter or abstract and she rescued the child and fed her in spite of the growls of the children of Israel. There was another time, many years after, when she behaved in the same way to an old man. She had torn the Poppy of Remembrance from his coat one Armistice Day and then paused in her stride when he said, looking up at her sadly. 'You know, that was for my son. He was killed on the Marne.' Shamefacedly she picked up the red paper flower and pinning it on his breast again, walked away.

She may by such touches be distinguished from the sterner, more arid members of her sex who went with her through the inferno of the years that followed – and should be since for her softness, her weaknesses, her humour, her follies, which they had crushed out of themselves, Dublin always refused to take her as seriously as them. Dublin has always been cynical about Constance. They made a joke of her 'afternoon teas' with the strikers' children. They pretended that the existence of two odd countesses in Dublin – she with her radicalism, Lady Aberdeen with her anti-tuberculosis campaign – was too much for one city. They pretended all sorts of confusions occurred as a result, such as that Cassie would find himself by error in the vice-regal lodge, and Bellingham, the A.D.C. to the Lord Lieutenant, would be stirring the soup with Constance in Liberty Hall instead of sipping it up in Phoenix Park. Even in 1916 they mocked at her in the same way; she was playing Rosalind in green tights, they said, among the flower-beds in Stephen's Green. A bitter city. A city to breed insensitiveness in anyone naturally less insensitive than she.

But however the *flaneurs* might joke about her, it was no joke to have to be in that basement day after day all through the winter of 1913–14. When the English trade unions sent specially chartered food-ships up the Liffey, as to a second Londonderry, she was relieved of the unpleasant task of begging food from unwilling friends, but she was kept doubly busy ladling out what she got. She must have welcomed such occasional forays into the open air as that described by Captain Jack White, the founder and first trainer of the Citizen Army. He and she had got into some scuffle with the police which ended with a baton charge. The mob, as mobs will, turned tail and left the street to the Captain – and beside him, only the Countess. Taken in hands by half a dozen police he was dragged, bleeding profusely from the head along the street to the station. 'But she followed me all the way,' he testifies, 'hammering the police on the back with her fists, or dodging between their legs in the vain effort to release me. In the end they got me inside and slammed the door on her. Did she go? She remained there hammering on the panels and they could not get her to go away until she was permitted to come into my cell and dress and wash my wounds with some disinfectant lent her from the kitchen.'

Her mind was kept active, too, by her meeting with Larkin's lieutenant, James Connolly, a man of an analytical and constructive turn of mind in matters political; and her old, or perhaps it would be better to say her first impulse towards nationalism was revived when this Captain White, late of the Gordon Highlanders, a South African D.S.O., and the son of Sir George White who won his spurs at Ladysmith, began to organize the strikers into a Red Army. For the time being she was unable to do more than lend her Fianna Hall in Lower Camden Street as a drill-hall, but she made her mind up to join that army later if they allowed her. For the rest she stood loyally by the women and children until the spring of the New Year, eight months after the beginning of the strike, the men began for very hunger and hopelessness to steal back one by one to work, and some of the unions refused in a body to fight any longer for the rights of the Transport Workers. As to the major issue of the strike ended indecisively; some men signed the required pledge that they would not join the offending union, some did not, and the masters were by now more or less indifferent. Murphy, no doubt, had reason to feel content enough in that he had for the time being at any rate effectively put a halt to Larkinism. The strike, on the other hand, had a powerful effect in awakening Labour throughout the country and from its date may be said to date the consolidation of trades unionism in Ireland. Who won the strike, it is hard under these circumstances to say.

Larkin stood his ground until October, 1914, when he left for America, where, almost at once, he was sent to Sing Sing. Connolly carried on when he left, extending his policy in a manner to be described in the next chapter. After 1916, profiting by the spiritual influence of Connolly's death and the association of the workers' army in the Insurrection, Labour was able to begin a heavy period of reorganization. But its new leaders were men of a softer race and they reverted to more regular and conservative methods. To-day[1] they have become a purely opportunist party, so timid that the word socialist does not occur even once in their printed programme; they possess large funds, fine premises, a moderately forward policy, but little courage. One Larkin was apparently enough for a lifetime.

1. This was written in 1933-4. Labour in Ireland is still pretty conservative but in 1967 it did ask the electorate to vote 'Left' and called its policy socialist. For this conservatism two things have been responsible since Larkin's day : the Church, to whom the merest breath of the word Socialism is suspect; and the natural conservatism of a country largely agricultural. In these 1967 local elections Labour made considerable headway – in spite of the words Left and Socialism.

CHAPTER V

REVOLUTIONARY POLITICS: 1914–1917

§ 1

BUT, now, in allying herself with Connolly, as she did when the strike was a thing of the past, she put her finger into a much more serious and sinister business than anything she had hitherto touched.

So far she had acted more or less as a free agent, feeling her way down and down to the core of Ireland, by her instinct for lost causes. Heart outward, she radiated a magnetism that reacted to the same kind of magnetism in others. Wherever she felt the attraction she had propelled herself towards it without thought. Henceforward she came within reach of the antennae of men acting deliberately where she acted by instinct, men searching consciously and deliberately for their own type where she searched with blind feelers. Through Sinn Fein, Griffith, the suffragettes, the Fianna, the strikers, Larkin and Connolly, she had worked her way deeper and deeper into the innermost circles of Irish politics; until, finally, she was caught – as everybody in those days who was seriously of an extreme turn of thought was caught, in the toils of the small but powerful society, the Republican Brotherhood, that secretly manipulated revolution in Ireland from 1905 to 1922.

Her alliance with Connolly dates from 1914. Up to then the only contact she had with these men was when her Fianna was used to cover the activities of their organizer, Mellowes. Once in the Citizen Army her will was deflected by their will from what, according to the view of this biographer, was her true vocation.

To understand what happened one must go back quite a long way into the history of the Brotherhood. Around the nineteen hundreds these men numbered, perhaps, a dozen effectives, and these were the younger legatees of the old tradition. For after the debacle of the '67 rising and James Stephens' flight to Paris, the Brotherhood lapsed into inactivity for several years. It was reorganized in '73 – two men still live who were present at that reorganization, Dr. Mark Ryan, and Robert Johnston, both now very old men – and then, though the question nearly split the organization, it flung itself behind Parnell. He, however, while using them never acknowledged them, and in '82, from his cell in Kilmainham Jail, disowned them, partly under the influence of his mistress who was then bearing him his first child and was anxious to get him out of jail, if not out of politics, partly because he had raised a storm that he would not ride, a revolutionary spirit that he could not or would not control. After the Parnell split the Brotherhood faded out again and during the last years of the old century it may be said to have degenerated into a body of talkers. The founding of the Gaelic League, however, raised a new spirit among young Irishmen and a different type of recruit came into the ranks of the secret society. The old men were, in too many cases, conservative, ineffectual, and weary – the kind of men that liked to whisper darkly in tavern corners about the Republic; the new generation was fanatically idealist, or fanatically realist, often puritanical – non-drinkers, some even non-smokers. The inner history of the Brotherhood from 1900 to 1912 is the history of a fight by the young men to take over control from the old.

In some cases the older men, like Neal John O'Boyle in Belfast, or Tom Clarke in Dublin, were cordially with the young bloods. Clarke illustrates in his life a good deal of the history of the movement. He was sent over in 1883 in the most callous and irresponsible way by the Clan-na-Gael, the American corollary of the Irish Republican Brotherhood, to 'help' Parnell by further dynamite activities in England – this the year after Parnell's repudiation of the Fenians, and the Phoenix Park murders by the Invincibles! Clarke was caught and with some eight or ten others sentenced to jail for life. Parnell saw no reason to fight for his release; after the split he and his comrades in Chatham, or Portland were forgotten, though it must be remembered to Redmond's undying credit that he stood by the prisoners and did what little he could for them. One by one the unfortunate men went mad in jail under the brutal treatment deliberately meted out to them, or were released with shattered health, until, finally, Clarke found himself isolated in a row of empty cells. After fifteen and a half years he was released, went to America, returned to Dublin and opened a little tobacconist shop, first in Amiens Street and later in Parnell Street – a frail-looking prematurely old man, peering at you over his spectacles as he handed out your tobacco or cigarettes. His shop was open from morning to midnight, a centre for every nationalist-minded person in Dublin, and as he had the idea of stocking two or three copies of every local newspaper in Ireland, a meeting-place for men from all over the country who happened to live in the capital. For the young men in the Brotherhood he was an inspiration as well as a comrade – they all liked him and some loved him. 'More than any other man he was responsible for the insurrection, for he was the mainspring of the group which from 1911 on had worked and planned for an insurrection.' His fifteen years in jail had not shaken his determination one jot.[1]

Other live members of the old Supreme Council of the Brotherhood were Fred Allan and P. T. Daly – already mentioned in connection with Larkin and Connolly. Typical of the younger men with drive and organizing power were Jack O'Hanlon, Bulmer Hobson, P. S. O'Hegarty, Sean MacDiarmada, Denis McCullagh, Dr. McCartan. Pearse did not come in until quite late – either in the last few days of 1913 or early in 1914, in fact. Michael Collins is an example of the rank and file who came to the front in the later stages of the fight; he had been sworn in by MacDiarmada, in 1909, while working in London.

With such men began the new revolutionary movement. Their policy was the old policy of working for the control of every kind of extreme nationalist thought, and their methods the old methods of quietly planting as many members of the Brotherhood as possible into these movements and especially into their executive-committees; not a very difficult task at a time when there was small competition among able men for membership of unpopular organizations. Thus, Hobson was president of the Dungannon Clubs, and McCullagh secretary. On Cumann na nGaedhal they had William Rooney, the co-founder with Griffith – whom they never could control – and P. T. Daly. On Griffith's National Council they had Hobson, O'Hegarty and others – enough to outvote Griffith when they could not persuade him.

By 1905 Griffith had launched Sinn Fein. That was at a

---

1. P. S. O'Hegarty. Introduction to *Glimpses of an Irish Felon's Prison Life* by T. S. Clarke. Dublin 1922. P. xiii. Clarke's unfinished little book is one of the most terrible and moving, without being in the least bitter or vindictive, indictments of British treatment of Irish political prisoners during the nineteenth century.

public meeting in the Rotunda in March. Shortly after, his *United Irishman* was killed by a threatened libel action – Griffith having calumniated a priest named Father Humphreys in the columns of the paper. As he was to do with many other papers similarly or otherwise threatened by the law, Griffith simply closed down his paper and re-christened it in May, 1906, as *Sinn Fein*. (The name had been floating around Dublin for several years.) But the practical work of the establishment of Sinn Fein was an I.R.B. activity. Griffith could invent movements, but he could never move them. The incarnation of his thought came when the young men proposed to him that all existing nationalist organizations should be amalgamated. This event resulted from a visit of Hobson to the Clan na Gael in 1907. There Devoy and others to whom he outlined the home situation saw at once, with the clearer perspective of distance, the waste of energy involved in having several small and disparate organizations and persuaded him to try, at any rate, on his return, to amalgamate the larger bodies such as the National Council, Cumann na nGaedhal, and the Dungannon Clubs.

But to make them coalesce was one thing – to make them agree in action another. Griffith was all out for a mild policy of the resolution of the old pre-union parliament, the Kings, Lords and Commons of Ireland, under the gentlemen's Constitution of 1782; they aimed at an Independent Republic. Griffith, while not denying the power of the gun, was not, as they were, committed to the use of it. Griffith believed in open propaganda and open organizations; they believed in propaganda, open and secret, but pinned their faith to their own secret organization of the Brotherhood. Griffith was a bourgeois; they were democrats. Griffith had no quarrel and desired no quarrel with the Church; they were condemned and feared by it. Griffith believed in and was mildly supported by the middle-classes – people like John Sweetman or Edward Martyn, for example, they believed only in men of determination, and they expected to find them mainly among that 'large and respectable class – the men of no property'.

The chief difficulty they had to contend with was Griffith's objection to organizations in general. A journalist of great talent, he hated meetings, he hated argument, he would not tolerate any kind of contradiction, and he believed in his own word and his own pen as against every other form of persuasion. It was this distaste for organizations that undid him – for the Brotherhood were adepts at intrigue; they had small difficulty in packing and persuading his own committees to his disadvantage, and when it came to his amorphous National Council, such constituents of it as the Celtic Literary Society, Inghini na hEireann, the Ninety-eight Clubs, the Gaelic Athletic Choir, the Catholic University Medical School over whom Griffith had no influence but his personal appeal, were 'bottled' even before their representatives began to listen to him.

The first result of Hobson's activities was a meeting of the disparate bodies at 11 Lower O'Connell Street. The second was an active Sinn Fein organization, which, in spite of general agreement on policy, forthwith threatened to break into Left and Right. The third and ultimate result, seen only after 1916, was the Republicanization of what had before that been little more than a liberal movement. This later alteration in the outlook of Sinn Fein was due partly to national feeling, partly to Griffith's conversion, partly to De Valera's and Collins' capacity for persuasion.

Meantime Griffith went his own way. In his paper *Sinn Fein*, now the mouthpiece of a real movement, he continued stubbornly to express his own views, and with such effect that the Brotherhood could make no headway against him. In fact Griffith held them in a cleft stick. The harder they worked to spread the new organization, the more listeners he got for his policy. None the less they laboured so manfully that, when in 1910 they saw the futility of their efforts and decided to abandon Griffith – though in the most friendly way – Sinn Fein had some one hundred and thirty branches throughout the country. The year after there were about six. The year after that there was one. The break into Left and Right had begun.

Turning in on itself the Brotherhood now came to a crisis in its career. The younger men, chiefly Hobson, wanted a paper of their own. (They had learned at least something from Griffith.) The older men, accustomed to the hocus-pocus of whisper and the general conspiratorial atmosphere of secrecy, were aghast; but Hobson had his way. He threatened to start a paper on his own if the Supreme Council would not help him. Rather than give him so much influence, the older men surrendered; but they refused to allow him to become editor. Tactfully he suggested McCartan – then in his final year as medical student – and the Council agreed. Very naturally, in the event, it was not the hard pressed student but Hobson and O'Hegarty who wrote most of the paper between them. This paper was *Irish Freedom*, and it was managed by MacDiarmada, a friend, also, of Hobson.[1]

The following editorial from the new paper illustrates the alignment; it is couched in the typical I.R.B. mixture of diplomacy, firmness and astute political insight:

'Under whatever name we propagate our ideas the Irish Nation must be built on Sinn Fein principles, or non-recognition of British authority, law, justice, or legislature. That is our basis, and the principles of the Sinn Fein policy are as sound to-day as ever they were. The movement is temporarily suspended because ... some of its leaders directed it into an '82 movement, thinking they could collar the middle class and drop the separatists. But when the separatists were dropped there was no movement left.'

Sinn Fein refused to take the hint, and two years later Griffith was just as adamant as ever. 'We do not care a fig,' he snapped, 'for Republicanism as Republicanism.' The third party – Labour – listened with impatience to both, the *Irish Worker*, still hopefully socialist, saying 'The revival of the Irish language (for example) is a desirable ambition and has our whole-hearted support; but the abolition of destitution and disease, and the conditions that cause them, are even more necessary and more urgent. What use,' it snaps, 'is bilingualism to a dead man?'

In short the Republican Brotherhood had not achieved a great deal by its amalgamation of the small parties. At most the amalgamation had clarified the position.

The position remained unchanged from that one until after the Rising of 1916 – a Right Wing Sinn Fein, a Left Wing Separatist movement, partially above ground but mainly burrowing underneath the whole political stratification, and a

---

1. MacDiarmada was a young man of very pleasing manner and good appearance who, as a pupil-teacher, quarrelled with his manager – a cleric. Emigrating to England he became 'curate' in a public house, returned to Belfast where he got work on the trams, and was there chosen by the Dungannon Clubs as Sinn Fein organizer at a salary of thirty shillings a week; his salary to be made up by a shilling-a-week subscription from thirty members. As manager of *Irish Freedom*, MacDiarmada applied the same methods to the finances of the paper by levying a shilling a week on the members of the society. He was executed in 1916.

Socialist Party of small proportions – so small, indeed, that the Brotherhood never gave it much attention until well after the Dublin strikes, when Larkin and Connolly between them had made it into a weapon worth stealing.

The young men, in and around 1910, have felt very satisfied with their general progress, or felt that they had proven the old men wrong; for it was the last hey-day of the Irish Party with high hopes of Home Rule. They simply saw themselves revolving idly on a calm keel. Still, in 1911, they felt that things were not as bad as they seemed; the labour unrest of that year had heated the public mind; the hopes of Home Rule in the South were exciting the Orangemen in the North where the Unionist Clubs and the Orange Lodges were already passing violent resolutions against Asquith and the Liberal Party. Then, at last, they heard the rumble of the tide for which they had been so long waiting. The resolutions gave way to threats, the threats to action, and Carsonism and the Ulster Volunteers followed. The young men rose against the old and overthrew them; the entire Supreme Council of the Brotherhood was altered in a week.

Not a moment too soon, either; for while the new council was casting about, in its usual astute way, for somebody, not of their number, who would start an open Volunteer movement in the South, there appeared a letter in the Gaelic League organ, *An Claidheamh Soluis*, from Prof. Eoin MacNeill of the National University, under the title 'The North Began', urging the South to follow Carson's example. At once Hobson, who was the moving spirit in those years before the war, arranged for a meeting of representative men, the invitations coming from The O'Rahilly (then secretary of the Gaelic League, afterwards to be killed fighting in the Rebellion). The meeting of the Provincial Committee gathered at Wynn's Hotel in October, 1913; the public meeting to enrol volunteers was held in the Rotunda on November 25th; four thousand men joined that night. Yet, only a little time before Dillon was excitedly, and one may imagine delightedly, writing Redmond not to stay at the Gresham when he came to Dublin – 'it is uninhabitable; beset by a swarm of office-seekers from early morning till late at night'. Carson, that same September at Coleraine, was shouting treason to the Ulster mob, adding in his fury that he did not care two pins whether it was treason or not. 1913 was, of a surety, an exciting year, what with the Dublin strike, the founding both of the Citizen Army and the Volunteers, and the formal establishment of the Ulster Volunteer force. The pace became even more furious with the landing of some thirty thousand rifles at Larne for the Ulstermen on April 24th, in the year following; and of fifteen hundred rifles and some forty thousand rounds for the Southern volunteers at Howth and Kilcool three months later.[1]

What happened with Sinn Fein, the I.R.B., was resolved, must not happen with the Volunteers. They set themselves to strain every nerve to control the latest movement. Again Hobson, now a member of the Supreme Council, was effective; he managed to gain MacNeill's confidence and to the end they agreed on a deliberate policy of cautious advance. But it would appear that he underestimated the pace and, as he and his comrades had ousted the more conservative members before him, so in his turn he lost the confidence of the more ardent colleagues, of Clarke and even of MacDiarmada, and later even of Pearse whom he had, as recorded, sworn into the Brotherhood in 1913-14, and who was now as extreme as he had before been moderate. In brief, Hobson soon found himself suspect by his own colleagues in the Brotherhood who were eager to advance to an insurrection, suspect by the Redmondites in the Volunteers who were eager to advance nowhere, suspect by Connolly and the Citizen Army, for whom even the most eager of the Brotherhood were not eager enough, and suspect lastly by the authorities who disliked the entire movement, and disliked everybody connected with it, sometimes even Redmond himself.

For Redmond and the Party had now come into the game, and were to split the triumvirate of Sinn Fein, Labour, and the Republicans – all connected with the Volunteer movement – by establishing, ultimately, a volunteer faction of their own. The Party Leader, in sum, demanded control of the new movement, intimating quite clearly that if he was not allowed large representation on the Provisional Committee he would at once call on his followers within the movement to leave it. That was in June, 1914. Hobson fearing the effects of a split at this early date managed to persuade his colleagues on the

1. It may be mentioned here that at the Howth gunrunning the Fianna took charge of a quantity of the ammunition and got it safely home, even to the extent of fighting off the Volunteers themselves who wanted to use it against the police. They buried the 'stuff' in a manure heap at Artane, it was dug out the same evening and safely stowed. The boys were proud of their share in the exploit, and Madame Markievicz even more so.

committee to accept the inevitable, and for that he was and has ever since been bitterly criticized; in the end, however, the split came six months later. The Irish or Republican Volunteers, controlled by the I.R.B., went their way to insurrection, in spite of Hobson's early and Casement's last-hour efforts to restrain them; the National or Redmondite Volunteers continued also to meet and drill, or they enlisted in the British Army on Redmond's advice – but there was no reality in their movement and they dwindled into what Connolly, in his impatience for action, speaking of the whole body of volunteers indiscriminately, called in contempt 'comic-opera revolutionaries'.

One can sympathize with men like MacNeill or Hobson or Casement, who had worked early and late in the Nationalist cause, and might well have expected a little more trust and sympathy from their colleagues than they got. But Clarke, MacDiarmada, and Devoy were not the type of man to be patient either with circumstances or men that disagreed with them. In the light of subsequent events Devoy's comments on Casement, who was the incarnation of unselfish chivalry, make unpleasant reading to-day.

A last example of the astute methods of the Brotherhood may be given here – an example of their method of quietly controlling such bodies as the Volunteers. Secretly, at the beginning of the volunteer movement, they drilled their own men – using Madame Markievicz's Fianna as drill-masters, boys like Ryan, Lonergan, and Colbert (afterwards executed in 1916) – the only trustworthy instructors available who had any knowledge of drilling. When instructors were subsequently enlisted by Volunteers in the regular way – ex-British army men for the most part – it was an easy matter to have instructions issued to them from H.Q., that officers were to be chosen from the ranks *solely for efficiency*. In this way it 'happened' that some ninety per cent of the officers were members of the Brotherhood.

Here, around the opening months of the war, we return to Constance Markievicz, her connection with the Citizen Army, and the man under whose influence she moved with, and was moved by the Brotherhood towards the Revolution. Here, too, we leave Casimir for the time being: he drops out of her life for several years from 1913 onward, heard of only at rare intervals when a brief message from him reaches her, after 1914, from the zone of war.

§ 2

James Connolly was a very different type from Jim Larkin. There was terrific force in the man, great drive and energy, but outwardly, except in his heavy physique, he showed small sign of it. Heavily-jowled, heavily-shouldered, ball-faced, with straight clipped moustaches and thin hair, he looked more like a quay-side publican than a social revolutionary and patriot. His speech was slower, his gestures more restrained, his manner had far less wild nervousness, picturesqueness, or flamboyance than Larkin. His thought was more solid, deeper, and more patient than Larkin's; he moved more slowly to more distant ends. He naturally made no appeal to people who felt that romantic Ireland was dead and gone – 'with O'Leary in the grave'. And yet it was his emotions and his love and his hate that in the end betrayed him.

He appeared in Ireland before Larkin and he left it after him; without him Larkin could hardly have been the effective force he was. But before that, he had, like his friend, 'done everything'. Born in Monaghan in 1870, he spent his first ten years in Ulster, then emigrated with his parents to Scotland where, in Edinburgh, his father became a Corporation dustman. At eleven he was a printer's devil – it was illegal to have employed so young a child; he was a baker's 'devil' at twelve; he worked in a mosaic tile factory at sixteen; and after that he was by turns tramp, navvy, pedlar, and what-not, before at the age of twenty-one he married in Dublin and returned to Edinburgh to follow his father's trade as street-scavenger. He loved books, and loved them not merely for their content but their format, handling them with a physical delight in their fine craftsmanship. He read widely. He wrote a good deal – mainly pamphlets and articles. A play of his *Under which Flag?* was produced at Liberty Hall in March, 1916. One serious historical study he completed – *Labour in Irish History*, published in Dublin in 1910. He was a man who might well have felt, though he was too modest a man to say it publicly as Jim Larkin did: 'I'd rather paint a picture or make a book if I could do it, than be a strike-leader. If I became a demagogue, who made me one but the Dublin bosses?'

From the beginning he was not only a Socialist but an Irish Nationalist; a faith imbibed from his old Fenian uncle, John Leslie, and developed by his own readings in Irish history. Leslie was a propagandist and speaker for Socialism as applied to Irish land troubles, and Connolly, at the age of twenty-five, was himself a frequent speaker at Socialist meetings, and actually threw up his job as a scavenger to stand at the municipal elections as a Socialist candidate. But he was of the generation of pioneers and he only received three hundred votes. He turned to shoe-making and failed at that. He made plans to turn farmer in Chili and was on the point of concluding his arrangements with the Chilian government when old Leslie persuaded him to try Dublin once more, enticing him – this was 1896! – by the idea of starting an Irish Socialist Party there. And anyone who knows even a little about the condition of the Irish Labour movement in 1896 – and no guess however modest is likely to underestimate the apathy of the workers of those days – will deny the apparent hopelessness, however much they may admire the courage of that adventure.

Once settled in Dublin, where he first became a navvy and then a proof-reader, not only did Connolly found his Irish Socialist Party, but he flung himself against political apathy as well (it was the height of the Parnell aftermath) by founding an Irish Socialist Republican Party. He thus combined at the very beginning, as he combined in his death, the two finest causes for which a man can work – the emancipation of his country and of his fellow-men.

One naturally thinks of such a man as an idealist; and he was an idealist if to persevere in a cause too realist for one's contemporaries is idealism. In the eyes of Griffith he was certainly an idealist and a mad one, as he was an idealist, and a magnificent one, in the eyes of Constance Markievicz. But he was as unfortunate in his followers as in his enemies, for if the one, like Griffith, or, if the collocation is not unseemly, Mr. William Martin Murphy, understood but were repelled, the others were attracted but did not understand. It was, as somebody pointed out at the time, fit story for an Ibsen – a leader without lieutenants; and the fault is undoubtedly with the lieutenants, for he was neither so original nor so deep, unless by comparison with the shallows babbling about him, that a mature woman like Constance Markievicz, now in her forties, and his lieutenant since the strike, could not with a little study have grasped firmly both the import and the meaning of what he taught.

His doctrines were an amalgamation of everything he had read that could, according to his viewpoint, be applied to

Irish ills, a synthesis of Marx, Davitt, Lalor, Robert Owen, Tone, Mitchel and the rest, all welded together in his Socialist-Separatist ideal. He favoured Industrial unionism as the method of approach to what he called variously, the Workers' Republic, the Irish Socialist Republic, the Co-operative State, the Democratic Co-operative Commonwealth. The workers' unions, that is to say, would, in his plan, organize in advance, according to their generic industries rather than their particular crafts; later they would be the means of popular representation in the Workers' Parliament; and they would be the power controlling the national wealth and the national industries outside it. In a word he believed in vocational representation combined with 'all power to the Unions'. To this end he advocated the confiscation of surplus wealth, and maybe of all wealth – his teaching on the point is not beyond doubt – and he would do this by organizing and agitating for Reform in and out of the capitalist Parliament while it lasted, and by armed revolution when the time was ripe to overthrow it.

This is not to suggest that a mere outline does justice to Connolly's thought, though its merit was not so much its thoroughness of its detail as its courage and necessity at the time in which he appeared on the Irish scene. Had he lived on, he would have been forced to elaborate his ideas and to defend his programme point by point. He would have been faced by the practical problems of the day in all their apparent complexity and interdependence, and it is not possible to say now whether his mind would have been powerful enough to contain such problems without confusion. But as he was not answered in his lifetime, nobody can answer for him now against his opponents. He was never given the opportunity of applying his principles even on a small scale, and so his reputation is far less than that of men like Horace Plunkett or George Russell, who worked in a smaller ambit and whose ideas could never have had more than very restricted results, but who were able to produce some results however small. He would have been obliged, too, if he had lived, to abandon much of what he held – particularly his idealistic and unscholarly notions about the old Gaelic State and all its appendages; and it is very doubtful if in the highly technical intricacies of modern economics his doctrines would not have been ineffectual against the compulsion and necessity of the moment. But he had at least a point of view, and he had a definite idea of what he meant by terms such as 'a Republic', 'Freedom',

'Emancipation', 'Autonomy', 'that, like trinkets to children, satisfied his contemporaries with their dazzle.'

Everybody who knew the man seems to have been impressed by him. Æ, who had met him during the Dublin strike, writes: 'He was a sombre, concentrated man of great ability, all his faculties under complete control, ready for use, a fine speaker, very impressive by his mere mastery over his matter. I heard him speak at a meeting in the Albert Hall at a meeting where there were many famous speakers and he was to my mind the most impressive of any. The surgeon who attended him when he was wounded and a prisoner was immensely impressed by Connolly's strength of character. He liked him so much that he became a kind of guardian to Connolly's son, Roderick. The English general who received Connolly's surrender told me he felt he was *a man*, and said, I wanted to shake him by the hand, and he was so impressed that he told Lloyd George that these were the real people of Ireland and he ought to give them complete Dominion Government at once. I regretted his Nationalist obsession because by his death Ireland lost the only labour leader it had with brains and high character. His mind, too, was capable of growing. I had hopes of making him a guild socialist rather than a state socialist as I thought the guild idea was more flexible and in accord with Irish possibilities, and in his book on Labour he refers to these ideas of mine. But with his death there was really nobody to guide Labour, nor has there been since.'

Unhappily there is every reason to believe that Connolly was to Constance Markievicz not a teacher but an hypnotist. Whoever else might test his doctrines she was certainly not the person to reinforce them by analysing them, still less to rehabilitate them after he was dead.

For while one may be satisfied that she heard and read all that Connolly said in his paper, the *Irish Worker*, and in his published pamphlet, as well as his own solid conversation, and heard a good deal more of it from her sister Eva, who was secretary to the Salford Trades Council, she shows no sign in anything she herself wrote about him of having bestowed an adequate amount of thought on his matter. Even by 1924–5 when she published a pamphlet on *Connolly's Teachings and the Catholic Church*, it is clear that she gave those teachings, on which she finally came to pin her faith, nothing like the careful examination they deserved. To her it was all so simple that she seems to have wondered if there was not 'a catch' somewhere. 'Looking at his programme', she wrote of his first manifesto of 1896, 'we are inclined to wonder at its simplicity; that it is so short, and that it contains so few items.' But then she sails on in a whirlwind of oratory: 'But if we take it in conjunction with his further writings we will realize that it only gives the first points to be aimed at, indicates, as it were, the first battles that must be won and the first positions to be captured in the campaign against the conglomeration of horrors that greedy capitalists have forced on our people.' As a sample of her superficiality it will suffice here to note that the single sentence, 'No sudden seizure of the wealth-producing processes is contemplated *but a gradual reorganization and reconstruction of the whole system of production and distribution*,' is her sole explanatory comment on a programme whose first two articles call for:

'1. Nationalization of canals and railways.
2. Abolition of private banks and money-lending institutions, and establishment of State banks under properly elected boards of directors, issuing loans at cost.'

It is outside the scope of this biography to examine Connolly's doctrines in detail; we are only interested in him in so far as he affected Constance Markievicz. But one feels satisfied by the impression both he and she left with independent observers that he was a moderately careful student and that she really did not understand, and did not try to understand, what he talked about. Writing in 1924, three years before her death, Professor Clarkson comments on her exposition of Connolly: 'Countess Constance de Markievicz is enthusiastically but not over-intelligently engaged in attempting to revive, through the medium of the Glasgow *Forward*, and of Socialist lectures at Republican Headquarters in Suffolk Street, Connolly's interpretation of Irish history. With peculiar but characteristic emphasis she has seized on his quite untenable hypothesis of the Gaelic State as the keynote to which to pitch the recital of his great epic. Mme Markievicz improves on Connolly in her fervent desire to overthrow what she calls the present "Feudal Capitalist State".'

She was ingenuous. She had accepted Sinn Fein *con amore*. When Hobson told her of his Belfast Fianna, she said, 'I'll start them here.' When she read about Ralahine, she decided first to emulate it at Raheny – and then went into figures. When she saw the strike starting in Dublin in 1913, she said, 'Of course!' – and went at once in search of Larkin. So with Connolly and the Citizen Army. 'The first and last principle of the Irish Citizen Army,' said the constitution of the army, 'is the avowal that the ownership of Ireland, moral and material, is vested by right in the people of Ireland.' She read and accepted. *'Que de bruit pour rien!'* was her attitude. Discussion was unnecessary, examination superfluous, analysis pointless. Her position was: 'Let's do it!' A woman of action, invaluable in a revolution. But, afterwards . . . ?

It was hard to expect more. 'All her mother gave her,' said a woman who knew her since she was a child, 'was her lovely nose, and all she got from her father was his foolish head.'

'She was', Æ recalls, 'a fine breathless character, straight as a lance, truthful, and devoid of fear more than any human being I ever met. But she, like her sister Eva, was too much in a hurry to get somewhere and they neither of them had the pure aroma of thought these get who sow their flowers and wait for them to come up. Constance was like a child who dibbles down flowers without root to make a ready-made flower-garden. I suppose she was gifted with energy which would never let her be still. She should have been born in America.'

Another danger for her in Connolly's influence has already been mentioned, and allows us here to merge his story and hers into the secret history of the revolutionary period; he was always at least as much a Nationalist as a Socialist and he became more and more Nationalist towards the end. This is quite clear from his 1897 reprint of articles from Miss Milligan's *Shan Van Vocht* and the *Labour Leader* – a pamphlet called *Erin's Hope*, where he says: 'The Irish Socialist Republican Party was founded in Dublin in 1896 by a few working men whom the writer had succeeded in interesting in his proposition that the two currents of revolutionary thought in Ireland – the socialist and the nationalist – were not antagonistic but complementary, and that the Irish socialist was in reality the best patriot. But to convince the Irish people of that fact he must first learn to look inward upon Ireland for his justification, rest his arguments upon the facts of Irish history and be champion against the subjection of Ireland and all it implies; that, also, the Irish question was at bottom an economic question, and that the economic struggle must first be able to function freely nationally before it could function internationally and as socialists were opposed to all oppression so they should ever be foremost in the day's battle against all its manifestations, social and political.'

In the first number of the *Workers' Republic* (August 13th, 1898) he says again:

'We are socialists because we recognize ... in (socialism) the only principle by which the working-class can in their turn emerge in their divinity of freemen with the right to live as men and not as profit-making machines for the service of others. We are Republicans because we are socialists and therefore enemies to all privileges, and because we would have the Irish people complete masters of their own destinies, nationally and internationally, fully competent to work out their own salvation.'

Connolly recognized at the very end that his position was open to misunderstanding, if he did not actually admit that he had, in point of fact, gone over to nationalism and away from socialism. The night before he was shot – not for being a socialist but for being a nationalist – he said to his daughter, Norah: 'The socialists will never understand why I am here. They forget I am an Irishman.'

It is clear now, that from 1914 onward, when, in the circles in which he moved, talk of revolution was open and frequent, he became rather a nuisance both to the I.R.B. and Socialist Labour, in both cases by reason of his extreme fervour. Daily he urged in his paper, and in conversation and speeches, that the time had come for a Rising, and, though he could be ignored at first, things became serious when he actually threatened to lead out the Citizen Army on his own, and showed by his actions – open drilling and manœuvres – that he meant it. So it happens that Connolly was doubly an influence, leading Constance Markievicz away from the cause of the living people to the cause of the abstract nation – firstly, thanks to *her* failure to grasp the primal importance of his socialist beliefs, and secondly, by *his* virtual abandonment of Labour about the time she met him. That this statement of their respective positions is a fair one is clear from the judgment of his contemporaries on his actions at the time – the judgment of the extreme section of the I.R.B., such as Pearse, as well as of the more deliberate section, such as Hobson, that he was something very near to a hothead (and most of those who still remember him testify to the occasional violence of his temper and the sudden force of his passion;) and the judgment of the socialists as represented by such as Sean O'Casey, who sums up his own attitude by writing that 'Connolly was no more an Irish Socialist martyr than Robert Emmett'. As for her, when all the hurly-burly was over, it was not to Griffith or to Pearse she returned, but to him and the remnants in print of what he believed.

Here she was then, fighting beside a man who not only believed, as she had been taught to believe from the beginning, that all things came from Freedom, but who was flesh of the flesh of Hunger and Want, a man to implement Freedom just as she would have liked to do, in terms of the poor lives she loved. Had Connolly lived, her dream might have come true and hand in hand with him she might have trod on roses through the Coombe, and seen the sweaty nightcaps soar in Kevin Street for the end of Poverty. But he died, and not under the Plough and the Stars, and while they sang songs to him they forgot what he had taught – and she, faithless soul, forgot it, too. Nor did she, it is clear, begin to have any idea at all of the complexity of Irish problems, or the complexity of the Irish mind, until after the Civil War – in her last two or three years of life, that is – when hard thinking followed on disillusionment, and she realized that life was really much more difficult and much more sad than she had ever imagined in the days of her abandon. One could almost regret that she ever awoke – she was so lovable and so light-hearted in her role of the gay and gallant rebel, riding to her death, as, thirty years before over the Sligo uplands, she rode to the hounds, hell-for-leather over the double-ditches and the stone walls, her wild hair flying to the wind.

§ 3

Her formal connection with Connolly, the Irish Citizen Army, and the Labour movement – to which, hitherto, she had stood in the position of a rare sympathizer from the ranks of the bourgeois Sinn Fein (she was also a member of the Irish Volunteers) – dates from March, 1914. By that time the little 'army' of working men had dwindled, like the strike, to nothing. In that month reorganization began and she found herself one wet night in a back room in Liberty Hall, with Connolly, O'Casey, Captain Jack White, Councillor 'Bill' Partridge – to die after 1916 – and P. T. Daly, the old Fenian and strike-organizer, the inevitable secret envoy from the Brotherhood. They were there to frame a Constitution for the army. A few days later, on the 22nd, she was on the stage of the Concert Room in Liberty Hall, watching a public meeting of labouring men elect their Army Council. With Richard Brannigan she was elected joint Honorary Treasurer. Connolly, one observes, was given no post.

She made herself a uniform of dark green, high-collared to the chin, glinting with brass buttons, caught about her middle by a leather belt, and she wore a wide-awake hat whose leaf was pinned up on one side by the flaming badge of the Red Hand – the insignia of Larkin's union: on her left breast was an immense Tara brooch of beaten silver intended to catch a bratta swung over the shoulder *con brio*. There were deep pockets high and low; she wore high knee-boots; sometimes a holster was held to her side by the leather belt – and this was not merely braggadocio for she was a crack shot. It was a fine uniform, and had she been dressed so when she was twenty or twenty-five years old they would have called her the Diana of Dublin; even as it was, and her beauty was in its full – she was in her middle forties – there was something noble in her line, and she walked among the men like a man.

There was plenty to do in those months. Sean O'Casey tells (in his pamphlet on the Citizen Army) of typical days spent with her, recruiting in the little villages outside Dublin, Clondalkin or Lucan, or Coolock, or Finglas. He describes the little village street, empty when they arrived, the tea at the local 'restaurant' that did service for lunch, and then Captain White standing in the car and the village people standing a long way off, gazing fixedly towards the car as if it were some dangerous machine calculated to upset for ever the quiet rhythm of their lives. The speakers would exhaust themselves in trying to waken a spark in the passive eyes staring up idly at them, and then there would come, at last, a ripple of excitement when they heard the 'nervous and impassioned eloquence' of Countess Markievicz.

He tells, too, of lighter evenings in the big marquee in Croydon Park, Fairview – well inside the city's bounds – where on Sundays in summer there were concerts, if the tent was not being used as a dormitory for the week-end camps held there in fine weather. There would, in that case, be a little bell-tent for the commandant – at that time, Jim Larkin, and another tent for the officers of the Army Council who could attend. The men paid a shilling apiece as they turned in from Saturday night work; at reveillé, six a.m., they received a bowl of porridge and milk, then at eight they sat down to bacon and eggs, bread and butter, and tea; then came church parade, followed by drill, or rifle-practice, or a route march into the country where the men ate their sandwiches and water by the road-side, ending up with the long march home, weary enough to be sure of a sound sleep before the sirens called them to the new week's round of work in the factories or on the quays.

She took all possible share in these affairs. At a sports meeting she would be like Boyle Roche's bird, in ten places at once, arguing with the stewards who had let order crumble into chaos; on a route march you saw her in her place beside the men; or you found her toiling down in Lower Camden Street, at amateur theatricals to raise money for guns or uniforms. And this in addition to her work with the Fianna, to whom the outbreak of the war had also brought ample opportunities for rebel propoganda. For since the Defence of the Realm Act had made commercial printers wary of printing sedition, the boys had to print their own; with the result that her secret press at Surrey House was busy as a mill-wheel, from 1914 on, turning out anti-war posters, anti-recruiting handbills, pro-German leaflets, Sinn Fein leaflets, and all the rest of that revolutionary propaganda which became so common in the ten years that followed that one walked on sedition, drove over sedition, leaned against sedition, sat on sedition where it was painted on every wall, road, asphalt, pillar, shutter, and garden seat, from length to length of Ireland. And these handbills and posters had to be distributed and pasted-up, mainly after dark, and hecklers had to be gathered in for recruiting meetings. Finally, sedition gathered such momentum that she scarcely needed to intervene at all. Having helped to create the pace for revolution, everybody ended by being whirled helplessly if willingly at its heels.

Nor was that the end of her activities. With her title and her unusual name and her eloquence, she was frequently in demand for lectures. Once at least the police closed an entire county on her when in the March of '16 she was due to lecture in Tralee on the Fenians. Otherwise it is clear from their secret reports that they watched her carefully and wondered what to make of her – a wonderment that is evident from their habit of referring to her at times, with dislike, as 'The woman generally known as the Countess Markievicz'. A few pages further on is given a detective's report in which she figures; another private report of the time lists her under the heading,

SEDITIOUS WEEKLY PAPERS

Name	First Published	Owner
The Spark	7.2.1915	Marianna Perolz

Address	Editor
10 Nth. Gt. George's Street	Supposed: Countess Markievicz. 49B Leinster Rd. Rathmines.

(The Mme. Perolz referred to was her friend, and lectured in her stead when the authorities forbade her to enter Kerry.)

But wherever she supposed all this must lead her, Connolly was thinking that it was leading nowhere. He grew restive, then fretful, and at last angry. A war involving England had always been the unconcealed desire of Irish rebels; yet here was England more seriously threatened than at any period in her history, not excepting the period of the Napoleonic wars, and although the Republican Brotherhood had decided on the outbreak of the war in August that there should be an insurrection before the war ended – this he may or may not have known – there was Hobson openly intriguing with these wretched Redmondites, and the rest of the Volunteers apparently inactive. Even with Pearse orating at the grave of O'Donovan Rossa he must have felt exasperated; while as for Hobson, the pages of the *Workers' Republic* testify to his fury.

Continually he incited his readers, in language that should have caused his paper to be suppressed a dozen times over; as other papers were, unfailingly, in those years – his own *Irish Worker*, suppressed in October, '14, resurrected as *The Worker*, suppressed again and resurrected as the *Workers' Republic*; or *Irish Freedom* which ended in October, '14; or Griffith's progeny, *Sinn Fein*, which sank in August, '14, rose as *Ireland* in October, sank and rose as *Scissors and Paste* in December, only to sink and rise again as *Nationality* in June, '15, to sink again after the Rising, and rise again for another chequered career in the years following.

Perhaps he had more skill than Griffiths in skirting the edge of sedition, perhaps the authorities thought him small game; but one can imagine that his readers knew well what he meant by saying, in October, 1915:

'Neither Home Rule, nor the lack of Home Rule will make the Citizen Army lay down its arms. However it may be for others, for us in the Citizen Army there is but one ideal – an

Ireland ruled by Irishmen from the centre to the sea, and flying its own flag outward over all oceans ... The Citizen Army will co-operate only with a forward movement. The moment that forward movement ceases it reserves to itself the right to step out of the alignment and advance by itself if needs be.'

And unless Con was asleep in those months she must have understood, too.

The only reason other than those given why the paper was not suppressed must have been that the authorities simply did not believe that Connolly meant to use his guns. But Connolly did mean to use his guns, and he meant to lead an attack somewhere or other, unaided by the Volunteers, if need be. Indeed, since there are several police reports in the published minutes of the *Commission on the Rebellion in Ireland* referring to whole nights spent in skirmishing under arms about the sleeping streets of Dublin (and there were probably hundreds of others like these), one wonders why the authorities ever even doubted it. 'At 12.45 a.m.', 'at 12.15 a.m.', 'at 5.20 a.m.', 'at 12.5 a.m.', 'between 10.30 and 11 p.m.' – the reports always commence and go on in terms similar to the following:

'5th December, 1915. At 12.15 a.m. 76 members, 62 with rifles, assembled at Liberty Hall, Beresford Place, under the command of James Connolly, James Mallin, and Countess Markievicz, and proceeded to Cross Guns Bridge, Phibsborough, where they broke up into sections – some going along Whitworth Road and others along the Canal Bank to Newcomen Bridge – and went through manœuvres as they went along They returned to their hall at Beresford Place, at 3 a.m. and broke off there.'

Another night they manœuvred 'in the vicinity of Dublin Castle' – or so the weary-eyed policeman reported, though his superiors declared afterwards that they never credited it.[1] Another time it was about the slums of the Coombe, another time about Stephen's Green.

One would wish to picture 'Madame' – they called her nothing else nowadays, a compromise with equality and fraternity – tramping about the city on these nights, if there were not always the fear of being falsely dramatic, always the

1. Evidence of Lieut.-Col. W. Edgeworth-Johnstone. Royal Commission on the Rebellion in Ireland. Minutes of Evidence. London 1916, p. 52.

fear lest the serious woman turn and grin, with you, at herself. And so she does on one of those marching nights. One is just beginning to note the silent and dimly lit streets, the odd curtain corner being raised where a woman who leaves off nursing her sick child, or the old woman who cannot sleep rails in a whisper down at this unwomanly woman out at so late an hour among rough men ... And you are just beginning to defend her, when suddenly, you observe with dismay that your drama has been exploded by a pop-gun: solemnly she marches with the childish toy sloped on her shoulder and as she wheels about a corner across the tram-rails you note, too late, the smile of the ungrown imp.

But pop-gun or no pop-gun, these skirmishings (about places, be it noted, that were ultimately attacked or taken in the Insurrection) were a serious business, if not for the authorities who 'could not credit it', for her and for Connolly; and even more so for the Republican Brotherhood who could credit it, and did. So much so, that in the end, somewhere about September or October of 1915, Pearse seems to have met Connolly and tried to come to an understanding with him – MacDonagh having previously met him on the same errand. (Of these pourparlers, incidentally, the police heard something through their usual channels, a very curious thing considering the secrecy of the affair and the more frequent ignorance of the police with regard to matters far less private.[1])

Connolly was appeased for the time being, as a milder and even more friendly tone in his edition of November 27th shows, but, though Pearse's latest biographer, Leroux, says categorically (though without quoting his authority) that 'a kind of alliance was concluded between the two', his impatience and anger soon flared up again. On Christmas Day and Boxing Day of 1915 the secret military council of the I.R.B. decided, definitely, that Easter Sunday of the following year was to be *the* day, only to hear that Connolly was purported to have decided on going out on his own against the Castle in January, and they remembered that he had actually paraded his men, in full view of the enemy, in one of his nightly manœuvres, about the precincts of the Castle itself. They kidnapped him on the 19th of January and held him prisoner for three days.

1. See Minutes of Evidence, Royal Commission, p. 3, par 4. See also questions 338, 340, 341; also questions 167 to 169. Evidence of the Right Hon. Sir Matthew Nathan. Events show that such pourparlers took place some time in 1915.

They had not reckoned on his association with Madame. Pearse learned from her, to his dismay, on the night of the 22nd, when he met her on his way to Tom Clarke's in Parnell Street, that the 'Reds' were going to rush the Castle that night, with or without their commandant. How much of it was her *blague* one cannot tell, and no documents are available to show how much she knew or guessed at this date of Connolly's relations with Pearse or the Brotherhood; but Pearse, at any rate turned white and implored her to tell Liberty Hall not to stir until they heard from him. (It seems clear at least that she was now more or less accepted by both camps as a serious revolutionary.) Returning home she found Connolly before her, in a state of intense emotion. (He lived in Surrey House at this period.) 'I have been through hell,' he told his daughter, Norah. 'I have walked forty miles to-day,' he told his friend William O'Brien. It was as if Emmet, the night before the Thomas Street debacle, had been forced to abandon his insurrection. Finally the Brotherhood solved things by taking Connolly into their confidence; in February, behind the backs of the Hobsonites (wheels within wheels), they swore him into the society.

It was a more or less willing surrender on both sides but it amounted to a victory for Irish Nationalism. From the point of view of Connolly's subsequent career and final fame, from the point of view of the subsequent career of Irish Labour, and Madame's career as an apostle of the downtrodden, it would surely have been far better if Connolly, since he *would* die, had gone out that winter night against the Castle, since even if he did no more than wave his sword like Emmet and call the loungers to follow him, he would at least have died for the poor. As it was, one must concur, from the point of view, with Sean O'Casey – 'The higher creed of international humanity that had so long bubbled from his lips was silent for ever. Irish labour lost a leader.' And Constance Markievicz, one may add, once more lost a cause. She had become the creature of the Republican Brotherhood.

All that Connolly was able to contribute to the new tradition was the memory of his name and the oblivion of his faith. His humanitarianism influenced many at the time, including Pearse, who shows the immediate effect of it in his *The Sovereign People*, a last pamphlet in which, for once, he descends from Sinai to acknowledge the 'material basis of Freedom.' But all it amounted to in the end, since Pearse died before coming to that intellectual maturity which might, conceivably, have developed his pity for men above his love for 'Ireland', was a vague and ambiguous phrase in the Proclamation of the Provisional Government of the Irish Republic in 1916, a phrase long afterwards to be mouthed by everybody, examined by few, and honoured by none, that article which declared 'the right of the people of Ireland to the ownership of Ireland and to the unfettered control of Irish destinies to be sovereign and indefeasible.' The only man of all those revolutionaries who had a shred of a social policy, the only man who knew what he meant by signing his name to that article, the only man who might have known, that is, what to do with success if it had come to them, flung away his life in one magnificent gesture of waste – *waste* since the only one of his lieutenants to survive him was a woman who, with the best will in the world – 'ignorant good-will' is Yeats's phrase – had only the vaguest idea as to what her leader had for so long been talking about.

Two weeks before the Rising, as if to signalize the merging of the cause of Labour in the cause of Ireland, Connolly had hoisted the Green Flag over Liberty Hall, and in the *Workers' Republic* of April 8th appeared what could be taken as Labour's apologia:

'Where better could that flag fly than over the unconquered citadel of the working class, Liberty Hall, the fortress of the Militant working class of Ireland. We are out for Ireland for the Irish. But who are the Irish? Not the rack-renting, slum-renting, slum-owning landlord, not the sweating, profit-grinding capitalist, not the sleek and oily lawyer, not the prostitute pressmen – the hired liars of the enemy. Not these are the Irish upon whom the future depends. Not these but the Irish Working Class, the only secure foundation upon which a free nation can be reared. The CAUSE of Labour is the CAUSE of Ireland, the Cause of Ireland is the Cause of Labour. They cannot be dissevered. Ireland seeks Freedom. Labour seeks that an Ireland free shall be sole mistress of her own destiny, supreme owner of all material things within and upon her soil. Labour seeks to make the Free Irish Nation the guardian of the interests of the people of Ireland, *and to secure that end would vest in the Free Irish Nation all property rights as against the rights of the individual* ... Having in view such a high and holy function for the Nation to perform, is it not well and fitting that we of the Working Class should fight for the Freedom of the Nation from foreign rule, as the first requisite for *the free development of the National powers needed for our Class?'*

It was Connolly's last appeal to Irish Nationalism, the last expression of his hope that by joining forces with the Nationalists they would combine hereafter the practical with the ideal. But the man's heart was too big, his faith in his fellows too generous. It was not so much a hope as an illusion. Madame read it in the same hope and illusion.

A last view of Surrey House sees it now the haunt of every accepted rebel in Dublin, perpetually under observation by the police, and raided more than once: one of those 'open houses' that were a characteristic feature of almost every town in Ireland in those days of fellowship and common cause.

A picture of life there, just before the Rising, has been communicated by a frequent habitué, Mr. Frank Kelly (afterwards one of Collins' trusted men, and associated with him in the famous release of De Valera from Lincoln Prison). He writes:— 'I used to come down to it from Kimmage where I was in Camp with Pearse's army before 1916. Crowds used to gather into it at night. We had tea in the kitchen; a long table with Madame cutting up slices of bread about an inch thick, and handing them around. The bread was eaten as quick as she could cut it. She had lovely furniture and splendid pictures. When we used to go into the sitting-room and someone would sit at the piano and there would be great singing and cheering and rough amusements. She had lifted her lovely drawing-room carpet but had left her pictures on the walls and on the bare boards there was stamping of feet. In one corner James Connolly would sit at the fire and take no part in the pranks of the juniors. I remember him one night. He sat at the fire, looking into it, hour after hour, and never saying a word. Then he got up and went home. That same night Collins was reciting at the top of his voice Emmet's Speech from the Dock. A few weeks after we were all in the thick of the fighting.'

And Surrey House, even as they were being scattered over the jails of England, reverted, with the help of raiding soldiers, the auctioneer, and the painters and renovators, to the peaceful daily round of a suburban villa. From that on Madame Markievicz had neither child, nor man, nor roof, that she could call her own. Her friends who said that in Surrey House she lived 'in a pig-sty' simply shrugged their shoulders; for them her decline could go no further.

§ 4

The Rising broke out on April 24th, a bank-holiday – a day like Sunday – very quiet, very empty, very dull. Once the cars had taken the people out to Dalkey or Kingstown or Howth or to the foothills of the mountains at Rathfarnham, it was very silent on that Easter Monday of 'Sixteen when Constance walked with under a hundred men and women of the Citizen Army into the public gardens – really more like a city square – of Stephen's Green. There as second-in-command under Mallin, a silk-weaver and secretary to the Silk-weavers' Society, she was to hold an outer position of a double circle of positions taken simultaneously by the rebels that morning. In Stephen's Green they were to command the nearer approaches from the South and South-East to the centre of the city.

One must visualize Dublin as divided, East-West, by the Liffey. All about the southern half of the city runs the arc of the Grand Canal, as to the North – though only a partial arc there, the Royal Canal. The insurrectionists were far too few in number to hold a circle as widely flung as these two segments; all they could hold was a number of buildings well within the canal bounds, and then not even enough to keep more than occasional contact with one another, not even enough, as it transpired, to prevent the enemy from walking down between the outer positions to the Headquarters in O'Connell Street. When the fighting began, for example, a squad of Lancers gathered undisturbed at the top of O'Connell Street and galloped – rather insanely – into the firing-line from the buildings about the Post Office, the centre of the rebel circle; then they retired and reformed at the end of the street again, with the populace standing about, watching them as if it were the start of a race.

The insurrection, therefore, as far as her position in Stephen's Green was concerned, consisted chiefly of sniping, day and night, with occasional skirmishes or raids. These street-raids were the really exciting part of the fighting, for them. For the men at the centre, on which the British decided to concentrate, it was different. Here the thing was a siege, with day and night made horrible and dangerous by the perpetual battering of shells against the house-fronts, the gradual closing in of fires that crept from abandoned forts or leaped up afresh under the hot rain of incendiaries. Then there would come the point when the rebels found themselves battered in and in from the windows, down and down to the cellars, and lastly forced by the crackling of flames all about, and the exploding of their own ammunition overhead, to dash from their last position in a block, out under machine-gun fire and snipers' bullets, over a death-raked street.

That Monday morning, however, all this was yet in the future. The Green contingent set to work in feverish haste. Trenches began to play havoc with the shrubs and flower-beds. Houses along the sides of the Green were picked out by Madame and Mallin, who simply smashed in the windows with hatchets and bundled their men through to fortify every aperture with sandbags and furniture. The College of Surgeons, a heavy, limestone fort of a place, on the west side of the Green they made their headquarters. Here there was perpetual activity. Commandeered food, largely from Jacob's, gelignite, ammunition, water to quench fires (in every conceivable kind of container from fire-buckets to milk-churns), sandbags, – filled with earth from the Green – went in the wide doors all that afternoon. A detachment was off at the double to take Harcourt Street railway station where there was a similar to-and-fro for hours. Another squad went farther south still to the bridge near Portobello Barracks. Along the other sides of the Green barricades were flung up, man-high, across the streets – every car, of every type, motors, drays, trams, horse-vehicles, – as they ran unwittingly into this city that, to their occupants, must seem to have suddenly gone mad. There was small time for thought all that afternoon and when dusk fell the rebels must have been too weary to feel even the exhilaration of seeing, on the flag-pole above the college, the tricolour flapping in the evening breeze. They had closed the gates of the Green; they had flung out their outposts; they had manned their barricades; their snipers lay watching in the gutters of the roofs. They now retired to the centre of the park, and to the inner rooms of the buildings they must defend. At a safe distance the sight-seers waited too. Rifle-fire was cracking from the direction of the Castle and O'Connell Bridge. The insurrection had begun.

It was about this hour that Constance got in her first shot at the enemy. It was a queer little incident. Watching from the shelter of some kind of erection in the Green she saw a khaki uniform in the window of the University Club (T.C.D.). It was, actually, an Irishman, Dr. de Burgh Daly, watching the movements below him from the window of the reading room. The page-boy from the lower floor was also watching and saw the woman raise her rifle and fire. She missed. It was somewhere around two o'clock, for the hall-porter was at lunch. Afterwards at the trial of the Countess the boy told what he had seen and it was largely on his evidence that she was sentenced to be shot.

That Madame Markievicz was armed and fought as a man is not unique. In the Citizen Army the women were given rank and duty just as if they were men. In Stephen's Green there were upwards of twelve or fifteen women besides the countess, including Miss ffrench-Mullen, Mrs. Donnelly, and Miss Margaret Skinnider. They were divided as to their work, some on the commissariat, some at Red Cross work, some working and fighting shoulder to shoulder with the men. During the period actually spent in the Green the work of all three branches was almost equally dangerous. The food-table was sheltered from sight in a corner of the Green, but water had to be fetched from the caretaker's, whose hut could be reached only by dashing across an open space with the bullets smacking the earth about their feet. In the College of Surgeons, later, because it was a strong fort they were not so exposed, and, short of being shelled out, comparatively safe. Madame was merely one of the more colourful figures; she had several women comrades who did as much and acted as bravely as she did. Margaret Skinnider was wounded while taking part in a raid during the week.

It so happens that James Stephens lived hard by the Green and he has left an eye-witness's account of events in this quarter as they appeared from the outside; and it is clear from his narrative that everything began very quietly. The tempo increased with an ominous and deliberate slowness. He writes of Monday afternoon:—

'We stood a little below the Shelbourne hotel (which overlooks the Green) looking at the barricade, and into the Park.

'We could see nothing. Not a Volunteer was in sight. The Green seemed a desert. There were only the trees to be seen and through them small vistas of greensward.

'Just then a man stepped on the footpath and walked directly to the barricade. He stopped and gripped the shafts of a lorry lodged near the centre. At that instant the Park exploded into life and sound. From nowhere armed men appeared at the railings and they all shouted at the man. "Put down that lorry. Let out and go away. Let out at once."

'These were the cries. The man did not let out. He halted with the shafts in his hands and looked towards the vociferous palings. Then, and very slowly, he began to draw the lorry out of the barricade. The shouts came to him again, very loud, very threatening, but he did not attend to them.

' "He is the man that owns the lorry," said a voice beside me.

'Dead silence fell on the people while the man drew his cart down by the footpath. Then three shots rang out in succession. At the distance he could not be missed, and it was obvious they were trying to frighten him. He dropped the shafts and instead of going away he walked over to the Volunteers.

' "He has a nerve," said another voice beside me.

'The man walked directly towards the Volunteers who, to the number of about ten were lining the railings. He walked slowly, bent a little forward, with one hand raised and one finger up as though he were going to make a speech. Ten guns were pointing at him and a voice repeated many times.

' "Go and put back that lorry or you are a dead man. Go before I count four. One. Two. Three . . . Four. . . ."

'A rifle spat at him and in two undulating movements the man sank on himself and sagged to the ground.

'I ran to him with some others, while a woman screamed unmeaningly, all on one strident note. The man was picked up and carried to a hospital beside the Arts Club. (Cassie's club in the days that were.)

'There was a hole in the top of his head and one does not know how ugly blood can look until it has been seen clotted in hair. As the poor man was being carried in, a woman plumped to her knees in the road and began not to scream but to screech.

'At that moment the Volunteers were hated. The men by whom I was and who were lifting the body roared into the railings: —

' "We'll be coming back for you, damn you!"

'From the railings came no reply and in an instant the place was again deserted and silent, and the little green vistas were slumbering among the trees.'[1]

That was a quiet evening for the women in the Green. Even a pleasant evening. They still had easy access to the houses they had taken and in the College of Surgeons they had makeshift beds and plenty of coal to keep them warm through the chilly April night. Their only serious trouble was a shortage of food. For the moment they were only rebels in name; the night was calm and the populace was still free to come and go as if there had never been an insurrection.

So, all through the evening the holiday-makers were straggling into the city, attracted by the faint crackle of rifle-fire reverberating at intervals over the harbour-waters to the beaches as far as Howth, and all along the shore to Killiney and Bray. Long after dusk they were wandering in and around the city, too excited by rumour and the heavy tension of the unknown to retire to sleep. The lights went up as usual but there were no police abroad – not in uniform at any rate, for several had been shot already and the authorities in the Castle had taken the remainder off the street. After dark detectives and looters prowled about the city like night-cats. Around the Green the barricaded houses seemed oblivious of everything.

But the rebels' positions were too scattered and too isolated; before, at dawn, the low rain-clouds began to weep on the roofs of the city, military had crept into the Shelbourne Hotel, whose windows now dominated and made futile the trenches below. They were part of the two thousand troops rushed up from the Curragh on Monday night. From daylight they sniped continuously into the Green, too cautious to attack a position that might, in turn, be protected by an enfilade from other houses along Baggot Street. So, that morning people rose to find soldiers resting under arms in side streets; residents sent out tea for the troops; the servant girls and the street gamins joked with them. A queer kind of insurrection, this, these soldiers must have felt. One said it reminded him of the Sidney Street anarchists.

The sudden morning salvo from the Shelbourne was the first indication to the entrenched rebels that the plans of the week

1. *The Insurrection* in Dublin. James Stephens, Dublin and London, 1916. pp. 16 *seq*. The man was a well-known Sinn Feiner and Madame, furious, threatened to court-martial the man who had shot him; but nothing was done in the end.

were gone awry. It made Tuesday an unpleasant day. The sniping was good enough to make the Green untenable; proved that the Green no longer dominated the eastern and southern approaches to the centre of the city; and showed the rebels that they were now on the defensive. All they could do for the time being was to reply to the Shelbourne snipers and skirmish now and again to the south in the direction of the canal. That would keep a free area behind them at any rate. Mallin had a narrow escape that day, a bullet passed through a badge in the front of his hat and ruffling his hair hummed through the felt behind. Madame, who believed in luck, kept the badge for years.

Even yet, however, the populace was merely curious.

'I went to the Green,' writes Stephens of this Tuesday morning. 'At a corner of Merrion Row a horse was lying on the footpath surrounded by blood. He bore two bullet-wounds but the blood came from his throat which had been cut. Inside the Green four bodies could be seen lying on the ground. They were dead Volunteers.

'The rain was now falling persistently, and persistently from the Green and the Shelbourne Hotel, snipers were exchanging bullets. Some distance beyond the Shelbourne I saw another Volunteer stretched out on a seat just within the railings. He was not dead, for now and again his hand moved feebly in a gesture for aid; the hand was completely red. His face could not be seen. He was just a limp mass upon which the rain beat pitilessly and he was sodden and shapeless and most miserable to see. His companions could not draw him in for the spot was covered by snipers from the Shelbourne. Bystanders stated that several attempts had been made to rescue him but that he would have to remain there until the fall of night.'

Such an extraordinary freedom of observation as this suggests a riot rather than an insurrection. Stephens actually says that he halted a while in front of the hotel to count the shots that had struck the windows. And, in fact, since the rebels had shut themselves up in houses and blocks of houses – boring a way through the wallpaper from house to house when the artillery, like a scythe in a cornfield, began, later, to force them in and in – the military continued to approach in safety quite close to individual positions. The populace, too, could, with a little ingenuity, transverse the city from end to end in safety. Only the wide open spaces of the river-approaches were impassable. It was the big guns whose deep, trembling, discharge began to sound from Tuesday night on that began the real drum-beat of war.

In the Green on Tuesday evening Mallin held a conference with his lieutenants. It was stupid to remain exposed there, Constance argued; as it was stupid ever to have gone there. And it was characteristic of her to say it like that; she would have said the same thing to Connolly separated from her by a barrage of fire and smoke down in O'Connell Street. So at dark they decided that the Green was too hot to hold: but if the electric lamps did not go up that night, there was a bright moon. Sleepless with tension they waited until it sank and then in the pitch-dark just before dawn they clambered over the railings on the west side, away from the Shelbourne snipers, and stole across the tram-lines to the College of Surgeons. The rest of the night passed quickly. They tore up the carpets into strips and the men slept in them rolled like mummies. Broken chairs and the coal in the boiler-house made excellent fires for cooking. They laid out their dead on old benches from the House of Lords and a rough crucifix, fashioned out of metal breast-plates, hung heavily over the bodies. Not until the sun spread dimly into those barricaded rooms did she have time to notice, staring down at her from the wall of the Board-room, a woman who had once smiled at her beauty. Afterwards, when the place was surrendered, the English military found the features of Victoria Regina lying in torn fragments on the floor beneath an empty frame.

For the men, that night was a little more comfortable than the nights before it in the Green. Mallin, an ex-army officer and a fine leader of men, saw to it that life in the College was regular and disciplined. Wisely he kept his men and women hard at work. He allotted duties with care and planned work in relays. Boring through the block of houses of which the college is the south-eastern corner began at once. Food was short and contact must be made with Jacobs biscuit-factory; and the military must be prevented from taking up positions in the abandoned Green. To do that he must be able to enfilade the street on which stood the Shelbourne – North Baggot Street. One by one during that night and the day following they gnawed their way through the neighbouring houses until they reached South King Street, which conveniently possessed a slight advantage over the wider North Baggot Street which it continues westward; from the corner house of South King Street, that is to say, one can look sidewards down at the Shelbourne front, and dominate that side of the Green. The south he commanded as long as he held Harcourt Street station; and Harcourt Street he retained by skirmishing in squads about it and along the canal. As to the shortage of food and information which were both troubling the rebels sorely, a sweetshop, tapped by the miners boring through to northward through the block, gave them a supply of chocolates; and they were also able to send out scouts, the women and the boys mainly, through the lanes behind their position. Indistinguishable from the sightseers, these, with patience and pluck, managed to reach even as far as the headquarters in the post-office. Contact with Jacobs' was made by them in the early morning of Wednesday and some food – flour and biscuits – brought relief to the besieged.

That Wednesday and following, the women slept in the caretakers quarters, and they munched through the chocolates as they talked and hazarded guesses as to what was happening elsewhere. They could now hear the rumble of the guns to the north, where one of the oldest and noblest streets in Europe was being battered to bits. From the roof they could see the search-lights at Fairview lightly fingering the clouds. In an odd and rather frightening silence they heard the crumble of tottering masonry. The rattle of rifle fire was almost incessant and came from three different points. Constance did not sleep much that night. Many of the garrison were little more than boys and all were unaccustomed to the thunder of war; wandering among them during that week, she made friendships that lasted to her death, cherished by her as the most precious fruit of her life's work. With her, was Councillor Partridge, of that first Army Council of the Citizen Army; as they talked in low tones, partly from a natural feeling of awe, partly not to waken the sleeping lads about, he confessed that he had left at home a wife who was near to her time and that he could not keep his thoughts from her. Madame promised him that if they should come alive out of that place she would see that the unborn child was never left to want. She did, after, manage to get a message out to her sister Eva asking her to stand sponsor for her to that child of revolution: it was called after her, Constance. To such a woman, reared as she was so far from the real people of Ireland, there was a genuine exhilaration in such intimacies among the simple folk she loved. With emotion she watched them at their prayers. This alone separated her from them. The only woman there marked off by difference in religion although of the men several were not Catholics. From that moment she desired to become, and ultimately did become a Roman Catholic – the last barrier, as she saw it, down.

The next day was sunny. To their east there was terrific firing all that morning. Several thousands of military had been landed at Kingstown and were marching towards the city; the rifle fire came from the direction of Ringsend and Bolands Mills where the flour-moted garrison under De Valera, and his outposts at Mount Street bridge, contesting the advance, decimated a whole detachment of Sherwood Foresters; then guns mounted on lorries battered the rebel fort into flames and with one exception every man there was burned to death. From the College roof they saw the fire; what it meant they could not tell.

The quays to the north were murderous, that sunny day, with cannonade. There, again, they could not know that the gunboat Helga was hammering Liberty Hall into a ruin. All day the noise grew in intensity and black motes of soot and burning paper came flying on the air. The women in the Stephen's Green position were glad when there was food to be prepared for the men, or work to be done about the sleeping quarters, for when there was nothing to do the strain began to tell. At dark, clouds of coloured whitish smoke could be seen rising like balloons over O'Connell Street and then bursting into tongues of leaping fire. The College, they now found, was a good position to hold, but a poor one for active attack; there was little to do but snipe from the roofs by day and watch by night the red sky and the rising sparks and the stars made pale by contrasting flame.

Through Thursday it went on; and Friday, and Saturday. A weird routine had established itself inside the College. They lived there as if they would continue to live there for weeks or months yet to come. Mallin ruled them well: the place was as ordered as a factory. Life had become mechanical and their bodies were adapting themselves to a regime. The jokes with which they had first met fears of death or hunger had ceased. They were exhausting their sense of wonder; their reactions were purely physical. The exhilaration of having come out under arms, the pride in fighting under the rebel flag had died down. They could still see a flag over Jacob's factory across the slum-roofs; it was the only sign of comradeship with their fellows. They could guess, too, that the centre of the assault was O'Connell Street, and when that was finished, their turn would probably come. Otherwise, they were becoming cut off with no way of knowing what the rest of the city, let alone the rest of Ireland, was thinking or doing. They just went up to the gutters and watched and sniped by the hour. Then they came down, wondered, and tried to sleep. Not even Mallin's vigour and ingenuity could find enough to do now. If it were not for the occasional raids – become very occasional by the end of the week as their scouts reported larger and larger numbers of military, and above all the presence of mobile armoured-cars in the streets – they must have choked emotionally. Then over the rifle-fire and the crackle of the machine-guns they heard the slow quiet tolling of the mass-bells. They had been there a week.

Stephens' memoir for Sunday morning tells its own tale of the College of Surgeons, by now an isolated and all but silent building. 'There is much rifle-fire,' he observed, 'but no sound from the machine guns or the eighteen pounder and trench-mortars...' As the Insurrection began gently and then mounted to its mid-week crescendo, so it was dying out to a gentle close. 'I met D.H., and, together, we passed up the Green. The Republican flag was still flying over the College of Surgeons. We tried to get down Grafton Street (where broken windows and two gaping interiors told of the recent visit of looters), but a little down this street we were waved back by armed sentries. We then cut up by the Gaiety Theatre into Mercer's Street, where immense lines of poor people were drawn up waiting for the opening of the local bakery.'

This means that Mallin had withdrawn his men from the corner of South King Street – where the Gaiety stands. It means too, that the interested observer is again free to roam, though within limits. Stephens had seen the volunteers at the beginning of the week waiting for the attack. He now saw the silent houses waiting for the end. For him, free to roam and pick up news, the surrender was a matter of hours. For Mallin and Madame, and the men and women under them, there was only that deepening silence. They listened to it and looked at one another, and looked away.

They had breakfast as usual; the snipers went to their usual posts; an occasional crack or two overhead indicated that they were getting something to shoot at. But there were long patches when no crack sounded. The mass-bells told them the quarter hours, ringing as they did the usual fifteen minutes before mass. A bell from SS. Michael and John's for half-past ten mass, and a bell from Clarendon Street for quarter-past eleven mass measured off shorter periods of time. From the roof they saw the flag still flying over Jacob's to their north-west. From O'Connell Street there was little sound at all. They had dinner as usual. That was their last siege-meal. Silence closed about them like a darkness. Then a loud and sudden hammering on the great central door resounded through the entrance-hall. A man came down from the roof almost simultaneously to say that a motor car had driven up from the mouth of Grafton Street with two Volunteers in it and two British military, and they whispered that a small white flag fluttered by the wind-screen. It had halted opposite the college. They saw four men alight and come to the door.

It did not take either Mallin or Madame Markievicz by surprise. Already that morning they had foreseen the end, and with a strange optimism they had gone about the halls of the college, room by room, looking for an unlikely place to hide their revolvers. Hers was a costly and excellent German automatic. Later, when peaceful days returned, they might, they hoped, get a chance to retrieve the guns. Some of the men, too, had been ordered to take French leave – not difficult where they were in plain-clothes and egress possible by the back-lanes into the poor quarters about. Three minutes sufficed to allow the envoys to enter and deliver their message from Moore Lane where Pearse had already surrendered and whither Connolly had been removed, badly wounded in the leg. Then into the empty street they filed, Mallin and Madame leading. The door remained open behind them; their arms rested wherever they had laid them down. In the street Mallin gave them his last command to fall in. They marched past the Green, stiffly, to meet their captors. Only a few remained behind, with the wounded, to await arrest. The envoys and the two Englishmen came out and watched them go, led by the man who was about to die, and the woman in slouch hat and green uniform who was doomed to live. That was about two o'clock on the Sunday afternoon, of April 30th, 1916.

They were met by a Major Wheeler. The rank and file were herded with the bulk of the rebels in the grounds of the Rotunda. Not one of them but will tell you that they did not care what happened to them then. Indifferently they sat there while the detectives wandered to and fro, staring into their faces, picking out the men they had seen on route marches, or on platforms calling youth to arm, or entering and leaving such houses as Surrey House. She was taken to Kilmainham Jail, overlooking – if that high walled place can be said to overlook anything – the wide range of the Phoenix Park north of the Liffey. She was put into a separate cell. Parnell had lain in his cell there when she was a child.

By dusk every rebel flag over the city had been hauled down. The police emerged once more. Business resumed its way – except where, as in O'Connell Street, the city lay in smouldering ruin, a tangled mass of fallen stone, crumpled ironwork and brick. Fine buildings like the Royal Hibernian Academy, the Linen Hall, the General Post Office, were mere smoke-blackened shells. As for the cost in human blood, in one cemetery alone, between April 27th and May 4th, there were 415 burials, 216 of them being deaths from gunshot.

Up in Kilmainham, they could hear faintly the sounds of the city returning to its work, and the cries of children returning to their play. It is safe to say that, excepting a very few people, the city thought of them as a crazy rabble who had upset normal life for a whole week, caused a lot of destruction and many deaths, and fully deserved everything they were now going to get.

§ 5

In Kilmainham Madame Markievicz was segregated from the rest of the women prisoners, about seventy in all, took her exercise separately, was kept in a separate cell, and spoke only to the wardresses. Court-martial began on the Tuesday, for not until Monday night could one say that the last shot was definitely fired. Individual snipers, unaware of the surrender, continued the fight, sporadically through Sunday evening, and the military remained on the watch for them all through Monday. The trials were brief – there was no defence. They took first the three best-known of the signatories to the Proclamation of the Provisional Government – the old Fenian who had spent so many long years in jail in his youth, Tom Clarke; Pearse, the mouthpiece of revolution for several years; Thomas MacDonagh, the poet, and university lecturer, all of the Republican Brotherhood. They were tried and condemned to be shot out of hand.

They were sentenced on Tuesday and on that night a wardress passed the word to Madame Markievicz. The next morning, May 3rd, she was awake to hear the firing squad clank into the yard below. Too far to hear spoken voices, all she could do was sit up on her pallet and listen out for any little sound, other than the sound of a chance footstep, closing her ears to all tiny internal noises of the prison beyond her door. The sun rose a little before half-past five. At six it was quite bright. Then, just as she was beginning to wonder at the long silence, there rang out a volley. She spoke of it many times afterwards, how she found herself rigid and tense as the reverberation died, and how, just as she began to sink into herself, an awful single shot of duller tone ran through her like an iron rod – the dispatch. She heard it three times and then the silence returned as before. Three gone.

She was in that jail all through the week, hearing a bit and a scrap from her friendly warder about each new decision. She woke each morning to hear those same volleying sounds – and the heavier isolated revolver-shots. That morning died Pearse's brother Willy, the sculptor; they were the only sons of their mother. With him died The O'Hanrahan, Joseph Plunkett, Count Plunkett's son, and Edward Daly, who was brother-in-law to Clarke and the son of the old Fenian Edward Daly of Limerick. Seven gone.

That day she was tried herself. All the official records of the trial are in the possession of the British Government, for obvious reasons not available for publication. The following brief particulars, however, I am permitted to quote from them:

'*Constance G. Markievicz was tried by Field General Court-Martial held in Dublin on May 4, 1916, on the following charge: "Did an act, to wit did take part in an armed rebellion and in the waging of war against His Majesty the King, such act being of such a nature as to be calculated to be prejudicial to the Defence of the Realm and being done with the intention and purpose of assisting the enemy." The accused pleaded not guilty but was found guilty and sentenced to death by being shot. She was recommended to mercy by the Court solely and only on account of her sex.*'

Major MacBride, the husband of Maud Gonne, was evidently tried the same day. He was executed the following morning. Eight gone.

There were no executions on Saturday or Sunday, but her friend, and chief in the rising, Mallin, was shot on Monday. With him went her Fianna captain, Con Colbert, Edmund Kent and J. J. Heuston. Twelve gone.

The last executions, there, took place at the end of the week, when they shot her best friend and her real master, Connolly. With him went young MacDiarmada, one of the last and most active of the Republican Brotherhood. Fourteen gone.

Three days before that Thomas Kent was shot in Cork. The following August 3rd, Sir Roger Casement was hanged in Pentonville Prison, London. That adds up to our sixteen dead men. To be remembered for ever.

How she received her sentence we do not know, but shortly after it was announced B. records that she, also in Kilmainham during that week, managed to get a glimpse of Madame Markievicz. She was sitting on her plank bed and looked radiant. On the pretext of borrowing a comb B. stepped into the cell for one second, and as Madame took it she looked up and said, 'Oh! Have you heard the news? I have been sentenced to death!' This, with such a smile of rapture that it sounded as if she were announcing some tidings of great joy.

Her sentence commuted – to penal servitude for life – she was moved to Mountjoy with some twenty women and girls, the residue of the Kilmainham prisoners who had not been released. Finally only five other women were retained and sent for 'internment' to England, first to Lewes and then to Aylesbury. Madame Markievicz, being a prisoner undergoing a life-sentence, was sent direct to Aylesbury. In those days prisoners were simply prisoners; treatment as politicals only came much later. She was a life-convict and they treated her accordingly.

The journey was not uncomfortable, but her thoughts cannot have been pleasant. She sat all the way between two wardresses; people stared at her; she could not move without a wardress at her side, watching the little towns roll past, the English fields, so quiet and so lush that it was hard to think this country was at war. Her country was being broken behind her. Her best friends were dead. Her life was to end in jail.

§ 6

When the great outer double-door of Aylesbury Prison rumbled to behind her she found herself in a wide passageway closed in front by another double-door. When this second door opened – never were both doors opened together – she was led to the prison offices. Her name and all the necessary details about her were entered on the prison rolls; the regulations were read out to her; she was told to undress, given a bath, and put on the convict dress she was to wear from that time on. Then she was led to her cell. A pallet-bed, a table fixed to the wall, a three-legged stool, a few utensils for her toilet.

The next morning introduced her abruptly to the regime of the prison. With the other convicts she rose at 6.30, washed, dressed, and was marched to chapel, fasting. An hour later she was given one pint, or about two cups, of tea, rather chill, without sugar, and five ounces of bread (which amounts to about three good slices of ordinary baker's loaf). This, she found later, was less than the usual amount allotted and represented war-rations. Then came the day's work, each to her own task, scrubbing, laundering, rope or twine making, cooking, carrying, mending. She was given at ten o'clock a piece of cheese and bread. At twelve o'clock dinner was served – two ounces of meat with thick gravy, mainly flour, two ounces of cabbage, one potato, and again three slices of bread. Back to work again until 4.30 or so – earlier in winter – when supper came, a pint of tea, without sugar, and two slices of bread. Meals were eaten alone in the cells. After supper the convicts were locked up for the night.

Such was her daily round. In the course of time she learned the variations, she found that there was no meat on Thursdays – only suet pudding and treacle; on Fridays only boiled fish and potatoes; on Saturdays there was a stew, and on Sundays cold corned beef.

Madame Markievicz's comment on the regime suggests a world of misery, although while she was in jail she smiled her way through to the end. 'A jail is a veritable sweater's den where the poor prisoners unwittingly help to keep down the rate of wages. They are packed together in unsanitary, ill-ventilated cells. The food is insufficient and of bad quality and the limit to work is ten hours a day.'[1]

A vivid account of life in that prison while she was there comes from the pen of a swindleress named Mary Sharpe, 'known,' as a policeman interjected during one of her many trials, 'to the police of the civilized and uncivilized world as Chicago May.' She, too, found the food inadequate and bad. 'My principal suffering,' she wrote, 'was hunger. I would be so famished that I would gobble down (all) my bread for breakfast and dinner. When supper came, I would, then, have nothing but a pint of awful cocoa. Sometimes, another prisoner, not so voracious as I was, would slip me a hunk of bread ...

1. *The Voice of Labour.* May 1st, 1919. 'Down with the Bastilles.'

When I got this extra food I would soak it in water until it became twice its usual size. Then, when I ate it, I tried to kid myself that it was filling and satisfying.'[1]

As to the unhealthy condition of the prison, the limestone walls easily held and exuded the damp. The drinking-water was always pale with lime. The floors of the cells, also of stone, did not make the cells any the drier in the wet weather. The ventilation consisted of a box-like, grated, insertion in the wall which provided a meagre light. (At night, until lights-out, a gas-flare outside in the corridor lit the cell through an immovable glass-window over the door.)

It was not the only prison that Madame Markievicz found unsanitary and unhealthy. Maud Gonne, who went with her in 1918 to Holloway, reported that she, Madame, and Mrs. Clarke were kept there in solitary confinement for several days after arrest, 'in small cells with little or no inlet for air.' The only association at first was in the yard but presently they were 'allowed to meet in a passage-way near open lavatories from which, in the warm days, there came an appalling stench.' Madame McBride developed lung trouble here as a result of the ill-ventilation and the noxious atmosphere.

The general treatment of the convicts by the authorities, happily, bears no comparison with the treatment suffered by Clarke at the hands of the male warders of Chatham in the 'eighties. Even Chicago May had no complaint against the warders, and she did ten years and two months in Aylesbury, as a hard-labour prisoner, and was given to pitying herself rather more than befitted a woman who ruined scores of men without the slightest trace of pity. She even acknowledges that little transgressions were overlooked, as when prisoners boiled water for tea with fat and a bit of rope for a wick, or when a prisoner burned in the main hall an anti-Catholic book that she had been given to read by mistake. Reading was encouraged in the jail. The allowance was two books a week, but prisoners exchanged books surreptitiously and some read as many as a book a day. In summer they were free to read from about 5 p.m. until the light failed, which was about 10 p.m.; in winter until the gasflare sank outside the cell about the same hour.

One feature of prison life there was, however, which got on Madame's nerves, as it did with every prisoner – the peephole in the door. Painted inside the door of the cell was an

1. *Chicago May; Her Story.* May Sharpe. London, n.d., p. 187.

eye, with eyebrows, eyelashes, iris and all complete; and not merely was it painted but it was carved to look the more lifelike. Outside the door was a tiny slide which a warder could move aside and there the prisoner would suddenly see the glint of a real pupil. Never at any hour of the day or night was a prisoner sure of her privacy, and Madame confessed that she used to walk up and down in her cell madly, trying to forget that awful staring eyeball. But, again, she might thank her fate that she was spared the two worst features of the older surveillance – the devilish rule which forbade any convict, for any reason whatsoever, to speak to another convict – 'the silent system' – and that other torture which drove nearly every one of the Fenian prisoners in Chatham to insanity, periodic inspection at night, accompanied by doors clanging back into place, just as the wearied wretches were dropping into a light sleep.

But in spite of the blessed relief of books and occasional conversation, the round of life in that jail was exhausting as a treadmill. A visitor was a great event, even if it was only a Salvation Army general, or a bishop preaching in his robes. So small a thing as a bright sermon at church was something to turn over for days in the hollow tooth of the brain. Even for a woman like Madame Markievicz, whose mind was filled with many ideas and many memories, the death in life of that tomb soon began to exhaust the pleasures of remembrance, and the movement of her thoughts gradually became more slow. The conversation of professional prostitutes, thieves, blackmailers, ended by becoming a bore. And yet it is interesting to note that when she met the woman Sharpe several years after in America, Con ran up to her and greeted her as an old friend.

For all that one must feel, from what one knows of her own nature and from what is known definitely of her life in jail, that she managed to remain cheerful throughout the ordeal of her first imprisonment; and that, even though those first months after the rising were a severe test, harsh and wearing, for all the prisoners; and much more so for the women, far more than the men.

In the internment camps at Frongoch where there were hundreds of men freely conversing, it was not at all comparable to her life in Aylesbury or to the deliberately cruel life imposed on the older political prisoners of the nineteenth century. Even in Lewes, Dartmoor, Maidstone, or Portland where the sentenced men, like de Valera, Desmond Fitzgerald, Prof. MacNeill, Griffith, W. T. Cosgrave, and the other leaders were being treated as ordinary convicts, there was no comparison with the life old Tom Clark had led for fifteen and a half years in Millbank and Chatham. Never could they say, and never has any of them said, as Clarke said, that if the future appeared as black and appalling as the imagination could picture it, 'the worst the imagination proposed to the body was outdone by the horrors of life in English jails.' Besides, the first feeling of indifference to life or death, which was common to all who took part in the insurrection, naturally waned as the desire for life asserted itself again. After all, they had fought; they had kept to their vow; they were not dead. True their people hated them – as far as all outward appearances could tell. The press execrated them. Public bodies denounced them. But on the other hand they were many where the old Fenian prisoners had been few, and the very sight of comrades is in itself invigorating. They were able to break rules, circumvent rules, defy rules. And they ended by winning the right to be treated not as murderers but as political prisoners. Besides their punishment only lasted, in the event, only a little over a year.

But Con had no comrades, and therefore had not the power the men-convicts had when banded together in defiance to make life troublesome for the authorities. She could not even speak with the few comrades who were also in Aylesbury. They – Winifred Carney, Helena Moloney, Nell Ryan – were kept in a separate wing. They saw her often, in the yard or at mass, filing past in her convict dress among all the other convicts, and for a second she would see and smile at them, but no more. As even young 'lags' can, however (especially Irish lags), they did manage to communicate with their comrade, in spite of the rules, and with the outside world as well. For the rest she was kept to her solitary cell, and lived in silence, prepared to accept the life before her, the lot of an entombed prisoner, the broad-arrow dress, the coarse linen, the rough work.

In that acceptance her first summer in jail passed slowly. She was entered in the prison books as a Catholic and was permitted to dress the altar in the chapel. She also worked in the prison library, helped to catalogue it and make selections for the prisoners. Here she found relief from the routine of jail by meeting a friendly Irish wardress. With her she could

talk a little, and from her gather something of the Irish news –
learn for instance that two thousand five hundred men and
women had been sentenced and deported since May, learn
news of the war, news of English politics in which, already in
the autumn, the Asquith–Lloyd George rivalry was coming to
a head. She does not appear to have impressed this warder
greatly. In her vague, aery, Irish way, she probably made no
effort to control her tongue – and it may be agreed that
Madame Markievicz did not, at first meeting, tend to impress
people who were unacquainted with her background and her
personal history. But that she was cheerful and a 'good'
prisoner – one who took things as they came, obeyed the rules,
and was neither fractious nor sullen – is admitted. She was
also, this woman says, slatternly in her ways. Always a petticoat hung down, a stocking was twisted, her hair was for ever
astray. But she could be counted on for a smile and a quip in
the roughest weather.

Mr. Alfred Byrne, M.P., now the Lord Mayor of Dublin,
visited her in the winter of that year to investigate conditions
in the prison. He was taken to her cell by the head warder,
but found it empty; and it was only after some little search
that they found the countess in the kitchen on her knees over a
bucket of steaming water, scrubbing out the floor. She was
pleased to meet Mr. Byrne. (Only the previous May she had
smuggled out a pencil note from Mountjoy thanking him for all
that he had done for her; and adding, 'I wanted to tell you
how glad I was to hear of the great work you are doing – we
may meet again in happier days. I believe great good will come
out of all this pain.') Now she met him, if not in the days she
still hoped for, at least in days made slightly less poignant by
the passing of time. She did not appear, he says, to mind the
work she was doing. 'I am better pleased,' she smiled, 'working
than being idle.'

Two other visitors found her less friendly, but otherwise
in the same mood. These were Lady Battersea and Adeline
Duchess of Bedford, who were among the official visitors.
Madame Markievicz was brought in the usual way to the
waiting-room, and as usual her dress was hitched up and
crooked, and an inch or two of underskirt showed beneath;
and as usual, also, the prisoner stood (on one leg) and the
visitors sat. Perhaps it was this that ruffled her.

'What are you doing now, Constance?' asked the duchess,

and she told her, with a gay smile, that she had been scrubbing when they called.

'Oh?'

There was a slight pause.

'That is rather hard work,' sympathized the duchess.

'No!' protested Constance quite seriously.

'Well – eh – you don't *like* scrubbing out your cell?' smiled the duchess.

'Why not?' asked the countess in genuine surprise. 'Wouldn't you?'

Presently the duchess asked, perhaps probing about the rumoured change to Catholicism. 'Do you say your prayers at night, Constance?'

'Yes, of course,' was the reply to that. 'Don't you?'

The dowager was not fluent. She looked to her friend for help, but Lady Battersea was silent.

After a few more awkward words they rose. 'Well, goodbye, Constance.'

(It is well that she did not adopt the form of address more usual with prisoners – Good-bye, Sharpe, or Good-bye, Markievicz.)

'I suppose you wish you were out of this place?'

'Why, yes,' admitted Constance. And then she prodded with a little smile as they fumbled for the door-handle. 'Wouldn't you?'

To Chicago May she was 'the grandest woman I ever met,' and as the two women went through some rough times together May knew what she was talking about. 'She was Irish to the backbone ... No kind of hardship ever feazed her ... I think it was when the Germans were making their last successful push and General Haig was telling the English Tommies that their backs were against the wall and they would have to fight, that the prisoners were ordered to go to the Anglican chapel to pray for the success of the troops. I knew the rules and I knew they could not force me to go. I slammed my door shut. The Irish countess and the German spy Bertha (Wertheim) would not go. For spite they made the three of us women carry enough gruel around the prison to feed the entire three hundred convicts. We had to carry immense, heavy cans, up winding stairs.

'While we were doing this, the Countess recited long passages, in Italian, from Dante's *Inferno*. The place looked like Hell all right with the lights dimmed and musty-smelling bags tacked across the windows, as a precaution against bombing.' Strange but warm friendship – 'Poor, dear, Countess Markievicz,' sighed the 'badger', from Philadelphia, in 1927 when, down and out after a life of crime, she heard that Madame was dead.

Apart from these few witnesses to her life in that jail, we have only her own words as to the kind of inner world she built up for herself as a defence against the challenges of those unhappy days. She thought a great deal of her old friends, of what they must be doing, and of what they might be thinking. Of Eva she thought frequently. To Miss Edith Roper, Eva's friend and the writer of her memoir, she wrote, in 1926: 'Her human presence was so beautiful and wonderful, but with her the spirit dominated every bit of her and her body was just the human instrument it shone through. It is so hard to put things like this down in a way that anyone can understand. When I was in Aylesbury, we agreed to try to get in touch a few minutes every day, and I used to sit at about six o'clock and think of her and concentrate and try and leave my mind a blank, a sort of dark still pool. And I got to her. And once I told her how she sat in a window and I seemed to know what she was thinking. It was a great joy and comfort to me. When I got out, I lost this in the bustle and hurry of life, but now just the last few days I seem to get in touch again. . . .'

§ 7

In the months following the Rising, opinion had been changing everywhere with regard to the Irish question. In Ireland it seemed to change overnight. The executions awoke old and forgotten emotions in the hearts of the people, disturbed and aroused the sleeping racial memory in which every Irish patriot has his niche and his votive lamp. Ever since Parnell's day a dust of oblivion and unreality had settled on those old pictures of Emmet raising his sword, and Tone with his narrow lips and his hooked nose facing the west. Now those memories became freshened and real. Honour, like a King, was come to earth. The ruins of Dublin took on glory and were a pilgrimage. The names of the very streets sang with inspiration. To the litany of old sorrow the young added the names of Pearse and Connolly, MacDonagh and Mac-Bride. The poets began to put their names into their verses. Thinking of Constance Gore-Booth and the old days in Sligo, Yeats wrote:

> 'That woman's days were spent
> In ignorant good will,
> Her nights in argument
> Until her voice grew shrill.
> What voice more sweet than hers
> When young and beautiful
> She rode to harriers?'

Thinking of Pearse and others he wrote:

> 'This man had kept a school
> And rode a wingéd horse;
> This other, his helper and friend
> Was coming into his force;
> He might have won fame in the end,
> So sensitive his nature seemed,
> So daring and sweet his thought.
> This other I had dreamed
> A drunken, vain-glorious lout.
>
> He had done most bitter wrong
> To some who are near my heart,
> Yet I number him in the song;
> He, too, has resigned his part
> In the casual comedy;
> He, too, has been changed in his turn,
> Transformed utterly;
> A terrible beauty is born.'

And to those who, unmoved, argued with the cold voices of wisdom, he said:

> 'You say that, we should still the land
> Till Germany's overcome;
> But who is there to argue that
> Now Pearse is deaf and dumb?
> And is their logic to outweigh
> MacDonagh's bony thumb?
>
> 'How could you dream they'd listen
> That have an ear alone
> For those new comrades they have found,
> Lord Edward and Wolfe Tone
> Or meddle with our give and take
> That converse bone to bone?'

Thinking of some story they had told him about Constance Markievicz, he wrote the poem, *On a Political Prisoner*.

'She that but little patience knew
From childhood on, had now so much.
A grey gull lost its fear and flew
Down to her cell and there alit,
And there endured her fingers' touch
And from her fingers ate its bit.

'Did she in touching that lone wing
Recall the years before her mind
Became a bitter, an abstract thing,
Her thought some popular enmity;
Blind and leader of the blind,
Drinking the foul ditch where they lie?

'When long ago I saw her ride
Under Ben Bulben to the meet,
The beauty of her countryside
With all youth's lonely wildness stirred,
She seemed to have grown clean and sweet
Like any rock-bred, sea-borne bird:

'Sea-borne or balanced on the air,
When first it sprang out of the nest
Upon some lofty rock to stare
Upon the cloudy canopy,
While under its storm-beaten breast
Cries out the hollows of the sea.'

To her, in jail, Æ wrote:

'Here's to the women of our race
Stood by them in the fiery hour,
Rapt lest some weakness in their blood
Rob manhood of a single power.
You, brave on such a hope forlorn,
Who smiled through crack of shot and shell,
Though the world look on you with scorn,
Here's to you, Constance, in your cell.'

Eva wrote to her, under the title *Comrades*:

'The peaceful night that round me flows
Breaks through your iron prison doors,
Free through the world your spirit goes;
Forbidden hands are clasping yours.

'The wind is our confederate,
The night has left her doors ajar.
We meet beyond earth's barrèd gate
Where all the world's wild rebels are.'

Ledwidge, fighting with the British in France, sang the lament of MacDonagh, Seumas O'Sullivan the lament of MacDermott. Stephens remembered them, Colum, Dermot O'Byrne, all who had known them. And for the people there were those hundreds of older songs that become filled with new dignity as each time brings its meaning to their words. In those months there magically began an awakening of national pride whose fire can never have been foreseen, however wildly hoped for, by the men who had fought for it, because of its seed within themselves.

In America that old seed of fire was even more readily blown, where the memory of enforced exile, the emigrant-ship, the constant cruel fight for life, had raked the ashes year by year. They had risen step by step from the rags in which they landed on American soil after the Black Forties and were now a considerable political force. Immense *cortèges* following empty coffins through the cities of New England told British agents, manœuvring for American support in the war, that the Irish question had taken a new significance since the Insurrection.

'A man must be afflicted with blindness,' said Lord Curzon in the House of Lords, on May 21st, 'if he does not appreciate that the co-operation of America will be more hearty, more fruitful, if she could feel that Ireland, with whom she has so many associations, was pulling its full weight in the comity of free and allied nations. America realizes, as we realize, that to win the kind of victory which we are out to win in this war, the full strength of the British Empire must be turned to that purpose. A divided Ireland, a sulky Ireland, a rebellious Ireland, is a source of weakness.'

Even the Irish Party, who knew the rise of a new movement would threaten their long-held power, could not remain aloof. It was a difficult position. Public opinion if nothing else demanded that they should fight for the imprisoned men; even in self-preservation they must fight for them, since revolution thrives on suppression.[1] Daily during that first week of May, 1926, Redmond and Dillon pleaded for leniency and an end to executions. Sir John Maxwell had replied with new martyrs.

1. *The Life of John Redmond.* Denis Gwynn, pp. 472 f. London, 1932.

And at the same time that they thus pleaded for the rebels they were obliged to plead with an irate and disappointed England for an advance on her long-deferred promise of Home Rule. Weakened at home, and with prestige impaired abroad, they were treated on both sides of the Irish Sea as the weak party they were.

All through the summer Lloyd George deceived them with a series of double-meaning proposals for a settlement, based on the exclusion of the Six Counties under a Home Rule Act, a concession against which Redmond had always hitherto stood out; yet when he agreed to a temporary exclusion, he found that Carson had been persuaded privately that the exclusion would be permanent and final. The final exposé did little credit to the sagacity of the Party, or to its reputation. Their pleas for a relaxation of martial law were rejected; later a Unionist was appointed Chief Secretary at the Castle; and always the internees continued to be held – every one of whom, by remaining behind barbed wire, was fomenting daily pity and anger in his native village.

In December, the Asquith government fell and the Coalition took place. When it was too late the internees were released in a body – and, with that curious English sentimentality that makes no appeal to the cynical side of the Irish mind, they were released on Christmas Eve. They returned home just as popular pity was ripe to welcome them as heroes.

Collins took up the threads of revolution. Griffith simply began where he had left off, altering his policy, under the stress of circumstances, so that it now coincided with the policy of Republicanism. No more was heard of 1782. And, anyway, people no longer approached his movement in a spirit of inquiry or curiosity. Mass-emotion was king. They talked of Independence and the Republic and Liberty, now, with the simplicity of converts to a new faith, men for whom to question was to be disloyal to the faith of the martyred dead. In February of the new year Sinn Fein – the generic title from this on for all movements working towards Separation and a Republic – contested an election against the party in North Roscommon, and won easily. What was specifically at stake, what the candidate, Count Plunkett, the father of the executed Joseph Plunkett, declared he stood for, did not matter. It was the people's cry of 'Well Done' to the rebels. And as if the Government could not make up its mind as to its policy a fresh raid on the new movement followed immediately after, and a new bunch of martyrs were manufactured overnight; this even while Lloyd George was planning fresh overtures to the Unionists, the Party, (and even Sinn Fein) with a view to setting up a commission or Convention that would arrive at some solution of Irish difficulties.

When the new proposals were published in May, the Unionists and the Party agreed to meet; Sinn Fein held off, merely contenting itself with making conditions that were scarcely intended to be considered seriously. Nonetheless, to create a suitable atmosphere, the Government agreed to release all the prisoners unconditionally, and on June 17th, 1917, a little over a year since the Rising, the jails emptied. The following day the men arrived in Dublin, and drove through streets crowded with a cheering populace. They could now hold up their shaved heads as they passed the ruins of the houses where they had fought, high over the crowds that cheered them for that fight. No homecoming Fenian had ever been so welcomed. The new Fenians, it was clear, had not merely fought for an old cause but started a new movement.

Madame arrived in Dublin with the others and after the reception she drove to Dr. Kathleen Lynn's. On the way she had to pass the College of Surgeons. Here the car was halted and Maeve Cavanagh (the 'poet of the revolution', Connolly had called her), presented a nosegay of flowers. Her last welcome came from her dog Poppet, for whom over a year's absence had not been enough to obliterate the memory of the sound of a familiar step and voice. Flowers, and freedom; her dog capering madly about her; Balalley Cottage, and the sun of June on the Three Rocks, she almost wept to think of it. She would be up among the whins again, painting and reading and idling. Far below, the hum and bustle of smoky Dublin would sink to a silence, and far beyond the sunpools of the sea stretch out to divide her from England and Buckinghamshire – Aylesbury and the prison-bell, the steaming wash-house, the eye staring at her through her door, the sunless cells, the dank walls, all that entire dreadful death-in-life of the entombed.

The next morning she drove up to Clonliffe, to Holy Cross College, with her sister Eva, and asked the rector, Canon Mac-Mahon, to prepare her for formal reception into the Catholic Church. She was baptized there a few months later, made her first communion with the Sisters of Charity, Upper Gardiner Street, and was confirmed at St. Mary's in Haddington Road, by the late Most Rev. Dr. Donnelly.

CHAPTER VI

ILLUSION AND DISILLUSION: 1917–1924

§ 1

IT is hereabouts that the problem of The Fair Question, mentioned in the foreword to this edition, becomes urgent. How much is it fair to expect of her from this onward? Thus far she has had the interest that any personality might have for any novelist, since so much of her struggle has been with herself, her origins and background, and along the way this has meant personal conflicts with her family in Sligo, and with her husband, and there has been the interesting relationship with her stepson and her daughter, in which that with her stepson seems to have been much closer than with her daughter. The focus and main aim of her early life had been her longing to become one of what the Elizabethans used to call 'the mere Irish', or the old, native stock. Now, she becomes, inside this new world that was won, a public figure, a member of the cabinet of a revolutionary parliament, and whatever question was fair to ask about her personal achievement before this, must harden into questions of a public or political nature.

For the romantic poet, like Yeats, for the lover of the patriotic myth (using that word in its noblest sense), even for the biographer, and, one has reason to think, even perhaps for herself, it would have been ideal if she had been shot with the other leaders after the Rising. Yeats would then not have salted his poems about her with such phrases as 'ignorant good will', her voice that grew 'shrill' in nightly argument, her mind that became 'a bitter, an abstract thing,' or 'Too long a sacrifice/Can make a stone of the heart.' He could have written of her as warmly as he wrote of her comrades who died in the Rising, in *The Rose Tree*, and *Easter Nineteen Sixteen* and *Sixteen Dead Men*. Yet, supposing they, like her, had had to live on and cope, like her, with 'this pragmatical pig of a world' (his phrase) would not even they too have come within the ambit of other considerations in his poems about them?

She lived on as a political leader and it is in that role that we see and consider her from this on with, I trust, not unfairly questioning minds – always remembering that whatever we may decide to think about her as a political leader is, to a lesser or greater extent, equally applicable to all her associates. She is, *toutes proportions gardées*, a representative figure.

§ 2

If to live in action is to live in happiness, the next seven years of Madame Markievicz's life were happy years indeed. Chance was kind to her. It allowed her to burn her candle at both ends – to begin to live again when most people would have been doomed to relinquish action to others. Her continuing role, however, was action not thought. She was forty-nine when she came out of jail in 1917; she was fifty-six before the prison-gates opened for her at the end of her last bout of prison-life and she paused to think for the first time, one feels, in her headlong life – and thinking, become for the first time miserable.

She might well have expected now, after some eight or nine years of novitiate, to be accepted by the people whose acceptance she most desired, and to be free to do for them the work she had always wished to do when she broke from her own class. The acceptance was alloyed. In July, in Clare, after the election of De Valera for Ennis – another sad blow for Party hopes, followed immeditely after by another, the election of Mr. Cosgrave in Kilkenny, she was attacked by a mob; and, ironically, had to be protected by the police. On the other hand, that summer she had the gratification of being enrolled as an honorary citizen of Kilkenny, and presented with the freedom of the Borough of Sligo, her native county, where, beside her on the courthouse steps, stood old Larry Ginnell, the veteran Party member, one of the first of the old men to hail the new movement – a man who had seen Davitt greeted on the same spot, and Parnell howled at by an angry people. The two incidents, Clare and Sligo, must have shewn her that, as for herself, the work of finding herself was well begun, but that, as for others, total emancipation could only come when victory came to the cause she had chosen as her cause. In the end it must have seemed to her that Griffith was right and Connolly and Larkin wholly wrong. 'All things come to the victorious.'

In that way, politics first and armed revolution after – a more intensified repetition of her novitate – engulfed her once more. Still struggling for the whole-hearted love of the people, she set herself to do all that she could do in the work of reorganizing Sinn Fein until it became a purely Republican movement and reorganizing the volunteers until they became a guerilla army.

The words 'reorganization of Sinn Fein' and 'reorganization of the Volunteers' may seem to suggest two rather dull and cold-blooded operations. But ever since the Rising nothing was done in cold blood. Politics had become, since Pearse spoke, not politics but a cult. So if she lived externally it was because she was unable to live emotionally. The connection between the two is in an Irishman inevitable. She had taken no decisive action at any time which did not spring from an emotional condition; her very convictions were the sublimation of an emotion into a religion. And if she be taken as an average of the workings of the minds and hearts of Irish men and women at her period, it will be found illuminating to remember this emotional motivation of all her actions.

It was something utterly alien to the old Irish Party. True they had, in their day, also woven the most doleful atmosphere of pity and the most picturesque imagery about the question of Home Rule, elaborated it until a speech about Ireland in chains was all they needed to rouse the populace. But long attendance at Westminster, and long acquaintance with the English political mind, had also bred in them a thoroughly astute sense of tactics and values, a measuring capacity for what could be got and what could not be got, of what was worth taking at once and what was worth rejecting for the time being; so much so that, ultimately, Tammany Hall, may be said to have been fathered in the House of Commons. And because they fought for a people deep in poverty, they had come, also, to measure their ideals almost wholly in practical terms, and to deride all spiritual or visionary politicals as 'rainbow chasers.' They had developed, in spite of themselves, all the weaknesses inevitable to a party that was constantly suspected, sometimes feared, always yielded to with a bad grace, that had to fight against innumerable prejudices and won what it won against odds – until Sinn Fein, whose memory, with an adoration for everything extreme and an indifference to everything intermediate, leaped beyond the history of the Party, to figures and to a gospel far more spectacular, declared that the Party was capable of sacrificing all spiritual values for the most paltry material concessions.

This had not been Griffith's view at all times, nor even Pearse's. Both of them had at one period supported the Party. But with the passing of time Pearse had read more and more about the ancient wrongs, and the ancient glories, of Ireland which the Party was willing to forgive in the one case and forget in the other, if only a new Ireland might be set on its way by a repentant England. In reading of those aged things Pearse had formed for himself a vision that by his death (as well as by the exalted mood in which he wrote of it) became for ever after as sacred to all Ireland, and still remains as sacred to many as the treasure of David's ark. The result was the creation not of a political philosophy but of a heroic attitude. When the Party began to weep over Cathleen ni Houlihan, it was always a preliminary to a Finance Bill. When Pearse wept over Ireland's wrong it was a preliminary to martyrdom for Ireland's sake. It is a fate which every young Irishman felt at some time or other during those years. It had even overwhelmed the hardheaded Connolly. After 1916 it overwhelmed the entire populace.

It is true, however, that the new revolutionaries had learned something from previous suttees; with that often baffling mixture of the spiritual and the astute which is the composition of the Celt, a man like Collins, however much he might adore Pearse, had no intention of imitating him. There were no useless holocausts between 1916 and 1922. When, therefore, Constance Markievicz began to taste the quality of this second movement of which she found herself a member – and this time a prominent member – it is not surprising if she, by nature a highly emotional woman, felt the hypnotic influence in the glittering vision of Pearse, and forgot the rather humdrum and not at all spectacular ideas of Connolly.

Frankly, then, to this biographer, and it is possibly his misfortune, the following six or seven years of Constance Markievicz's life are of less interest than her life before the Rising. By becoming one of a mass movement, she loses much of her interest as an individual woman. The interest of her life during the period of the revolution is the interest of the revolution rather than the interest of her character. With the exception of her brief career as Sinn Fein, or Republican Minister for Labour, she had no opportunity to disclose her own peculiar virtues; for it was more in dream than in personal or self-realization, or self-assertion, that she suffered, drilled, preached, or organized all through the exciting years that followed on the Insurrection. She displayed in everything she did the courage and the resourcefulness that was only what one would have expected of her. Otherwise her weaknesses rather than her strength become evident during those years of thoughtless activity, excitement and danger.

§ 3

By contrast, during the autumn of '17 and the early portion of '18, Redmond was wrestling patiently, if rather hopelessly, with facts and figures in the Convention. His whole aim was to buy the support of the Southern Unionists against the North. He had seen the Home Rule Bill of 1914 passed and put on the Statute Book – but there accompanied by a suspensory clause, and also sent there by a speech by Mr. Asquith in which he gave the most solemn assurance to the Carsonites that, before putting the Bill into force, an Amending Bill would be introduced giving Parliament the power of 'altering, modifying or qualifying its provisions in such a way as to secure the general consent both of Ireland and the United Kingdom'. He realized, after the Insurrection, that this Bill could now never come into force without these modifications and alterations and qualifications; otherwise the North would never permit it, nor the Government coerce the North into accepting it. He tried now, for the last time, at the Convention, to labour for a settlement that at least a majority of those present would accept. All he had to go on was Lloyd George's ambiguous promise that if the majority vote was given for 'a substantial agreement', then 'the government would accept the responsibility for taking all the necessary steps to enable the Imperial parliament to give legislative effect to the conclusions of the convention'. (Which, from such a man, meant nothing whatever.)

For months the Convention continued to meet and argue, and, in the end, finance was the rock on which it broke. (We note that it was not finance, but, almost wholly, the matter of an Oath, and the extent of 'association' with the Empire, which divided Irishmen five years after – the measure of the different outlook of the old and the new movements.) Redmond, without any clear reason to believe that the North would abide by a majority decision, or that the Government would enforce it, was willing to give away fiscal autonomy to buy the Southern Unionists. His own colleagues deserted him on that and in the end the Southern Unionists would not be bought. Shortly after Redmond's death, a weary and disappointed man, the Convention dissolved. It was the last effort by the leader of the

Party to win Home Rule by constitutional means—and, be it noted, to win it for a United Ireland.

Here it is impossible to refrain from one comment. It has been said that the Party had its ideals. Redmond fought hard for a United Ireland. Time and time again, it is true, he proved accommodating on this point, and he virtually agreed to certain concessions as regards Partition, but he never agreed to permanent Partition, which is the essential point. It is an ironic commentary on those who held themselves to be more interested in spiritual values than material concessions, and it was they and not the Party – at any rate, not Redmond – who proved accommodating on the question of exclusion, for the sake of a good Exchequer.

§ 4

While the Convention was petering to its close, and the history of Irish Parliamentarianism with it, Sinn Fein was holding its own Convention or Ard Fheis. Here came delegates from the Sinn Fein clubs all over the country to elect the officers and executive committee of the revived organization, as well as to discuss the revised constitution and to agree on general policy. It met on October 25th (1917) at the Mansion House, Dublin, and represents Madame Markievicz's first important public appearance as a politician.

It was in some ways a memorable meeting. It was the first large public view of the new generation of politicians, largely young men. They came with their bicycle-clips still on their trousers, and the smell of the rain and the bogwater from their coats and boots. They were in the main raw and without experience, men of little knowledge outside the affairs of their own parishes. Her father's gardener might have been among them. But among them, too, were young men like Collins and O'Higgins who were to prove themselves able politicians later. In Dublin the people looked at them as they might look at any batch of countrymen, slightly contemptuous, scarcely interested. Even so must many a gathering of Irish members have brought smiles to the faces of the Tories in Westminster before they realized the force of a Parnell, an Egan, a Healy or an O'Connor-Power.

It cannot be said that Madame Markievicz disclosed any masterly qualities as a politician. She had not the patience necessary for that type of work, and people whom she had attracted and delighted by her ebullience and her vitality she merely annoyed now that the need was for solidity and detachment. She had only one quality that was valuable in these assemblies – she was outspoken and without fear. Where others paused for human respect or timidity, she never hesitated. Sometimes it was a quality that would have been as honoured in the breach as the observance, and often one feared that it sprang wholly from her love of the dramatic. Two small instances will illustrate. Her dislike for Bulmer Hobson, who had been opposed to the Rising, was unconcealed. She threatened to shoot him the first time she met him. One day she entered the same room as Hobson, without recognizing him. When he had gone she asked his name, and on being told it she appeared to be profoundly disappointed. 'If I had known it,' she cried, 'I'd have shot him.' At the Sinn Fein Convention she opposed the election of McNeill, who had also been averse to the Rising, but who had been imprisoned with the other suspects. She made a fiery speech when his name was put forward for the Executive. She declared he had signed the Proclamation of the Provisional Republic, and then deserted the men who fought for it. Only De Valera's intervention silenced her. He pointed out simply that she had her facts wrong, McNeill never signed the Proclamation. In the event McNeill was elected with 880 votes, the largest number given. She came fifth with 617. Collins came last with 340. There were twenty-four names between McNeill and Collins.

None the less she was probably at the height of her popularity at this time. Between Sligo, and Kilkenny, election to the new Sinn Fein, and several public appearances she found it a busy autumn and winter. On November 24th she presided at the Manchester Martyrs' demonstration in the Mansion House. Over the end of the year and into the new year, one finds her name mentioned several times in the Sinn Fein weeklies for meetings, demonstrations, or lectures. In February and March she was in demand for the three bye-elections of South Armagh, Waterford, and East Tyrone. In all of these the Party easily defeated Sinn Fein, a measure, possibly, of the popular feeling that while Sinn Fein was honourable, it was, so far, impractical. But the decision of the British cabinet to extend conscription to Ireland did much more for the Sinn Feiners than even the most practical kind of policy they could have offered the people. In April the Man-Power Bill received its third reading. A few days later the Irish Party left Westminster for ever. The Bishops at Maynooth had already solemnly pledged themselves to resist conscription by the most effective means at their disposal. The result was an extraordinary influx into the ranks of Sinn Fein and the Volunteers, who soon numbered some 100,000 men. Labour, throwing itself behind Sinn Fein, declared a one-day strike. In Offaly a Sinn Fein candidate was returned unopposed at a bye-election. And in the midst of this excitement, and, for many people, dismay, the Lloyd George Convention published its abortive report. Her party was in the ascendant.

Then, on May 17th, a sudden round-up of Sinn Fein leaders was made throughout the country, and on the following day a Proclamation was issued by the new viceroy, Lord French, and the Chief Secretary, Mr. Shortt, declaring the existence of a treasonable plot with Germany. The prisoners were scattered through various English jails. Among them was Madame Markievicz, who with Madame Maud Gonne McBride and Mrs. Tom Clarke, was sent to Holloway. There she remained all through that spring, summer and winter, until March 1919.

Holloway was not so bad as Aylesbury. She was treated as a political prisoner, and allowed to meet her fellow-prisoners. They were segregated, too, from the regular convicts; they had cells on a special landing, with a special bathroom, and they took their exercise at a special hour. All day she occupied herself as well as she might, sewing, embroidering, writing. Her chief distraction was her drawing: she filled an entire prison note-book with sketches for the decorations and end-pieces that later went into Eva's *The Triumph of Maeve*. They were not good decorations. Some of them would have been better fitted for a mural than the border of a book. All of them showed the old lack of discipline and control, and in their wild, wide suggestion of vasty spaces, demi-gods and god-heroes, were oddly typical of a mingling of Victorianism and the Celtic mist. Perhaps there was something of the same mixture in the artist, the Anglo-Irish lady in search of the picturesque, rather than the real Ireland. But as they were not permitted to receive visitors, letters, or newspapers, the old monotony descended on her after a few months, and above all that exasperating, nervous feeling that 'things were happening' in which she could take no part.

In all she spent a little over three years in prison – three years that must have stolen several more from her life at the end. Even the best jails, in her opinion, as a woman who had

experience of several both in England and Ireland, were not
fit for their purpose. Madame MacBride's opinion of Holloway has been quoted already (p. 160). She spoke of the experience there, during the hot weather, what with the smells
and the poor ventilation, as 'awful'. It was on her release from
Holloway that Madame Markievicz wrote her own attack on
the British prison-system – *Down with the Bastilles.*

From the little trickle of news that came into Holloway she
gathered that things *were* happening in Ireland. Arrests were
becoming more frequent. The first of several later spectacular
escapes from prison occurred in Cork in the November of
1918. Sinn Fein, having been suppressed in July, held its second
Convention in October. In December occurred the first General
Election since the war, the result of which, in Ireland, was to
give Sinn Fein, with its abstentionist policy, 73 seats, the Party
6 seats, the Unionists 26 seats. While in prison, the usual request to attend Parliament was served on Madame. She had
been elected to the Saint Patrick's division, in Dublin, the
first woman to be elected to the British House of Commons.
(The first woman to sit in the Imperial Parliament was Lady
Astor, elected for Plymouth a little later.)

The first Dail Eireann met in January, 1919. The De Valera
escape, engineered by Collins, took place, from Lincoln, in
February. Several other escapes followed, hunger-strikes, and
jail riots, and one prisoner died in Gloucester on March 6th.
The general release of the 'German Plot' internees followed,
and Madame Markievicz ended her second period of imprisonment on March 7th. On the first three days of April she
attended meetings of the Dail where De Valera nominated his
first cabinet. She was appointed Minister for Labour, April
2nd, 1919.

§ 5

In that same spring Casimir returned to Dublin. His visit
marks that April of 1919 as the last little fragment of not
only her, but his old, more or less normal life.

At the end of 1913 he had been in Albania, a centre of the
old Balkan troubles, where he made the acquaintance of the
Prince de Wied, chosen by the Powers in November, 1913, to
be the first sovereign ruler of Albania. Eight months later, on
the outbreak of war, rather in the spirit of those Irishmen
who enlisted in the British Army in 1914, he had responded to
the manifesto of the Grand Duke Nikolai 'to our nations'

which held out a promise of autonomy for Poland. Enlisting as a volunteer in the Twelfth Achtyrski regiment of Huzzars, he had been sent to the Carpathians to fight the Austrians. Here he received the Cross of Saint George for conspicuous bravery. In the winter of '15–16 he was badly wounded and almost died. He lay for almost twelve hours in the snow with a wounded arm and a shattered side until a private soldier – who happened to be a man of his own district – pulled him out by the legs, and carried him on his back to a railway siding where he lay for another bout among other casualties waiting in the hope of some passing train that might take them to hospital. Train after train rumbled by, overloaded with wounded, and about him dozens of men died from exposure. He developed a fever and attributed his salvation to it. Late that evening they managed to find a place for him in a cattle-wagon crammed with men sick of cholera, who, he used to recall, in spite of their condition kept eating canned food and cold sausages until half of them died of it.

After a lumbering progress of some hundred and fifty miles, the living and the dead were disembarked at Lwow (Lemberg), in Galicia. Here they put him into a hospital for typhus cases; he developed typhus himself; lost his hearing and suffered agonies for weeks with his wounds. From there he wrote to Constance, in the beginning of '16, a little message that reached her two weeks before the Rising.

'118, Field Hospital, Lwow.
'My Darling,
'I am not a bit sure that this will get to Dublin at all, as it seems that the Germans are playing lots of dirty tricks in the Irish Sea. However, I am glad to tell you that I am much better and in a week's time I am going to be sent to [illegible] for a couple of months.

'I am still very weak, especially my legs can hardly support my weight. My rib is almost covered up with new skin and I feel much less shaky although I am still very def (*sic*) and one has to yell to me.

'Gradually I am recovering the use of my left arm. Now fare you well my darling. Burn this as it is supposed to be covered with typhus bacillus and wash your hands. Best love to all yours.

'Dunin Markievicz.'

He had been through a bad time before he wrote that letter. Around him in the ward men had died of typhus by the dozen, many of them going mad in their death-fever. One poor wretch Cassie never forgot – a Jewish doctor who used to sit up in bed and grasp some object beside him, a candlestick or the like, and start telephoning madly to his wife three hundred miles away in Warsaw, his voice getting louder and louder as he felt she was not hearing him. 'Masha! Masha!' he used to shout. 'The children. Bring me the children. Nikolai! What are you doing with Nikolai? Bring me Nikolai! Masha! Do you hear me, Masha?' until his voice became a scream and he would fall back in exhaustion. Cassie used to say that after a quarter of an hour of that the sweat would be pouring off his own body and his temperature racing to fever-point.

From Lwow they moved him to Kiev in the Ukraine. Here, at first thin as a latch from his ordeal, he began to recover slowly, and he was soon living his old gay wayward life again. He had a brother in Kiev who helped him to earn a living, teaching in the School of Art. He began again to produce plays both in Kiev and Moscow – always in Polish theatres – such as his *Lilies of the Fields*, or *The Marriage of Martha*; usually with fair success.

It was in Kiev that he first met the young Ukrainian girl, a kinswoman of his, who recounts his life here and in Warsaw:

'In those days, 1916, Casi, after recovering, was full of joy of life and wrote plays, painted pictures, drunk like fish, was loved by all man and woman and known in all Ucraine as the best of pals and a regular sport. I was a schoolgirl, very much terrified by his rather wild reputation and although we were neighbours (about fifty miles) and related, our house, being very convent-like, was never visited by Casi and I never did speak to him until 1919. His love affairs were many and one' – here she mentions the niece of a well-known writer – 'nearly got him to the altar. But he really did not want to divorce Constance, he liked her and admired her in his own way.

'As the revolution broke out in Russia in 1917, Kazi stayed as long as he could, but as it began to be dangerous to stay in Kiev he, in 1918, went to Warsaw.

'I came there in February, 1919, with my people and we met in the house of our neighbours where we both took rooms – Kazi, a splendid man of forty-four, beautiful and surrounded by the romance of his life, and I, a girl well over twenty years his junior, and of a very old-fashioned and puritan stock. Casi was to me like a most wonderful event. We at once felt a current of mutual understanding, friendship and something that cannot be described.

'When we met we both had lost everything in the Ucraine and both had to work and earn, unless we chose to sit in some estate of some cousin, sponging on them, but we could not think of that.

'Kazi was stage-manager in the Polish theatre in Warsaw. I was in the Foreign Office, and after in the American Consulate. He came to work in the Consulate, too, where he soon became the most popular and indispensable member of the staff. He helped everyone, was good to all, overworked himself writing plays, painting portraits, and being correspondent first to a Polish paper and then to the *Daily News* and the *Chicago Tribune*, besides his daily work in the Consulate-General where he was a legal and commercial adviser . . .'

It was when his fortunes were at this low ebb that Cassie visited Dublin shortly after Constance came out of Holloway. His old friend Martin Murphy of the Gaiety describes the wanderer's return to the now all-but empty haunts of the Dublin wits. The Count was forty-five; his wife just turned fifty. Youth was over for both.

'I was sitting inside in Davy Byrne's, and as I wasn't working that day I had a good suit on me and a Burberry over my shoulder. I was talking to X, trying to get him to come home. He was merry, not too merry, you know, and I saw he was in company he oughtn't to be in. But I couldn't budge him. "Wan more, now, Martin," he kept saying and I would have to sit down with him and tried to pacify him and lure him home. Then, all of a sudden, I got a slap on the back and it was the Count. He knew me by my back. I hadn't seen him for years. "Glory be to God, Cassie," says I. "Martin!" says he. We were shaking one another by the hand. X knew him well. "Now, Miss Dunlea," he says, "Hand me that bottle of John Jameson and draw the cork." The three of us had a drink out of the bottle, then. "Have you seen the Countess?" said I then to Cassie. "I'll send a wire for her," said I. "She's down in Limerick at a political meeting. I'll do it this instant," and I jumped up to run for the post office. He held me by the arm and he whispered to me so that X wouldn't hear us, "No, no, Martin!" he said. "She'll be back in a day or two; I don't want to be mixed up in politics this time. I'm over on a diplomatic mission." "Oh, very well," says I. And we sat down again and went on with our drinks. Then we separated and I went off with X. "You know my address, Cassie, and you know where to find me any hour of the day or night," said I. And I left him.

'It was maybe four days after I went into Davy Byrne's again and there at the back of the shop was Cassie and Seumas O'Sullivan, the poet. "Hello, Martin! Hello, Cassie! Hello, Seumas!" Then after a bit I said, "Did ye see the wife?" "Not yet, Martin," says he. I started up. "What! You didn't see her yet and you four days in Dublin. She'll be mad with you if she hears it," I warned him. "I tell you what. You wait there now and I'll get her for you in one minute." I ran out and I got a bike outside the shop and I made off to get her. But I didn't get her in a minute. I went down to Mrs. Clarke's, down to Fairview, to the meeting-rooms, up to Suffolk Street, and at last I found she was addressing a meeting in the Mansion House. In I went. "You can't see the Countess," said a young fellow at the door. "I can't see her?" said I. "Now, you listen to me. I don't want to gate-crash into your bloody meeting. I was in meetings and in the movement before you were born. Take this note into the Countess and have no delay about it." And I got an envelope addressed to myself, and I wrote on it in pencil: "Dear Countess, Casimir is in town and is very anxious to see you. I'll arrange for him to be in the Bodega in five minutes. Go on with the meeting and you can ring him up then, Martin." There wasn't much delay then about interrupting the meeting. Out came Madame and she was very grateful to me. "He came to see me first thing," I said. "He would, Martin," says she. "He wanted to know where you were," said I. "And I told him you were in Limerick and he said he'd meet you when you came back. "Oh, thanks very much, Martin," says she. "I'll do as you say."

'Back I went hot-foot to Davy Byrne's and he was gone. I left the bike where I got it and I ran down to the Bodega and sure enough there he was with Seumas. "Stay where you are, now," said I, "and she'll ring up in one second." "Thank you, Martin," he says, and that minute the telephone bell rang. "Be sure, now, it's Madame," I said. And I left him to it. And it was Madame. And they had a long talk. And it was grand. And it was all right ...'

One would like to be able to take the good-hearted Martin's view of it. But if a husband dawdles about town for three or four days without making any effort to see his wife, it is hard to think other than that, on his side at any rate, not only love but affection had considerably waned. Where one is writing a biography with more oral than written material, one hesitates even to mention some of the gossip heard on the way. Yet, lest there be some truth in so important a matter, it may be better, in this case, to repeat, without prejudice, the not infrequently repeated rumour that at one stage Casimir returned to Dublin with the intention of asking Constance to agree to a divorce. When he saw and spoke to her, however, all his old affection, all his old respect, revived, and he confessed to his friend that he simply could not do it. If there is any truth in the story – this, perhaps, was one reason of that visit to post-war Dublin.

A simpler, ostensible, and equally probable reason was to collect the remains of his property from Surrey House. But Surrey House was gone, and Madame was living, now, where she could, in lodgings or with friends. What remained of her worldly goods had been removed from the ruin of Surrey House after the rising and placed for safety with Mrs. Tom Clarke at Fairview, though already much of it, pictures, lace, valuables, had been looted before some neighbour in kindness padlocked the door. Ultimately her linen and other effects went to Saint Ultan's Hospital, founded for the babies of the poor by her friend Dr. Kathleen Lynn.

One likes to recall that picture of the two elderly friend-lovers, now travelling out to Fairview on the tram-top, she talking gaily in her loud voice, he asking endless questions about their old acquaintances and about all that has happened to her and Dublin since he left it before the war; and the kind Martin listening with pleasure, a bit like a fond old godfather, to the pair of them. One would like, too, to be able to repeat even a few odd scraps of their conversation. But as if the very sight of Dublin bay, and the place where Larkin drilled his men, and the road to Raheny, has rejuvenated the pair of them, much of their loud talk is too personal, and too scandalous and barbed to be reproduced here. This is a different Dublin, already growing tense, about and below them. His memories clash with hers. For her a new significance that is foreign to him has already begun to attach to certain streets and houses on the way. In silence they alight and breast their way along the pavement to the house of her friend. They inspect the pictures, the odd sticks of furniture, the trunks of long folded clothes, creased, from so long a rest, like the clothes of a sailor home from the sea. That is their life – in those trunks and boxes and canvases – that will not return.

He gathers all that he wants, and he takes his load with him back to his new world. She takes leave of him, returns to Dublin and to hers.

§ 6

By the time he was back in Warsaw she was in jail again; this time in the Cork Female Prison, beginning, in June, a sentence of four months for a seditious speech in Mallow. Here, again, she was granted special privileges. Her meals were brought in from outside, cooked for her by sympathizers living near by. She was allowed, too, a privilege which gave her great mental relief: in an old rubbish-heap she began to make a little garden of her own with plants sent in from outside. She was always a good gardener, and had the reputation of being able to turn any old waste patch to use. People said she 'has a lucky hand', and most of her friends still have plants that 'Madame planted for me'. So that this or that is 'Madame's rose', or 'Madame's rosemary', or 'Madame's lavender' – and by them is she remembered when her summer blooms peep out again.

The effect of these repeated imprisonments must have been curious. She would be free for a period during which she could observe the gradual increase in the tempo of the Revolution, and then be immured away from it all for a long stretch of time. She would come out to find the drums beating louder than before; then she would be removed again and come out to find the whole scene thundering a *crescendo*.

So whereas in June there had been only sporadic attacks on police barracks, and individual shootings were still regarded as mere unorganized outbreaks of local feeling, and Dail Eireann scarcely taken seriously even by the mass of Sinn Feiners, she found on her release in September that De Valera's personal prestige, as a result of his visit to America, had done so much to increase the prestige at home of the Dail, and to turn the 'Republic' from a vague ideal into a definite objective, that within a few months a National Loan had been successfully floated by Collins, bringing in well over a quarter of a million pounds in Ireland alone and promising to bring in some five million dollars from America. Attacks on police barracks and patrols had also become a matter of such common occurrence that the people soon began to realize that the resistance to British rule was rapidly moving into a guerrilla war.

She came out in that autumn of 1919 just in time for the first stages of what was to become known as The Terror. In the August of her imprisonment the Volunteers had come under the Dail and the Minister for Defence – at that time Cathal Brugha, one of the most determined and fearless men at the Volunteer G.H.Q. As a result, with Collins as Director of Information tapping even the most secret sources of police intelligence, and the country brigades eager for fighting, organized attacks in Dublin and elsewhere became much more frequent and intensified from the end of that year onward. Raids for arms, ambushes on a large or small scale became the order of the day, and soon Madame Markievicz, like everybody else associated actively with the movement, found herself living a life that can only be called nerve-racking. From having no home, she came to the point when she did not even have a permanent lodging; for it became unwise to stay long in any house if she wished to be certain of avoiding arrest. She lived where she could; for some periods sleeping in different houses every night.

The actual period of the Terror began in mid-1920. In January 1920, the auxiliary forces known later as the Black and Tans were already being organized in England. In February that most unpleasant aspect of life in Ireland under the Revolution came into being – Curfew law. Then from midnight, at first, and later from ten o'clock, and during the summer as early on some occasions as five o'clock in the afternoon (this was in Cork city), every living soul was required to be within doors unless by special permit; and in the tense, excitable atmosphere of the times, when men were inclined to shoot first and question after, it was not even then safe to be abroad on the empty, white streets that suggested a plague or a desert. It was the nights, however, that were truly filled with fear. Then the entire civil population developed the sense of hearing to an acute degree. Long before a patrol entered a street people heard their faint tramp-tramp approach, and even the most innocent and the most trusting sighed with relief when the footsteps finally died away.

When the period of murder and reprisal came, in the first months of 1920, thousands took to sleeping from home. In March the Lord Mayor of Cork was taken from his bed by armed men with blackened faces and shot in the presence of his wife and sisters. On the other hand, in April, Mr. Alan Bell, an elderly man, a Castle official who was believed to be operating against the National Loan, was pulled out of a tramcar at Ballsbridge, Dublin, and shot dead on the open street. In April, over three hundred evacuated Royal Irish Constabulary barracks were destroyed by fire in a single night, and hundreds of Income Tax offices were either raided and their contents destroyed, or burned to the ground. By the summer one then saw for the first time throughout the country the Black and Tan recruit in his hastily assembled uniform, black trousers, a khaki coat, a police cap, a heavy revolver stuck in a military belt. With his arrival murder was let loose. The night became fearsome; the days were completely safe for nobody. As one listened then, after Curfew, for the tramp of marching men, one knew that death was on the creep. One heard it sometimes in the distance, the rattle of rifle fire, where the troops, on edge, let fly into the shadows of some darkened square or laneway; for, conniving with the 'gunmen', the local corporations often refused to light the city and plunged it into blackness from sunset to dawn. From this there followed the rumble of the armoured car with its crown of sweeping light. One heard its hum rise to a scream as its gears changed from low to high and it swept quickly through the streets. Then one heard it come to a purring quiet. The white finger of its searchlight would creep slowly from door to door, blaze outside a window, vanish into an alley archway, and then with the rising whistle of the engine whirl like a falling star on some other dark street. Sleep was difficult on those nights; sometimes it was impossible. Out of a light slumber a crash of a bursting bomb or the rattle of a machine-gun would send a man jumping into wakefulness until morning.

It was in that kind of Dublin that Madame Markievicz, now fifty-two, lived from pillar to post all through the winter of 1919 and into the autumn of 1920. If she had ever hoped for an exciting and dangerous existence, she was now granted her wish to the full. She loved disguises. When she went abroad, she became an old crone in a Victorian cape and a bonnet with a bob of cherries dangling into her eye. She enjoyed that – the mystification of her friends when she dropped in on them so disguised. She walked in on one of her Fianna meetings, password and all complete, and refused for a long time to disclose herself to the boys. But once she met, on a tram-top, a docker of more intelligence – or was it less power of flattery? – who hailed her so loudly through her disguise that she had to make a hurried departure from his too embarrassing friendliness.

Her courage and her ingenuity had its day-out that year. It was always a question with her of where she would sleep and where she could work. She lived in daily fear of raids and spent much of her time avoiding them. Once that summer she received a last-minute warning of a police visit to the house in which she did her work as Secretary for Labour. At once, with the sudden dispatch that had already become second nature to people like her, everything went pell-mell into a trunk, a cab was summoned, the trunk perched on the roof and off they drove. To the cabby's question, 'Where to, ma'am?' she just replied, 'Anywhere.' As he drove on she racked her brains to think where she could safely put that trunk-load of what, in those days, was always popularly known as 'stuff'. They drove out to Harold's Cross and they drove back. But still she could not think of a single place that could be called trustworthy – safe places had become rare as time went on. 'Where to, now, ma'am?' asked the cabby. And again she cried, 'Anywhere!' – and again he drove out to Harold's Cross and back. Then she hit upon the idea just as he was on the point of exasperation and she of despair. She directed the cabman to a second-hand shop directly opposite Lissonfield House, the headquarters of the Black and Tans. There she alighted and asked the proprietor, a friend of hers, to put the trunk in his window, marked 'For Sale, Three Pounds' (or for the times, some such enormous sum). The friend who remembers the incident and took part in it recalls that for days she had to pass that shop, always with a terror that she would find the trunk gone.

She was never missing, as far as can be remembered, from a meeting of her Fianna or a meeting of the Dail cabinet, and the cabinet met weekly at this time, always at great risk, and always in different houses. It seems to be the general impression that she was not really useful at such meetings. But it is also evident that she was not generally popular with men in revolutionary circles; and she was the only woman in that cabinet. It is natural, perhaps, that a woman's counsel, and even her presence, should be faintly resented by men like Collins and Brugha. At one cabinet meeting, D.F. recollects that she started some kind of discussion about the evil of capital punishment, not entirely tactful, nor even sensible at

such a time, and in such a place. Then, she started another
speech to the tune of, 'Of course all spies should be shot . . .' –
until Collins, who probably knew how easily innocent men
could be suspected, intervened and pointed out rather shortly
the dangers and difficulties that would follow from any indis-
criminate campaign of that nature. Another night she tried
repeatedly to cut across some statement being made by Cathal
Brugha, at best a brusque, definite man. Repeatedly he edged
her aside in the tone of a man holding himself in by willpower
rather than patience, with: 'If you will allow me, Madame,
to complete my statement,' or some such words, until it was
too late for her to say her say in the end. There are, unfortunately, no verbatim reports of those meetings, nor even of the
meetings of the Dail, when it dared, with attenuated numbers,
to meet at all. But the verbatim reports of Dail meetings from
August 1921, the period of the Truce, to June 1922, the period
of the outbreak of Civil War, will show that she received
scant ceremony, once or twice not even common politeness –
though one can understand how strained everybody's nerves
were at that time.

She had one complete year of active work – one cannot
say it was a year of freedom – after her imprisonment in
Cork, during which period she devoted almost her entire
energies to her work as Secretary for Labour. Then on September 26th, 1920, she was arrested again, tried by court
martial for being engaged in treasonable practices, and
sentenced to two years' hard labour. The trial took place in
Arbour Hill Barracks, where Emmet had been held prisoner
in his day, and the sentence was served, or rather begun, in
Mountjoy Jail, where innumerable revolutionaries were imprisoned from 1916 on, and were to be added to in the period
of the Civil War that brings the Irish troubles forward to 1924.
It was her third winter in prison; the other two she had spent
in Aylesbury and Holloway.

Of her sentence she served ten months and so at least escaped
the worst horrors of the Terror; for when she came out in
July, 1921, the "Troubles" were over.

§ 7

Subject, in these ways, to endless irritations and interruptions, her existence from her release after the Insurrection to
her release at the Truce had only two compensations. She was
absolutely and completely accepted at last by the mass of the

people, and she was allowed, when she was appointed Secretary for Labour, to work for them and to work with them in the way most dear to her. She must have been utterly and thoughtlessly happy during all that later period of the Revolution. Swept along in one great thunderous wave of enthusiasm, she must have felt as she sang her way with the ragged army of the Republic that she had found the road to the Land of the Ever Young. Like a tree that buds and branches in the final effort of the life-force, she had found within herself in her last prime, more of the pure vigour of nature, than at any time in the height of her youth and beauty. Her zest for life seemed endless in those four or five years between the Rising and the Truce.

Her work in the Dail cabinet was in itself both exciting and satisfying. To us it is interesting as an example of the power of a Parliament manned by men and women fleeing from the law to function in spite of it. It was as if Devonshire, or Wales, set up a rival Ministry, in Exeter or Conway, issued orders there from some back-room over a newspaper shop in a back lane, and by sheer force of obstinacy, backed by a few hundred guns, defied and to an extent thwarted the Imperial Parliament at Westminster.

It was not so much the practical success of the schemes of the Pretenders that counted. They had no money worth talking about – at most under two million pounds, and probably nearer half that amount. They had no control over the machinery of government, apart from the local urban and district councils. Yet they set up courts of their own whose orders were obeyed; instituted an effective boycott of Ulster manufacturers, in the course of which firms that disobeyed orders were fined; established consular representatives abroad; floated a National Loan with success; prohibited emigration; supported a guerilla army; established a Commission of Inquiry into Irish Industrial Resources which did some effective work, and published its results in a permanent form; and so on. Much of its work was inevitably barren, all of it partial and nibbling. A Co-operative Fishery Society was a complete failure. A Technical School taken over from Government control was not a success. A Department of Gaelic did no more than publish half a dozen useful textbooks. The Director of Agriculture managed to get some few thousand of trees planted, and established a Land Commission which considered about three hundred cases in dispute, but for the rest, in his own words, 'very little of a constructive nature' was done, nor could it, obviously, be done for agricultural industries. The main function of these banned Ministries was to produce a moral effect, and to give some earnest of the ability and enthusiasm of the young would-be governors of the new Ireland. Madame Markievicz's Department of Labour worked mainly towards the settlement of labour disputes, and co-operated in (later, took charge of) the Belfast Boycott. One incident has been recorded already which illustrates the conditions under which she worked – her sudden flight in a cab with all her office equipment. Miss Louie Bennett recalls another incident which gives an even better idea of those conditions.

A dispute on wages had arisen in a Rosary Bead factory run by a Dublin Jew who agreed to arbitration by the Dail Department of Labour. The Trade Union representatives met the employer in a Dail office in Harcourt Street under the chairmanship of a Dail officer. But they were warned that a raid by British military was expected at a stated hour, and they were told that they must come to their decision well within the hour. With their eyes on the clock they argued, and argued, with Madame butting in occasionally to say: 'Twenty minutes more' – 'Fifteen minutes more' – 'Ten minutes more' – until it was not so much a question of justice, then, as nerves. Finally the Jew surrendered and fled.

What with such raids and arrests her department changed hands four times in two years; it was taken over in turn by Alderman T. Kelly, T.D., Mr. Joseph McGrath, and Mr. Joseph MacDonagh. It worked on so modest a margin of expenses that, apart from the Boycott scheme, it cost between February and July of 1921 a bare £150. At the beginning it handled about eight cases per month, of which it would settle two, and find in the other cases that one or the other of the parties refused intervention completely, or refused to abide by the decision. By the middle of 1920, it was handling about ten cases per month, and settling about half. By the end of September, under Mr. McGrath, the number had risen to thirty per month, half being settled satisfactorily. On his arrest the total still increased – to about thirty-five per month, while the number of successful arbitrations increased from fifty per cent to approximately sixty-five per cent. But at the beginning of 1921, when the Terror was at its height, the scheme began to collapse and in six months only thirty cases were handled.

To her, this work meant infinitely more, however, than any results she could achieve. It made her part and parcel of the revolution. It gave her that kind of elation only possible where a multitude is moved by a feeling of oneness. Her elation was increased and sanctified by the ends towards which she worked, by the dangers she shared in common with others, and by the death, often suffered with heroism, of so many out of that multitude of known and unknown comrades, to all of whom she gave an equal admiration and an equal love.

§ 8

Then, literally overnight, it was all finished. Within a few months she was hurling epithets across the floor of the Dail at her beloved comrades. 'Oathbreakers and cowards!' she cried at them. 'Foreigners – Americans – English!' shouted Michael Collins. 'Lloyd Georgites!' screamed the Countess. She spoke of them as jugglers and tricksters. She sneered at the rumour (perhaps invented it) that Michael Collins was espoused to Princess Mary. She told him he was befogged when he met the British Prime Minister in Downing Street. She called one deputy 'an old woman'. She added her quota to the personalities, and bitter recriminations that make those months of December and January 1921–22, the most painful and pitiful in the history of modern Ireland.

To do more than turn the pages of the Dail reports is to re-live an extraordinary adventure. They begin, in 1919, with great public audiences in the Round Room of the Mansion House, with much oratory and ceremony, a Parliament of one party; then by degrees the attendance diminishes as arrests and raids interfere with the working of the abstentionists; finally there comes the time, in the January of 1921 when there is no President, and no business could be done in the absence of Responsible Ministers. Then, with the period of the Truce, in August, back comes all the old panoply and enthusiasm. Deputies have the greatest pleasure in proposing this, and they are honoured to be permitted to second that. 'I feel', said President De Valera, 'as a boy among boys. I hope that we shall win this Cause, as near to Heaven as boys are ... I have got credit for work which was not my work, but the work of loyal comrades like Arthur Griffith, Cathal Brugha, Michael Collins, and other heroes working with me. It is as a team that we have worked, and it is as a team that we shall work. ... Never at any time during the whole period of office has there been any difference of opinion between me and them ... With gratitude I turn to you, my comrades and colleagues who have conferred on me what I believe is the highest honour that could be conferred at this moment on any human being. Because here at an issue of peace or war, I have been chosen to be a leader ... We know our minds; we know that we have a straight road to travel; no by-paths to lead us astray ...'

At the first meeting of the same Dail, after the signing in London of the Articles of Agreement for the Treaty, virtually the next meeting of the same men and the same President, within ten minutes there is talk of unfairness, protests against secret sessions, and the Minister for Finance used, for the first time, the word 'traitor'. From that on the decline is swift. When the delegates come out from a secret session lasting three days the gloves are off. Sarcasms fly, interruptions, innuendoes. The President is charged with political dodgery. He says that Mr. Griffith brought something else besides the Treaty back from Downing Street. The Minister for Defence, Cathal Brugha, makes a painful personal attack on Mr. Collins, to whom he refers as 'this person'. Mr. Griffith speaks of Mr. Childers as a 'damned Englishman'. Mr. Collins tells Madame Markievicz that she has insulted his betrothed. Mr. De Valera has a very different kind of speech to make now. 'I am sick and tired of politics – so sick that no matter what happens I would go back to private life. I have only seen politics within the last three weeks or a month. It is the first time I have seen them and I am sick to the heart of them ... It is because I am straight that I meet crookedness with straight dealing always, and I have beaten crookedness with straight dealing ... What has sickened me most is that I got in this House the same sort of dealing that I was accustomed to over in America from other people of a similar kind ...' The climax comes after a solid month of talk when Mr. De Valera rises and leaves the House followed by the entire body of his supporters, and followed as they crowd from it through the doors by the loud voice of Michael Collins – 'Deserters! Deserters to the Irish nation in her hour of trial.'

With that body of men clustering about the doors is Madame Markievicz. As she comes out of that great hall into the fog of a Dublin winter's day, she is like a woman just beginning to feel a warm dream dispelled by the first shiver of her awakening.

§ 9

She had spoken well to the Treaty debate, and one might have thought, listening to her, that she, at least, unlike the majority of the deputies, had not been taken unawares by the sudden necessity for a practical articulation of her ideals. With all the others, or almost all, one felt that here was an exhibition of what results when a movement is a movement of emotion rather than of thought. One felt that if any old shell-back of the Irish Party were listening to the debates he must have chuckled sardonically in his beard to find Time revenging him and his methods on these idealistic young men and their methods.

They had spoken of a Republic as glibly as if it were a chemical formula. When even Mr. De Valera attempted to define the word in terms of what was practicable and feasible – in his famous Document Number Two – his own followers were unhappy, and several of them denounced it.

Indeed, they only were safe, as time showed, who stood upon the uncompromising rock of non-definition; and for such, not all Mr. De Valera's distinctions between the 'isolated Republic' he would surrender and the 'Republic' he would not, saved him from the charge of being unfaithful to his trust.

When she spoke, remembering at the twelfth hour all that she had imbibed from Connolly, she spoke as best she knew how, in terms of 'the material basis of freedom'. She protested in particular against the formation of an Upper Chamber in the new Dail. Speaking without mercy of her own class, she described the Southern Unionists as the people who had always 'combined against the workers ... who have used every institution in the country to ruin the farmer, and more especially the small farmer, and to send the people of Ireland to drift in the emigrant ships and to die of horrible disease or to sink to the bottom of the Atlantic.' (She was here surely remembering the story of Sir Robert Gore-Booth and the evicted tenants of the Seven Cartrons) 'I object to any Government whereby a privileged number of classes established here by British rule are to be given a say – to this small minority of traitors and oppressors – in the form of an Upper Chamber, as against all, I might say modern ideas of common sense, of the people who wish to build up a prosperous, contented nation. But looking as I do for the prosperity of the many, for the happiness and content of the workers, for what I stand,

James Connolly's ideal of a Workers' Republic – (A Deputy: A Soviet Republic!) – A co-operative commonwealth! – these men are to be set up to uphold English interests in Ireland, to uphold the capitalists' interests in Ireland, to block every ideal that the nation may wish to formulate ...'

It was not a great speech – and from that on it rambled sadly; but, however unjust, however inaccurate her prophecy of the functions of the Irish Senate may have been, what is interesting is that she at least was trying in her fumbling way to visualize the effects of the Treaty on the conditions of Irish life. Still hampered by her gallant, but unrealized idealism, she was not able to sustain her thought on that level. She wandered into vague warnings and into the usual detached and unsupported generalizations, and the usual declarations about the sanctity of oaths which characterized the speeches of all the other women deputies and of most of the men. Reading over the text of her speech again, one wonders what Connolly would have thought of it – what, indeed, he would have thought of all those speeches, not one of which, with the exception of a reasoned speech from Mr. Joseph McGrath – not even excepting hers – deigned to apply to the Treaty the test of the original Democratic Programme of Dail Eireann.

So, when she comes to answer the charge that she does not know what she means by the term Republic, her reply is of the feeblest. 'I know what I mean – a state run by the Irish people for the people. That means a Government that looks after the rights of the people before the rights of property. And under the Saorstat I don't wish to anticipate that the directors of this and that capitalist interest is to be at the head of it. My ideal is the Workers' Republic for which Connolly died. And I say that this is one of the things that England wishes to prevent. She would sooner give us Home Rule than a democratic Republic. It is the capitalist interests in England and Ireland that are pushing this Treaty to block the march of the working people in Ireland and England.'

She attempts only in one sentence to approach that practical question in a serious way; but she flies away from the problem as soon as she states it: 'In any case the thing is not what you might call a practical thing. It won't help our commerce; but it is not that. We are idealists believing in and loving Ireland, and I believe that Ireland held by Black and Tans did more for Ireland than Ireland held by Parliamentarianism – the road that meant commercial success ...'

Practical politics was not her line. The old Party shell-back in the gallery could have taken her by the hand back to Sligo and made her withdraw that last foolish statement in two minutes, as well as the still more foolish statement that 'we gained more in these few years of fighting than we ever gained by parliamentary agitation since the days of O'Connell'. He could have taken her on a high hill not two miles from Lissadell and pointed silently to the ruins of a dozen cabins. From some there grows on the very hearth an alder, or a lofty Irish yew. Its height and age is the measure of time since the fever-ridden creatures who lived there crawled over their threshold to die, in Forty-Seven. One might say each dying man planted on his earthern floor the seed of a tree that would in after time be a memorial to misery. Up on the wildest, poorest reaches of the mountain the low sun marks out the potato pits – on spots where no man would dream of tilling or sowing now. There are roads near by, too, and long, endless walls climbing the mountains, and dikes built like a Roman road, all at the wages of slavery. Every hand that built those works is rotten, who were the fathers and the mothers of the simple folk of the Ireland of her day. To their memory nothing stands but those great trees growing out of little ruins, and the Big Houses of the landlords who did *not* die of famine. If that is all changed, it is due solely to Emancipation, popular franchise, cheap education, and the Land Acts. If it was to be further changed ... but that would bring her back to the floor of the Dail and, who knows, to what kind of amended speech?

One thing – and one thing only – this woman said that was neither trite or superficial and that was when in concluding her speech she said brokenly, 'I have seen the stars ...'

She was fifty-four, and looked older.

§ 10

She was in Paris for the last week of January, 1922, for the Irish Race Convention; and if one wished to be dramatic one might play with that return of a disappointed, loveless woman to the city where she had been young, lovely, and loved. But as she is certain to have honoured those days, at most with a passing sigh, it would be false to her nature to dally over the return.

In Paris, too, it was, as at home, two weeks before, a divided Irish Race that met and argued in groups about the cafés. Every conversation returned to the Treaty, to the Republic that had been betrayed, to the Republic that must be upheld, to the men who had been trusted and proved weak, back over and over those days when all worked together, when this one met Mick Collins to discuss a friend's death, when that one had argued in jail with Arthur Griffith, back to the terrible nights when this friend sheltered and that friend had proved false. No room, yet, for thought or calm consideration where all was hate and disappointment and bitter disillusion. Her mind was rancid in those days. It took two years before it grew sweet again and she was her old gallant, lovable, dashing self. Two years – and in all she had only five more to live.

After Paris she went to America with the sister of Kevin Barry, the boy-student who had been executed in Mountjoy in 1920 and whose so early death had set all Ireland singing ballads in his memory. For four months she travelled without rest all over the States, addressing meetings on behalf of the Republic. Then back to Ireland in time for the whirlwind election drive of June, called the Pact Election because a Treaty and anti-Treaty Panel had been put before the electors by the Sinn Fein organization which was not yet officially split. The result was a majority for the Treaty, which with Farmers, Independents, and Labour, came to little short of a seventy-five per cent vote. Madame Markievicz was defeated at this election.

Meanwhile the country was in chaos. Civil war had broken out, Republican or Irregular troops – the intransigent I.R.A. – held barracks and towns all over the country, and in Dublin entrenched themselves in the Four Courts under Rory O'Connor. They were well armed and had ammunition in plenty, a good portion of which they got in a raid on a British tug that appeared, in a suspiciously adventitious way, off Queenstown early in April. The politicians were now entirely out of the running. The game lay between Collins as Commander-in-Chief and such men as Rory O'Connor and Brugha, at the G.H.Q. of the Irregulars. Pressed by the British on the one hand to implement the Treaty, and by the majority of the populace on the other to restore order, the new Provisional Government finally took the offensive. At 4 a.m. on the morning of June 28th, the Four Courts was shelled by Free State troops; on the 30th the occupants retired, blew up the building, and surrendered. There is no record of anybody having been killed in the engagement.

Madame Markievicz at once threw herself into the fighting

that immediately sprang up elsewhere around the city. The only Headquarters available was the Fianna Staff at Barry's Hotel, in Gardiner's Place, and with these she moved into position in one of the larger hotels in O'Connell Street – The Hammam. All along the street, as in the Insurrection, six years before, other positions had been taken and fortified, and as then also, a circle of fire began to drive the new 'rebels' in and in.

While in the Hammam, word came that a Free State sniper was doing great damage from a position in Arnott's tower in Henry Street and all efforts to dislodge him had failed. At that moment she was discussing plans at a table with the Officer in Command of the Dublin Brigade, Oscar Traynor, later T.D. in the Free State Dail. Saying nothing, she rose and took her Peter-the-Painter, went down by an underground passage they had tunnelled to Tyler's shop, and from its buttress that overhung the roof began to engage her man. The distance was under a hundred yards, and a Peter-the-Painter is accurate at nearly ten times the distance. For all that, she could not get him. They called her to stop after an hour, but she would not. They called her after two hours, but still she would not budge. So for several hours the duel went on until at last no reply came from the tower. She came down, cleaned her gun, and sinking into a chair fell fast asleep.

She had no command in this fight, and when the time came to abandon the position she had no option but to leave. Armoured cars rattling before the Irregular positions, and artillery battering at them from a distance, had thinned out the buildings from Findlater's Church to the Pillar until nothing stood but the Gresham Hotel where Brugha held out to the end. Not until August did that position fall. Then Brugha commanded his men to leave. Alone in the burning building he filled his magazine for the last time and from the doorway dashed out, firing as he went. He was shot down and though mortally wounded lingered on for two days. He was the most obstinate, and desperate, as well as one of the bravest of all those obstinate and desperate men.

From the Hammam Madame was taken to North Great George's Street where, exhausted and worn (she had not slept for five days and nights) she had to be treated as an invalid. From there she was taken to recuperate at Clontarf, and from there back to an old resort of revolutionaries, the Lawn, Peter's Place, in Dublin.

Meantime the old business of underground resistance had

begun in Dublin – Irishmen now resisting Irishmen; while through the country the Irregulars were forced from the towns they held until guerrilla warfare was resumed as of old. Griffith died on August 13th. Collins was killed fighting on the 22nd. Executions began that autumn, intensified by reprisals. In all during the winter and spring of 1922–23 seventy-seven Irregulars were tried and shot, including O'Connor, and Erskine Childers. Thousands were arrested. In the beginning De Valera moved among the Republican troops, armed exactly as they were (he had joined up as an ordinary Volunteer at a post in York Street) but now he had no authority and little or no influence. Later he retired to seclusion, 'on the run', formed a cabinet, and, as armed resistance began to peter out. resumed by degrees his position as leader. In April, 1923, he was able to issue a Cease Fire Order – the firing having in any case ceased by that date.

During this period, from the August of 1922 to the August of 1923, when a new election took place, Madame Markievicz was in Glasgow. There she helped to edit a Republican weekly-paper, *Eire*, which was smuggled into Ireland, and distributed either openly among the shops or by the usual underground methods of the Fianna or the women's organization, the Cumann na mBan. She returned after the election, in which she was again chosen for her constituency of South Dublin.

De Valera, arrested when he left hiding to address his constituents, in Ennis, in August, was now in jail, and with him many thousands of Republicans, scattered through Ireland in various internment camps. The armed resistance was over, the Free State was established, its Dail and all its machinery functioning. But at the August election a surprising number of Republicans had been elected, and as their propaganda still continued to defy the Free State Government, there was no reason to suppose that if released their resistance would be abated. These thousands of men remained in jail or interned until the end of 1923 when, in despair, they launched a universal hunger-strike in the autumn. In defence and support of the men Madame Markievicz came into the open. When speaking in Dublin from a lorry to urge the release of the prisoners, she was herself arrested and removed to the South Dublin Union, where she went on a sympathetic hunger-strike with the other women there imprisoned.

The strike, too immense to be controlled, and with the men already cowed and demoralized, broke down in November. At the best of time the internees had been existing under pitiable conditions. They were ragged, bootless, bearded, some half-naked. Most of them came from the poorest of homes and their relatives had no money to buy them clothes or food; and with the mass of the people out of sympathy with them, it was not now, as in an earlier period, possible to collect large sums to help them or their dependents. In batches they were released according as they abandoned the strike, and in batches one saw these bearded tatterdemalions wandering through the streets of Dublin to the railway-stations. Some of the more resolute men continued the strike up to Christmas. When two died of starvation, the strike was called off. A little before that with the other women, Madame Markievicz left jail for the last time. By the beginning of the new year the camps were empty and only a handful of men, including De Valera, remained in confinement.

It was the end of the civil strife in Ireland, as it was, in her time, at any rate, the end of the Republic. It was the end, too, for her, of the heroic life of a revolutionary.

She had entered Irish politics in 1908, at the age of forty. Now, at fifty-six, she had, for the first time, both the leisure and the inclination to pause and consider what it was she had done, and what she wished to do. 'I have seen the stars,' had been her cry, and she had added—'I will not follow a will-o'-the-wisp.' It began to occur to her that for many a dreamer the stars are little more.

CHAPTER VII

DISCOVERY:
1924–1927

§ 1

'WHAT I remember most about her,' writes A.F., who met her every week for years, 'was her shining intellectual honesty, her grand good humour, and her fine militant spirit. She was a good mixer, excellent friend, fine sport, and a loyal fighter in every weak cause.' That was the impression gained mainly in the last period of her life, and one feels that it was at every point a true impression. But from impressions a biographer is obliged to pass to that tiresome, and one sometimes feels, unprofitable process called analysis. So one baulks just a little at the phrase 'intellectual honesty' not because one questions for a second the honesty of her intellect but the quality of it.

There is a popular American phrase that says of things or people that they 'do not belong'. Having followed thus far the career of Constance Markievicz, one is certain that she belonged in two kinds of worlds. She belonged, without doubt, to the world where weak causes cry out for a bonny fighter. That brought her to the side of Eva in Manchester, to Sinn Fein in 1908, to the Rising in 1916, to the help of the Republicans in the years following, to the side of the 'Irregulars' in 1922, to the side of De Valera in 1924 when he was virtually a beaten man. She belonged, also, to another world where there is often not even the shadowy form of a cause to fight for – the world of the under-dog. So we find her in the cabins as a child; with the starving strikers in 1913; and in her last three years moving among the folk of the slums with her now wrinkled fingers always fishing in her pocket for a coin.

But while she belonged there, she had, also, two qualities, or they may be called two weaknesses, that prevented her from being really effective in either of these worlds. She would rally to a cause where there was something striking in the atmosphere surrounding it, and she would abandon a cause where the ordinary and the commonplace quenched the drama. On her own admission, the first thing that drew her in sympathy to the side of the unfree was the question of the franchise for women; yet to that fight she never devoted herself as she did to others. She entered and left the Gaelic League without having learned more than a few phrases of Irish. She left Eva's social work as soon as the excitement of the Manchester election was finished and done with. She left the social round, earlier, and later, in London and Dublin, as soon as the play had ceased to interest. Most striking example of all, as she drew away, with Connolly, from the hard social struggle to the excitement of the national cause. And after Connolly was dead, one could say, were it not for her wholly adventitious appointment as Secretary for Labour, she drew away from that kind of interest entirely. She was a woman who could work for weak causes and for lost causes, only where the drama of life was at its highest, but not necessarily at its deepest.

Her other defect was that she worked with blunted weapons; her mind was neither patient, nor trained, nor deep, nor able. Her intellect may have been shiningly honest, but it was not clear or powerful. It was not even reliable. The trouble with her was not that she was blind to the stars, but that she was deaf to such things as statistics. She was not unique in that. There have been thousands prepared to die for Ireland, for the ten who have been prepared to learn the irregular verbs in Gaelic or buy only Irish manufactures.

Here she is, then, with but three years of life left to her, staring at the fragments of a dream – an awakening that would have cured anyone who did not insist on living out her whole life behind the Mask. The shattering of ten dreams would not have changed her. Indeed there had been the dream of childhood, the dream of Society, the dream of Paris, the dream of the Art-Life, the dream of marriage – all broken before this one, and it had not altered her one iota. Nothing could. How childish it is in the face of such a story, to talk of anything but the most limited freedom of the human will.

The grand thing about this woman's life is that, although she did not alter herself, she did discover herself. She was right, in the first place, to have had her dreams. Without them she would not have been a whole woman. It was her fate to be broken and, like the gallant creature she was, she flung herself under the wheel of inexorable life. Wiseacres and cautious people could have said, at the end of all, 'We told you so,' – and she could have laughed at them because of the happiness she had found in rebelling against despotic fact. She was not one of those great souls who master life by self-knowledge; rather was she one of those brave souls who defy life in their ignorance. She had her reward, and life had its revenge, and both were surely satisfied.

Her self-discovery went farther than that. She learned in the last couple of years that were left to her, to take the measure of herself and of life. It is why one follows her career to the end with so much interest and without misgiving. The thunder and the confusion of her adventurous years had its reward in the melody that brings an ease to the heart at its close. Before that release came she had abandoned, virtually if not literally – she did not, unhappily, live so long – all interest in politics.

§ 2

She returned to her Fianna boys when the Republic collapsed. She had now an old Ford, an ancient wanderer that was the joke – though the kindly joke – of Dublin. Cassie's old friend, Martin Murphy, remembers the day she bought this tin-can of a car. In much noise and stink she drove up beside him in Grafton Street and cried out 'Martin!' (She would, of course, have said, 'Mawrtin!') 'I've bought a Flivver. Thirty pounds!' (She would have been tender with her *r's* – 'thi'ty.') 'Don't you think it's cheap?' And then off, before he could reply, in a whirl of smoke. In this car she would take her boys out into the country, or any group of ragged children she might have met, a veritable army clambering on every coign and corner of the car. She drove furiously, and as the thing was a mass of patches and wire-fastenings, it rattled without rest. The great hill for testing cars about Dublin is The Long Hill, County Wicklow – the old road from Dublin to Glendalough. She swore she always did it on top – and took the credit to herself. She did most of her repairs herself, it is true; she would doff her skirt and in her knickers climb under the carcass. If anyone, feeling it was a pose, quizzed her about it she just said, 'It's so much easier! Skirts are a nuisance when you want to work.' R.B. recounts that once on a lonely road, some such road as the Sally Gap, he came on a car by the road without a driver. All he could see was a pair of feminine legs and a scarlet petticoat. He chanced it and called out, 'Hello! Constance'. The legs wriggled and a head and nose, grease-spotted, craned about the wheel. It *was* Constance.

Both she and the Fianna boys were now fallen on evil days. There was no glory in it – all the adventure was gone – the numbers were very few. She stood by them to the end, and she took them wherever she could take them, marching, for all her fifty-six, or fifty-eight, years to do pilgrimage to the grave of Wolfe Tone at Bodenstown, or to attend the meetings of the minority Republican Party.

This minority Republican party was something of a mystery in Ireland after the Civil War. Nobody knew exactly what they purported to be and they had immense difficulty in defining their own position: indeed in their councils the President – then Art O'Connor – spoke once of 'schools of thought' with regard to their position, as if he were discussing a schism or a heresy. They had continued to meet ever since the outbreak of the Civil War, when the Irish Republican Army – the 'Irregulars' – created in 1922 an Emergency Government to give moral sanction to their own actions. From that on they had attempted to evade the feeling growing in their own minds, and in the minds of the people who supported them, that their position was unreal and absurd. They and their followers refused to recognize the Free State Parliament, and professed to co-operate in no way with the Free State Government. They refused to apply for passports, for example, and yet their consciences were sorely troubled by their constant use of Free State postage stamps. When their President, Art O'Connor, became a lawyer, practising in the Free State courts, which a loyal Republican could not recognize, he felt it his duty to tender his resignation.

Magnanimously, they rejected the power over life and death; and did not at the same time see that if they rejected that right, or any right, they acknowledged their lack of moral right in everything. Their position, as defined by Miss Mary MacSwiney, was that they were 'a symbol of a very important fact, that a people have no right to surrender their independence at the ballot-boxes; if you allow that you are raising a situation in which you are appealing to the majority'.

So they held on, attempting to continue the tradition and the authority of the Second Dail – the last Dail elected before the Treaty – long after the people had withdrawn their democratically-expressed support, long after their numbers as a schism or Rump had been reduced from their original 128 to a bare twenty members. They were an extraordinary type of historical curiosity. Their discussions as to their validities and invalidities would have delighted Sibrandus Schafnaburgensis, and may yet appeal to an Irish Sterne. They are an interesting example of the scholastic turn in the Irish mind.

The longer they existed the more absurd their position became. With an illogicality that did not strike them the only Dail they recognized was that Second Dail which rejected the Republic in favour of the Treaty. Since then there had been an election, the so-called Pact Election in 1922, followed by a Third Dail (Free State), and an election in 1923, when De Valera was arrested in Ennis, followed by a Fourth Dail (Free State) which sat until May, 1927. They had won seats at each of these elections, and were dismayed to know what to do with their new members. Madame Markievicz, for example, had been defeated in the Pact Election of 1922, and successful at the election of 1923. She asked plaintively for advice on her case. 'If I was beaten at the next election I would still remain on here, and if, at the next election, I did not go forward at all, I would still be here.' And Professor W. F. P. Stockley asked, in apprehension, 'What about the Second Dail members if they all die off? . . . It is a desperate state of affairs if there is only *one* surviving member of the Second Dail to hold on to the position.' While the position was worse for a member like Mr. Sean Lemass, who later (far later) became Premier or Taoiseach of The Republic of Ireland. He was never a member of the Second Dail, but was elected to the Third. The sacred Second Dail could not recognize him as a representative of the people at all.

In this impasse they set up in August, 1924, a body known as Cómhairle na dTeachtai, or Council of Deputies, to allow all elected faithful Republicans to take part together with the members of the Second Dail in discussion – though none but the members of the Second Dail were allowed to vote. This immediately began to tie them up in further knots, since the new Council of Deputies did things which, in counsel's opinion, it had no authority to do as a sovereign assembly. This became, for a change, a practical problem when some eight million dollars of Republican funds in America became a matter of dispute between the Free State Dail, which claimed direct succession, and these seceders who also claimed direct succession to the original Republican parliament that floated the National Loan. Any act that seemed to detract from the authority of the seceders had to be examined with much care.

In the middle of this confusion Mr. De Valera was finally driven to realize that metaphysical discussions led to a theological debating society rather than to practical politics. He found himself prating in the wilderness while the enemy functioned undisturbed. The only obvious course, he said, was to stop being an abstentionist party and enter current politics as a Left Wing Party.

Unhappily he had been vociferous in his denunciation of the Free State and of those especially who had taken the Oath of Allegiance as deputies in the Free State Dail; and he had pledged himself that in no circumstances would he take such an Oath. He now, after infinite hesitations, modified his attitude so far as to declare his willingness to enter the Free State Dail and participate in the work of government if the Oath were removed. The result was to throw the entire Republican movement into dismay. The I.R.A. withdrew its allegiance from all politicians in November, 1925. Cumann na mBan, the Fianna, and Sinn Fein drew apart in suspicion. Guarantees were asked of the new party – Fianna Fail – and refused. It seemed likely, certainly possible, that De Valera would actually recant his entire position, enter the Free State Dail, to overthrow which he had taken an active part in a Civil War, take the Oath of Allegiance, and so do everything that he could have done in 1922 and without any Civil War at all. The Council of Deputies withdrew their allegiance from him, and elected a new President of the Republic – President Art O'Connor.

In the event there was a further split. The extreme, intransigent, magnificently logical scholastics of the Left Wing seceded once more – or allowed De Valera to secede, though who were the hens and who were the eggs in these kaleidoscopic pretences at politics was something that kept fires burning as late into the night as when men argued over the verbum and the logos. At any rate, with less than the quorum permitted by the Constitution of the original parent Dail, the 'Faithful Survivors', as they called themselves, continued to meet for several years, denouncing Mr. De Valera to the end for being faithless to his trust.

Ultimately – though Madame Markievicz did not live to see it – Mr. De Valera and Fianna Fail took the last step towards recantation, forced to it by the decree of the Free State government after the assassination of Mr Kevin O'Higgins, the Minister for Justice and Vice-President of the Executive Council, that all deputies must sign the Oath before proffering themselves for election. Before this attempt to finish abstentionism, De Valera and Fianna Fail surrendered, entered Leinster House, took the Oath of Allegiance, and became part and parcel of the government of the Free State. Their theology was now useful to them: they declared that the Oath, taken under duress, was not binding. They adopted a policy of Republicanism within the constitution of the Free State. They set themselves to win power, remove the Oath, and quite frankly, indeed blatantly, to transmute the Free State Constitution, by virtue of its own powers, into a Republican Constitution pure and simple. It was a highly ingenious tergiversation, but that its authors will ever be able to clear themselves of the charge of common dishonesty is doubtful.

So it struck Constance Markievicz, who (1925-26) went no further than to join the new Party in its earliest stages. She was not at all happy about it, even then, and here is where that 'shining intellectual honesty' of hers does really appear. Though she had many sides, all were clear-cut. She was not a complex woman, and she did not possess a tangled mind. She knew quite well that almost all that she had said in the Treaty debates had been a condemnation of the social structure visualized by the framers of that Treaty; and she knew that no argument could now justify her in accepting the fruits of the Treaty that did not also stultify her and condemn her for her part in the Civil Strife that followed the rejection of it. If she were right then, she was right still – the thing was untouchable.

If she had been a false Sybil, then she must fall back on her secondary objection – that the Free State was contrary to Irish ideals, particularly in the matter of the Oath. Yet she knew well that in Mr. De Valera's original draft of Document No. 2 – which he had wished to move as an amendment to the Treaty – there was also an Oath. It was not the same Oath. It was that kind of verbal modification of the Oath which delighted the hearts of the theologians among the Republicans, but did not at all delight her. And that meant that she had taken her share of responsibility for the Civil War for the sake of a difference in words between two Oaths. And meant, worst of all, that she must rely for her present and future actions on just that one slender point. Her social beliefs must be sacrificed to it – her desire 'to do something for the people' – everything must be set aside and postponed once again, while she fought for a Party that based its right to existence on an argument about which she had the weakest convictions. (Later, when they had entered the Dail, they had many other planks in their programme, but for the moment the removal of the Oath was paramount.)

What she felt about it all we know only from her conversations with her friends, and they agree that she was miserable about it. Sometimes she showed her mind by open arguments, sometimes, unconsciously, by a note of exasperation in her voice when she seemed to realize the tyranny of the situation, and the absence of an honourable alternative. She was caught – that is all – by the world of the commonplace. Instead of drama she faced compromise. And there is neither adventure nor colour in compromise. It is merely a way of working with unpleasant facts.

None the less having joined the new Party, she did her loyal best for it. She toured the country in her old car, wrote propaganda, addressed those endless meetings that from being an excitement, had become first a bore, and now a routine. She had always been active and inventive at propaganda-work. She wrote many songs for the Fianna and for the Volunteers, and several plays and pamphlets. As to the plays, none were published – they remained, and properly so, for she had no illusions about them, in manuscript form, and their names sufficiently define them, *Blood Money, The Invincible Mother* (i.e. Ireland), *Broken Dreams*, – plays of all-too-heroic type with no pretentions to literature. As to the songs, written in haste, and probably without a great deal of real feeling, they rarely produced even as good a line as:

> *The storm-beaten rose lifts a pale green shoot*
> *To meet the rising sun;*
> *Young grass plants push up their sword-like blades*
> *To tell us The Day has come.*

More often they fell to the bathos of

> *We pledge ourselves by murders dark,*
> *In barrack, suburb, and in park. . . .*

to be sung to the air of *The Red Flag*.

Most of these were written after the Civil War and they mark the low-tide of her enthusiasm. What she did from 1922 onward, she did as a duty.

Politics were thus virtually finished for her. She continued, by force of habit, to dabble in them. At the election in June, 1927, which produced the Fifth Dail, she again won her old seat in Dublin South. She heckled at meetings – 'heckling' in Ireland meaning 'obstructing'. One typical encounter at Rathmines is remembered by a candidate at that election. Having, with Mrs. Sheehy Skeffington, and Miss ffrench-Mullen, determined to prevent the speakers from being heard, she stationed herself with her dog – now one *Shuler* – in the gallery. Her friends sat apart in the body of the hall, and interrupted alternately. The speaker referred to Miss ffrench-Mullen, as 'this woman'. Somebody else shouted back that Miss ffrench-Mullen was a lady. The speaker riposted that he regretted that he was not. Mrs. Sheehy-Skeffington interposed a remark about the Civil War. In the gallery Madame shouted some insult about 'traitors'. All the while her dog kept up an incessant and ear-splitting howl. In ten minutes the place was a bedlam, with the speakers trying to interject half-sentences between every pause. So the meeting progressed and concluded like every other such meeting at which she 'heckled' in the same way. A sorry business. It would have been very unlike her to have her heart in so inglorious a life.

§ 3

Time was, if one wished to get the true feeling for her life in her last years, one walked down Camden Street or Kevin Street, and went into the little shops, and houses of the poor, and into the memories of these old men and women, who still wander aimlessly, like sheep, or old grey snails, about the backstreets of Dublin.

The death of her sister Eva, in June, 1926, had left her very lonely and depressed. After it, as if in commemoration of Eva's life, she, too, began to seek among the slums for some little labour that would be not merely a communion of spirit with her sister, but that would be a refuge for her tired mind. Writing to Miss Roper, in July, 1926, she said how much she regretted having lost, 'in the bustle and hurry of life', that psychic contact she had been able to make with Eva when she was in jail after the insurrection. She said that she had thought of her from that on in connection with everything she did, and said, and thought. 'I was writing a play and doing a copy to send her; and so on through everything, though I didn't write often. And then everything seemed to be cut off all at once. But lately I've begun to see and feel her often . . . Last Sunday at Mass when I wasn't thinking of her at all, she suddenly seemed to smile at me from behind the priest – and I know it's real and that she, the real Eva, is somewhere very near. . . .'

Among the poor, she became strangely like Eva, even in

appearance, and far more like her in manner than like her own former self. She discarded something of her assertiveness; even her features softened as she drew near her sixtieth year; her voice lost some of its shrillness. In her dress she was now always shabby; her clothes hung from her as if they had not been pressed for years; her shoes were of the cheapest, sometimes mere rags of cloth; she would wear an overcoat from whose too-long sleeves her finger-tips would peep like a child's. Indeed with her cropped hair, and her little apple-cheeks that rounded above her lips a perpetual smile, she could look at times extraordinarily infantile.

She would not have been herself if she did not make of all this, in her own unique way, something in which she could find delight and even elation. Take her more than kindly interest in her poor folk during the 'Great Strike', sometimes called the 'Coal Strike', of 1926. With her own wrinkled hands she carried bags of coal on her own back up the tenement flights of the slums. It was a gesture that had something fine in it – like St. Francis, allowing himself to be pelted with mud by the street boys of Assisi. But she had no mission of Poverty to preach, and anyone would have delighted to help her to carry the coal. It is a very innocent and even a rather charming weakness, and one dallies with it only because it shows well how much her dramatizations aided, and did not interfere with the work she chose to do.

All this time from 1924 on she was living in 'rooms'. She seemed to pick out Zolaesque houses, of which Dublin has, in any case, a large number – the influence, partly, of two Universities, and several colleges, partly of the extreme poverty of half the population. Long after the rather squalid Joyceian Dublin vanished this lodging-squalor remained. A friend who lived with her in one of these ramshackle lodging-houses writes: 'The *ménage* was not so much squalid as topsy-turvy. Time was of no account – meals were served when hunger demanded. Con's room was bright, colourful and lovely – she had beautiful things – but at times it was so untidy that it would take a mountain-goat to get through it. This was due to political distractions and not laziness. The rest of the house was painfully ugly.' Of another North Side lodgings O. E. writes: 'Mrs. Mac. had a squad of kids; a woman for whom excitement was the breath of life. She was off down to the city at the first breath of rumour. She would throw on her hat, bang on the hall-door, and leaving a half-cooked dinner and nine hungry children, set out to see the fun. Madame Markievicz would come in, size up the situation, take off her skirt, command the kitchen in her knickers, fry herself a rasher over a dirty, smoky, greasy fire, and have tea out of a broken mug. Then she would set to work, and dish up a well-cooked dinner for the bairns.' Of one other resting-place of hers it is remembered that the poor people got into a crisis over the rent. It was a large bill, over a year's arrears, and Madame got quite miserable about it. Even after the death of old Lady Gore-Booth, she always had a small allowance, but towards the end she scattered it in charity without thought. 'As she had run almost completely out of money,' recalls A.F., 'she got out a ring her mother had left her – one of the few possessions she had stuck to – she had a large streak of sentimentality in her. She pawned or sold the ring and got £70 or £60 for it – it must have been a fine ring and so cleared off the rent. She never lent money. She just gave it away, like that.'

M.B. remembers that 'during the bad influenza there was a family living in one room in a slum. They were all down except the father. Con took over the *ménage*, nursed the sick mother, got the man his breakfast every morning before he went to work and did everything until the mother was on her feet again.' There was a dust-heap, too, in that backyard where she turned to making a garden. She used to trot in through the malodorous hallway if she were passing afterwards, to pick and pluck at the dried, crumpled earth, and to make a flower or two grow there under the washing and the trampling feet of the slum-cats.

She had touched that same world occasionally throughout her life, in Manchester, and with the soup-kitchen in Liberty Hall, but never, as now, to rest in it and find in it the image of herself. By day she was back at her childhood days 'in and out like a pet fox that you'd think somebody was after her'. By night she would take up her Connolly, and poring over him try to formulate his thought and apply it to the real things in Irish life which the Nationalists had totally neglected; or she was to be heard down in the Sinn Fein offices in Suffolk Street preaching the gospel, not of the tricolour but of the sickle and the hammer rampant.

As always since 1916 there was nobody to guide her, and she fumbled with her thought until it seemed to crumble and become shapeless in her hands. What could be expected of her? It was not her fault but the fault of the Irish people, if she, out of the Big House, one of the outcasts, Anglo-Irish in every line of her body and every tone of her voice, having taken the religion of the people, having taken their cause, having taken their manners, having tried to take their language found that when she turned to other tasks she turned to them almost alone. If, then, she mingled with her half-understood socialism, everything else that she thought dear to Irishmen, and made of it all a kind of Gaelic synthesis that was utterly impracticable, it is not so much her fault as the fault of her contemporaries. If her lectures in that little office in a sidestreet to a few dozen working girls and boys were a minor folly, it was the fault not of her ingenuousness but of our disingenuousness. She was not the first to go more Irish than the Irish themselves, not the first to take literally all that we blathered (with many but secret reservations). So she solemnly tried to link up with Connolly's thought her nationalist colleagues' rodomontade about a return to ancient Gaelic culture and the ancient Gaelic social world. It was amazing ragout – Marx, and the Brehon Laws, the encyclical of Leo XIII, the Seanchas Mór, Das Kapital and the Democratic Programme of Dail Eireann. Nobody could have done it but a woman who had not learned, for all her twenty years in Irish politics, that the native Irishman does not always mean what he says.

§ 4

It was well for her that she had other things to distract her – the tail-end of politics and her poor folk who were of all the things she touched the most real and satisfying. She would take holidays, too, packing lunch and her sketch-book and paints into the little car and rattling off alone into the mountains, usually Glencullen, or Tibradden, or Kilakee, and paint all day long. She might then drop into the cottages around so that you may still find in those cottages, here and there, a watercolour 'done by the Countéss'. (Always she was known to Dublin as 'the Countéss' – as Parnell was always called 'Parnéll'.) Her duties on the Rathmines Urban Council also kept her busy with committee work – Housing, Libraries, and so on.

She was busy for the last time with politics in 1927. The remnants of the old Irish Republican Army, now independent of all politicians, were becoming active in a sporadic way and there were many arrests. Coercion was inevitable and the Free State government applied it with a rigour that ultimately undid them. She could not, therefore, wholly keep apart from the doings of the new constitutional 'Republicanism' and when the election of June, 1927, for the Fifth Dail, took place she was in the thick of it, standing as usual with success, for her old division as a Fianna Fail candidate. That the populace stood by her so solidly at election times is a great tribute to them and to her. In her old car she did a whirlwind tour of her constituency, and helped other candidates in theirs, driving from village to village and stopping at the gates to address the crowds coming out from Mass. She broke her arm, one Sunday, cranking it. 'Just fix this up for me,' she said to the local doctor, full of pluck as always, 'It's lucky it's only my arm – I can still talk.' And she went on with her meeting, and addressed two other meetings that day, her shattered arm hanging limp by her side.

Towards the end of June she fell seriously ill; but fearing cancer she would not go to a doctor until the pain mastered her. Then she went to her old friend Dr. Kathleen Lynn, who ordered her into hospital for an operation. She chose Sir Patrick Duns Hospital which is situated on the edge of the Ringsend slums, but she insisted that she must be put into a general ward among the poor, and that none of her friends should be told about her illness. She remained there, in the long ward, with the poor about her until she died, and before her friends heard of her illness it was too late to move her (even if she had permitted it) to a private room where she might have had more comfort. After the operation, on July 5th, and a second operation on July 7th, a relapse set in. She rallied when her daughter was summoned by a broadcast appeal to her bedside. She spoke of seeing 'bright lights' – and she saw a 'bright place all lit up'. Her mind wandered a little then, and then again she said she was being borne upward, lifted up, and her hollowed and wrinkled face grew radiant. She sank into a coma at midnight and died at 1.25 a.m. on the morning of July 15th. Beside her was Cassie, and Maeve and her stepson, Stanislaus, and a few devoted women friends.

Out in the streets there were people crying for her – old basket-women, road-workers, women in shawls, tramwaymen, all asking the one question, 'How is she? How is the Countess?' And when they heard she was dead one saw them turn away and heard their loud lamenting, and saw even men crying because of her.

When they laid her in State in the Rotunda, the only place they could hire – a cinema – for the government loutishly refused to give the Mansion House, the slums poured in to see her, gazing at the small, contracted face under the glass panel in the coffin. One old woman brought two eggs and put them quietly on the coffin among the flowers. She said, 'I said when the little black hen would lay I'd bring the eggs to Madame at the hospital. Now she's dead, but I want to keep my word. I want her to have them.'

She lay there for two days and nights, with a guard of her own Fianna boys watching beside her. Then she was given a public funeral, one of those immense ceremonial funerals which had been for ten years, a feature of Irish life, with many bands, eight motor-tenders of wreaths, and every nationalist organization that existed following in the *cortège*. The Count and Stanislaus were there, and Sir Josslyn and Lady Gore-Booth, and Jim Larkin headed the Workers' Union of Ireland with a red banner inscribed in Russian. But at the graveyard there were uniformed soldiers with machine-guns to prevent a volley from being fired over her grave; and they did not bury her that day because the grave-diggers' union was not permitted to work on Sunday. The coffin was placed for the night in a vault, the Fianna sounded the Last Post. Mr. de Valera spoke a few words, and the crowd dispersed.

She is commemorated by a limestone bust in Stephen's Green, by a plaque in St. Ultan's Hospital; by the full-length portrait of her painted in Paris in 1900 by Szenskowsky, which hangs in the Dublin Municipal Gallery; by the Yeats' poem, *In memory of Eva Gore-Booth and Constance Markievicz*; and, one hopes, by the grateful memory of her people.

§ 5

Since that return to Ireland after the war Cassie had not, until now, seen Dublin or Ireland. He stayed for a little while after the funeral out at the Grange House, Rathfarnham, with Shamus O'Sullivan. Then he returned to Warsaw and never again came to Ireland.

Of his last years there his kinswoman whom he loved has written:

'Casi is now homeless. His instinct of wanting to protect, defend, and care for others, had no opportunity to develop. And I was so much like him in many ways – I loved painting and the theatre and I could listen for hours and hours to his life-stories (and besides he said the queerest thing of all, that I was like Alice who died in Paris about the time I was born) –that I never realized until long afterwards that Casi was a dreamer, a most delicate and susceptible soul, and very unfit for the hardness of life. I cried to-day remembering how Casi whom I called Teddie Bear took me every morning to the Consulate, holding my hand tight when it was slippery in the big garden we had to cross, and buying me four or five chocolates every day in a little shop going to the office.'

'He took me to the theatre, too, and it was during one of Childau's "Romance" productions, that Casi was staging, that I discovered how we both loved each other and that we must have met many times before in our previous lives. I remember so well the tune, *"Connais tu le pays?"* that Cavallini sang on the stage; and never will I forget it – I sang it to Casi two days before he died. But I do not know if he heard me.

'It would be hard to tell how good and how kind Teddie was – as everybody now called him.

'He loved shooting and it was on the estate of a friend, M. Fijalkowski, a man with whom he wrote several very good plays, that he suddenly got ill. He struggled in vain for a year with some dreadful disease which developed after influenza, got up, then back to bed, then up again, then to the Red Cross Clinic, then to the country where in spite of the best of food and care and good air he did not improve. Then he came to Warsaw again to the Holy Ghost Hospital because he had no money for the Red Cross Clinic. The mayor of the town requested the hospital to give him every care and he had a separate room and a private nurse. But nothing did help – in less than three months he was gone.

'In the country he had the company of the mother of his friend, the old Mrs. Fijalkowski who was his angel-guardian, and with whom he talked and talked and read lots of books as he was lying down. His mind became so very superior and detached from all earthen goods that Casi, or rather Teddie, was more like a saint or angel than a man during his last year of terrific sufferings (angina pectoris). His body was like a pincushion from over a thousand injections and his dear white hands, so white and thin. He looked very young and beautiful.

'I remember the day he came from the country to the Holy Ghost Hospital. I asked him "Teddie, why do you rather come to town? I thought the country was so very much better for your health?" He answered, "I wanted to see you once more before

I die." I did not realize then he could die. To the last moment I would not believe it. And then a terrible day came when he put his thin white hand in mine and told me – "Darling, forgive me, but I am dying." "Oh! Ted," I said, "You will not die – I will not let you." And then he said, "Promise me if there is something *there*, we will meet again." I answered, "I swear, Teddie, I will always be with you." Do you know, I feel him now always near me and am looking forward to the day he will come and take me by the hand like in the old days to help me, crossing some slippery garden to some place I do not know and where he is waiting for me.

'I cannot write more: tears are just strangling me. . . .'

He was fifty-seven when he died. Constance was fifty-nine. He left one son, Constance left one daughter. In Ireland he will be remembered by a portrait of Æ, and a landscape or two in the Dublin Municipal Gallery; by a few pictures in private ownership; by the Dublin United Arts Club which he founded; and by a few scraps of records in the manager's office of the Gaiety where he so often drank his uisge-baugh and treated Ireland and all its politics as the world's joke.

INDEX

ABERDEEN, LADY, 52, 59, 113
—— Lord, 52
Æ, 54, 55, 71, 77, 94, 116, 132, 134, 216
'Alice,' 38
Allan, Fred, 122
—— Maud, 55
Ashley, Lady Alice, 41
—— Hon. Evelyn, 41
—— (actor), 57
Astor, Lady, 179

BADEN-POWELL, 85
Barry, Kevin, 197
Battersea, Lady, 163
Baudelaire, 37
Bedford, Adeline Duchess of, 163
Bell, Alan, 187
Bellingham, 118
Bennett, Louie, 191
Bidgood, Capt., 27, 31
Biggar, Joseph, 63
Booth, Letitia, 21
Brannigan, Richard, 137
Bright, 15
Browner, C. J., 84
Brugha, Cathal, 188, 189, 192, 198
Bulfin, Edward, 71
Burke, Mr., Under-Sec., 65
Butt, Isaac, 69
Byrne, Alfred, M.P., Lord Mayor, 163
—— Davy, 61, 87, 182

CADOGAN, LORD, 68
Campbell-Bannerman, 52, 68
Campkin, Madame, 84
Carey, 64
Carney, Wilfred, 162
Carré, 84
Carson, Edward, 69, 126, 169

Casement, Sir R., 85, 128
Cavanagh, Maeve, 53, 170
Cavendish, Lord F., 65
Cézanne, 40
Childers, Erskine, 193, 199
Chamberlain, Austen, 68
Clarke, Tom, 64, 121, 128, 142, 156
—— Mrs., 160, 178
Clarkson, Prof. J. D., 11, 133
Coffey, Diarmuid, 47
Colbert, Con., 128, 157
Collins, Michael, 124, 144, 169, 176, 177, 179, 186, 188, 189, 192, 197
Colum, Padriac, 71, 91, 168
Connolly, James, 75, 101, 105 foll., 126, 129 foll., 158, 174, 202
Corkery, Daniel, 117
Coventry, Countess of, 43
Curzon, Lord, 168

DALY, P. T., 101, 122, 136
—— Edward, 157
Davitt, Michael, 63, 65, 69
de Burgh Daly, Dr., 147
De la Prade, Count Guy, 38
De Valera, Eamonn, 69, 124, 153, 162, 172, 177, 179, 185, 192, 194, 205
Devoy, John, 98, 128
Digges, Dudley, 113
Dillon, John, 63, 76, 126, 168
Donnelly, Rev. Dr., 170
Doyle, 'Toucher', 55, 61
Dubronsky, 56, 58, 61
Dunraven, Lord, 68

ELIZABETH, QUEEN, 20
Essex, Earl of, 20

FARREN, LADY, 90

217

Fijalkowski, 215
Fitzgerald, Desmond, 96, 162
Fitzpatrick, Norah, 84
Flanagan, 'Bird', 55
Foley, Edward, 29
Ford, Patrick, 66
French, Lord, 178
ffrench-Mullen, Miss, 147, 209
Furlong, 'Tommy', 56, 61, 87

GIFFORD, MISS, 114
Gilmer, Miss, 41
Ginnell, Laurence, 172
Gogarty, Oliver, 87
Gore, Francis, Sir, 20
—— Lady, 25
—— Nathaniel, 21
Gore-Booth, Constance, 15; childhood, 22–25; horsemanship, 25–31, 34; London, 32–35; painting, 35; marriage, 40, 41; *see also* 'Markievicz, Countess'
—— Eva, 18–19, 22, 35, 41, 55, 178
—— family, 15; history, 20 foll.
—— Henry, Sir, 22, 41, 63, 64
—— Josslyn, A. R., Sir, 41 50, 214
—— Lady, 17, 35, 41, 50
—— Nathaniel, Sir, 21
—— Robert, Sir, 21
Grattan, Henry, 69
Grenfell, Miss M., 41
Griffith, Arthur, 72 foll., 90, 108, 123, 130, 139, 162, 169, 173, 192, 198

HAMILTON, DUCHESS OF, 43
Healy, Tim, 63, 65, 66, 72
Heuston, J. J., 94, 157
Hill, C. J., Lieut.-Col., 40
Hobson, Bulmer, 85, 88 foll., 96, 123, 124, 133, 177
Hoey, Pat, 56, 59, 60, 61
Hone, Nathaniel, 93
Humphreys, Fr., 123
Hutchinson-Poe, Col., 68

JEFFARES, SEALY, 84
Jervis-White-Jervis, Sir John, 90
Johnston, Robert, 120
Joyce, James, 56, 80
Joyce's, 56, 87

KELLY, FRANK, 144
—— Pat, 56
—— Tom, Alderman, 71, 191
Kennedy, Hugh, 80
Kent, 157
Kilmarnock, Lady, 41
—— Lord, 41
Kingston, Countess of, Dowager, 41

LARKIN, JIM, 52, 75, 76, 83, 98, 102 foll., 126, 129
Laurens, Jean Paul, 37
Ledwidge, Francis, 54, 168
Le Fanu, Rev. F. S., 40
Leinster, Duke of, 43
Lemass, Sean, 205
Leslie, John, 129
Lloyd George, David, 169 foll., 175
Lonergan, 128
Lowry, Frank, 84
Lumley-Hill, Mr. C., 41

MCBRIDE, JOHN, MAJOR, 157
—— Maud Gonne, 80, 113, 160, 178
McCartan, Dr., 122
McCullagh, Denis, 122
MacDiarmada, Sean, 122, 125 foll., 158
MacDonagh, Joseph, 191
—— Tomás, 70, 118, 197
MacDonald, 'Wagger', 56, 61
MacDonnell, Anthony, Sir, 68
McGrath, Joseph, 191, 195
McKelvey, Joseph, 94
MacMahon, Canon, 170
McNeill, Eoin, 126 foll., 162, 177
MacSwiney, Miss Mary, 204
Mallin, James, 140, 145 foll., 157
Mansfield, Miss, 41

218

Markievicz, Casimir, 37, 40, 46, 49, 50 foll., 57, 84, 93 foll., 113, 139 foll., 213, 214 foll.
—— Countess (*see also* Gore-Booth, Constance); Dublin social life, 44–54; politics to 1916, 54 foll.; Fianna Eireann, 86 foll.; Raheny, 88 foll.; Surrey House, 97 foll.; James Larkin, 100 foll.; James Connolly, 129 foll.; Insurrection, 145 foll.; Aylesbury Prison, 158 foll.; Politics after 1916, 172 foll.; Secretary for Labour, Dail Eireann, 179 foll., 189 foll.; Cork Female Prison, 185 foll.; Mountjoy Jail, 190 foll.; The Treaty, 192 foll.; Civil War, 197 foll.; Post Civil War politics, 201 foll.
—— Maeve, 42, 50, 213
—— Stanislaus, 38, 42, 213
Martyn, Edward, 71
Maxwell, John, Sir, 168
Mellowes, Liam, 94, 96 foll.
Milligan, Alice, 71
Mitchell, Susan, 71
Molloy, Ray, 56
Moloney, Helena, 54, 80, 89 foll., 162
Montgomery, 'Jimmy', 59, 61
Moore, George, 40, 107
Mountjoy, Lord, 20
Murget, 37
Muncaster, Lord, 41
Murphy, Martin, 56, 58, 60, 61, 87, 203
—— William Martin, 107 foll., 130, 182 foll.

NEARY'S, 56
Nesbitt, George, 84
Nordgren, Anna, 36

O'BOYLE, NEAL JOHN, 121
O'Brien, Miss Nellie, 84
—— Peter, Lord Chief Justice, 45, 47
—— William (M.P.), 63, 63, 65, 66, 72
—— William, 142
O'Byrne, Dermot, 168
O'Casey, Sean, 136, 137, 142
O'Clery, Arthur, 80
O'Connell, Daniel, 44, 69, 76
O'Connor, Art, 204, 206
—— Rory, 197, 199
O'Donnell, Hugh, 33
O'Donovan, Rossa, 139
O'Grady, Stamer, 84
O'Hanlon, Jack, 122
O'Hanrahan, The, 157
O'Hara, C. K., Major, 29
O'Hegarty, P. S., 122, 125
O'Higgins, Kevin, 176, 206
O'Kelly, Seumas, 54
O'Neill, Hugh, 33
O'Rahilly, The, 126
O'Sullivan, John Marcus, 80
—— Seumas, 54, 87, 168, 183, 214
Owen, Robert, 88
Owens, Miss, 84

PARNELL, C. S., 63, 65, 69, 155
Partridge, W., Councillor 136, 152
Pavlova 58, 59
Pearse, Patrick, 79, 80, 118, 127, 139, 142, 156, 173
Perolz, Marianna, 139
Piggott, Richard, 63, 66
Pirrie, Viscountess, 47
Plunkett, Count, 70, 117, 169
—— Joseph, 70, 118, 157

REDMOND, JOHN, 22, 64, 68, 69, 168, 175 foll.
Rooney, William, 73, 122
Roper, Edith, 165
Ryan, Frederick, 71
—— Mark, Dr., 120, 128
—— Miss Nell, 162
—— Patrick, 128

SHARPE, MAY ('CHICAGO MAY'), 159 foll.

Sheehy-Skeffington, Mrs., 209
Sichalko, M., 41
nic Siubhlaigh, Maire, 84
'Skin-the-Goat', 65, 66
Skinnider, Margaret, 147
'Squidge', 17
Stephens, James, 54, 71, 117, 147, 168
Stockley, W. F. P., 205
Strafford, Earl of, 20
Sturgis, Miss, 41
Sweetman, John, 123
Synge, J. M., 54
Szenskowsky, 214

TRAYNOR, OSCAR, 198

USSHER, MRS., 41

VANDELEUR, ROBERT, 88
Victoria, Queen, 34

WATERFORD, EARL OF, 43
Wellington, Duke of, 44
Wheeler, Major, 155
White, Jack, Captain, 118, 136, 137
Wilde, Oscar, 44
Wyndham, Charles, 68 foll.

A NOTE TO READERS

We hope you have enjoyed this Cresset Library edition and would like to take this opportunity to invite you to put forward your suggestions about books that might be included in the series.

The Cresset Library was conceived as a forum for bringing back books that we felt should be widely available in attractively designed and priced paperback editions. The series themes can be loosely described as social, cultural, and intellectual history though, as you can see from the list of published titles at the front of this book, these themes cover a broad range of interest areas.

If you have read or know of books that fall into this category which are no longer available or not available in paperback, please write and tell us about them. Should we publish a book that you have suggested we will send you a free copy upon publication together with three other Cresset Library titles of your choice.

Please address your letter to Claire L'Enfant at:-

> Century Hutchinson
> FREEPOST
> London
> WC2N 4BR

There is no need to stamp your envelope.

We look forward to hearing from you.

THE CRESSET LIBRARY